ART BOOKS

FROM CRESCENT MOON PUBLISHING

Leonardo da Vinci
by James Pearson

Piero della Francesca
by Naomi Haskell

Giovanni Bellini
by Julia Davis

Fra Angelico: Art and Religion in the Renaissance
by Rosalind Mutter

Eric Gill: Nuptials of God
by Anthony Hoyland

Minimal Art and Artists in the 1960s and After
by Laura Garrard

Postwar Art
by George Knighton

Vincent van Gogh: Visionary Landscapes
by Stuart Morris

Max Beckmann
by Stuart Morris

Egon Schiele: Sex and Death in Purple Stockings
by D. Simon Eade

Mark Rothko: The Art of Transcendence
by Julia Davis

Jasper Johns
by L.M. Poole

Brice Marden
by Laura Garrard

Frank Stella
by James Pearson

The Light Eternal: J.M.W. Turner
by Jeremy Mark Robinson

Maurice Sendak and the Art of Children's Book Illustration
by L.M. Poole

Sex in Art: Pornography and Pleasure in Painting and Sculpture
by Cassidy Hughes

*Glorification: Religious Abstraction
in Renaissance and 20th Century Painting*
by Jeremy Mark Robinson

The Art of Andy Goldsworthy
by William Malpas

Andy Goldsworthy: Touching Nature
by William Malpas

Andy Goldsworthy In Close-Up
by William Malpas

Richard Long: The Art of Walking
by William Malpas

The Art of Richard Long
by William Malpas

Constantin Brancusi: Sculpting the Essence of Things
by James Pearson

Alison Wilding: The Embrace of Sculpture
by Susan Quinnell

*The Erotic Object: Sexuality in Sculpture
From Prehistory to the Present Day*
by Susan Quinnell

*Land Art: A Complete Guide to Landscape, Environmental,
Earthworks, Nature, Sculpture and Installation Art*
by William Malpas

Land Art In Close-Up
by William Malpas

Colourfield Painting: Minimal, Cool, Hard Edge, Serial and Post-Painterly Abstract Art From the Sixties to the Present
by Laura Garrard

Sacred Gardens: The Garden in Myth, Religion and Art
by Jeremy Mark Robinson

EARLY NETHERLANDISH PAINTING

EARLY NETHERLANDISH PAINTING

Rosalind Mutter

CRESCENT MOON

CRESCENT MOON PUBLISHING
P.O. Box 393, Maidstone
Kent, ME14 5XU,
Great Britain, www.crmoon.com

First published 1996. Second edition 2008 and 2013.
© Rosalind Mutter, 1996. 2008, 2013.

Printed and bound in the U.S.A.
Set in Book Antiqua 9 on 14pt.
Designed by Radiance Graphics.

The right of Rosalind Mutter to be identified as the author of this book has been asserted generally in accordance with sections 77 and 78 of the Copyright, Designs and Patents Act 1988.

All rights reserved. No part of this book may be reprinted or reproduced, stored in a retrieval system, or transmitted, in any form or by any means, electronic, mechanical, photocopying, recording or otherwise, without permission from the publisher.

British Library Cataloguing in Publication data

Mutter, Rosalind
Early Netherlandish painting. – (Painters series)
1. Painting, Flemish 2. Painters – Netherlands 3. Painters – Belgium
I. Title

759.9'492

ISBN-13 9781861713971 (Pbk)

Contents

	Illustrations 11
I	The Early Netherlandish World 17
II	Mysticism and Art in Mediæval Northern Europe 21
III	Space, Light and Aesthetics in Early Netherlandish Art 25
IV	Robert Campin–the Master of Flémalle 33
V	Jan van Eyck 37
VI	Rogier van der Weyden 55
VII	The Passion According to Rogier van der Weyden: *The Descent From the Cross* and Other Crucifixions 67
VIII	Petrus Christus 75
IX	Deiric Bouts 89
	Illustrations 94
X	Jan Gossaert 165
XI	Hans Memling 169
XII	Gerard David 181
XIII	Joachim Patinir 189
XIV	Bernard van Orley 195
XV	Hugo van der Goes 199
XVI	Geertgen tot Sin Jans 203
XVII	Jan de Beer 207
XVIII	Quentin Massys 211
XIX	Joos van Cleve 215

XX Anonymous and Other Early Netherlandish
    Painters   219
    Notes   231
    Bibliography   235

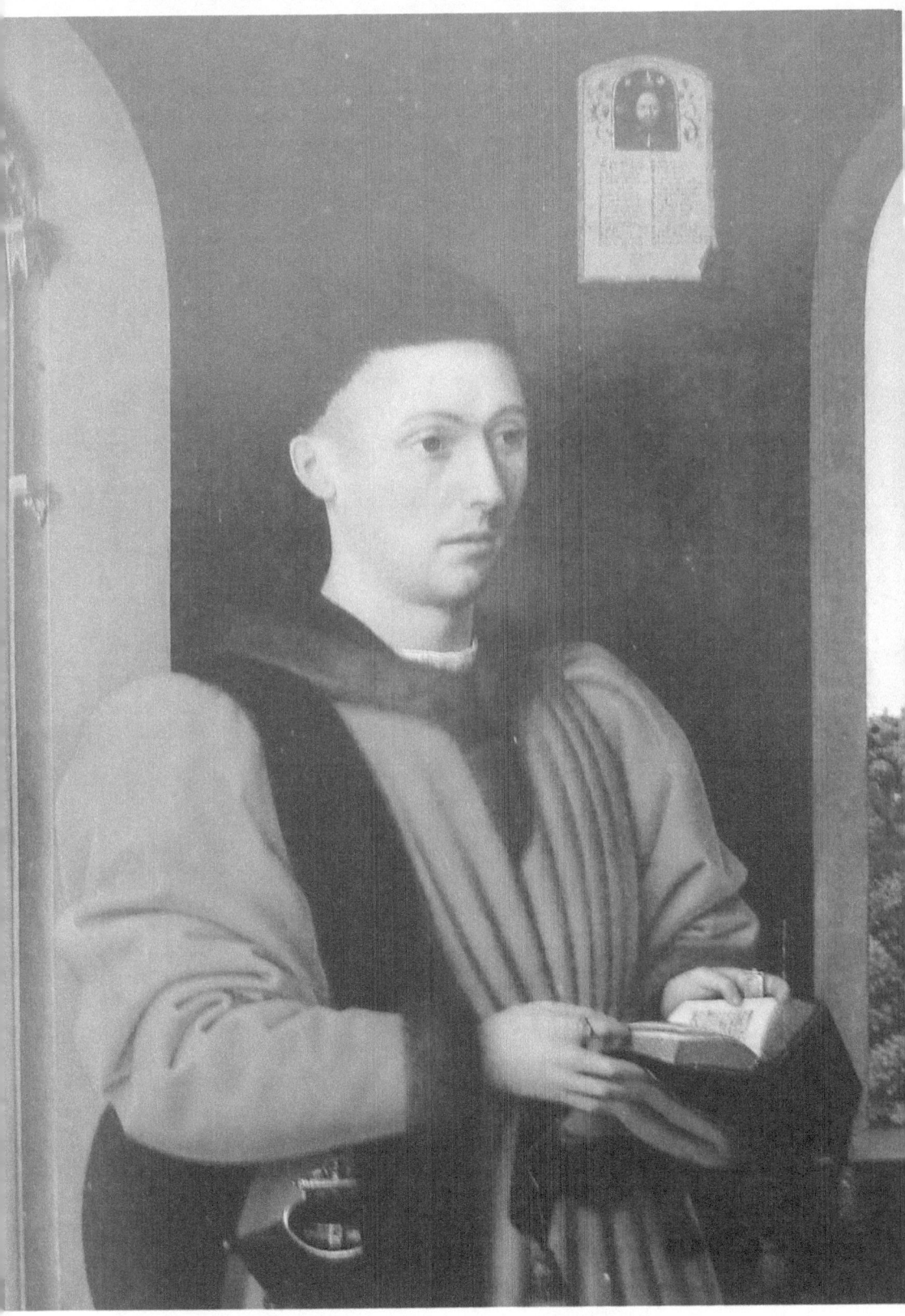

Petrus Christus, Portrait of a Man, detail

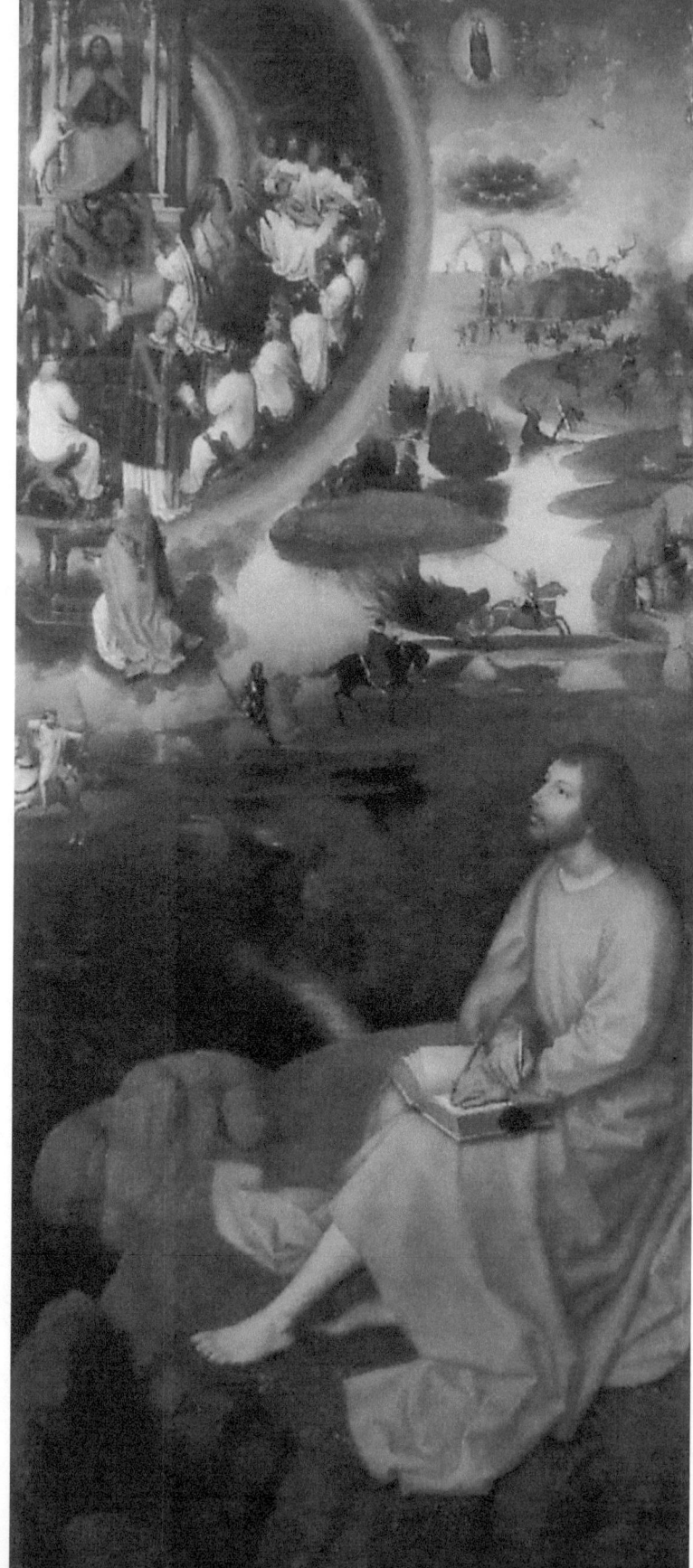

Hans Memling,
John On Patmos,
Bruges

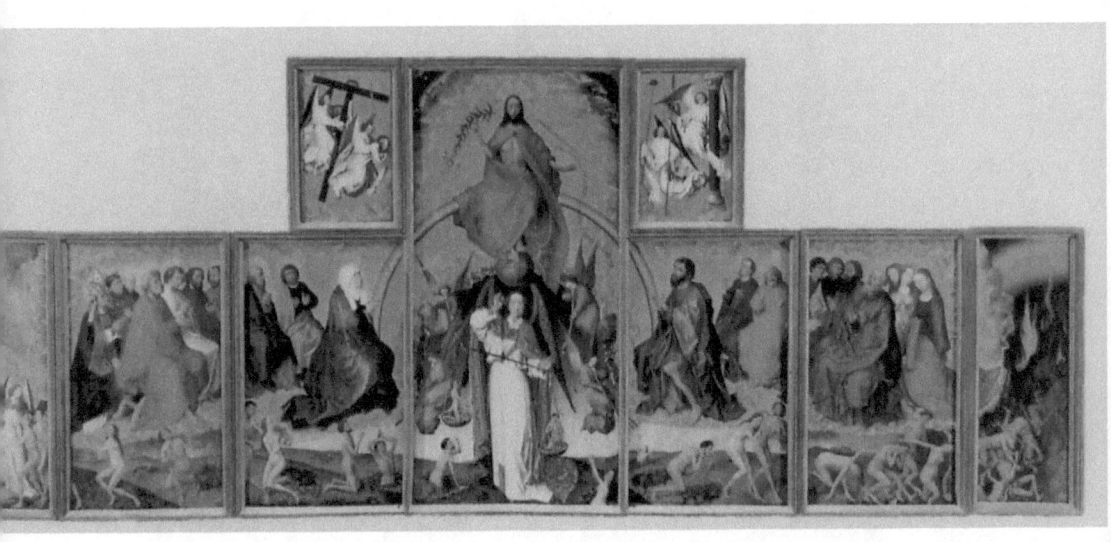
Rogier van der Weyden, The Last Judgement, 1445-49, Beaune

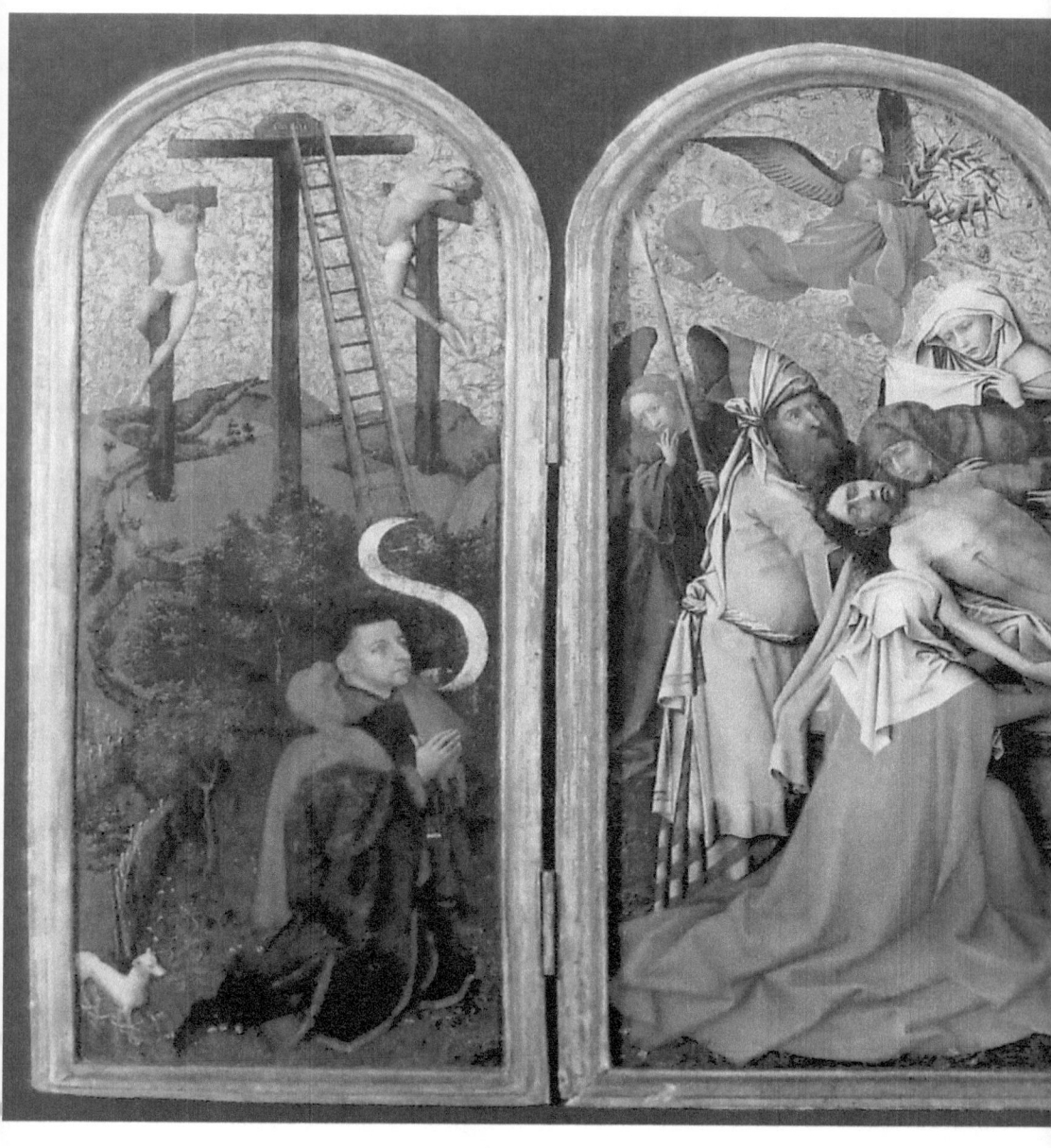

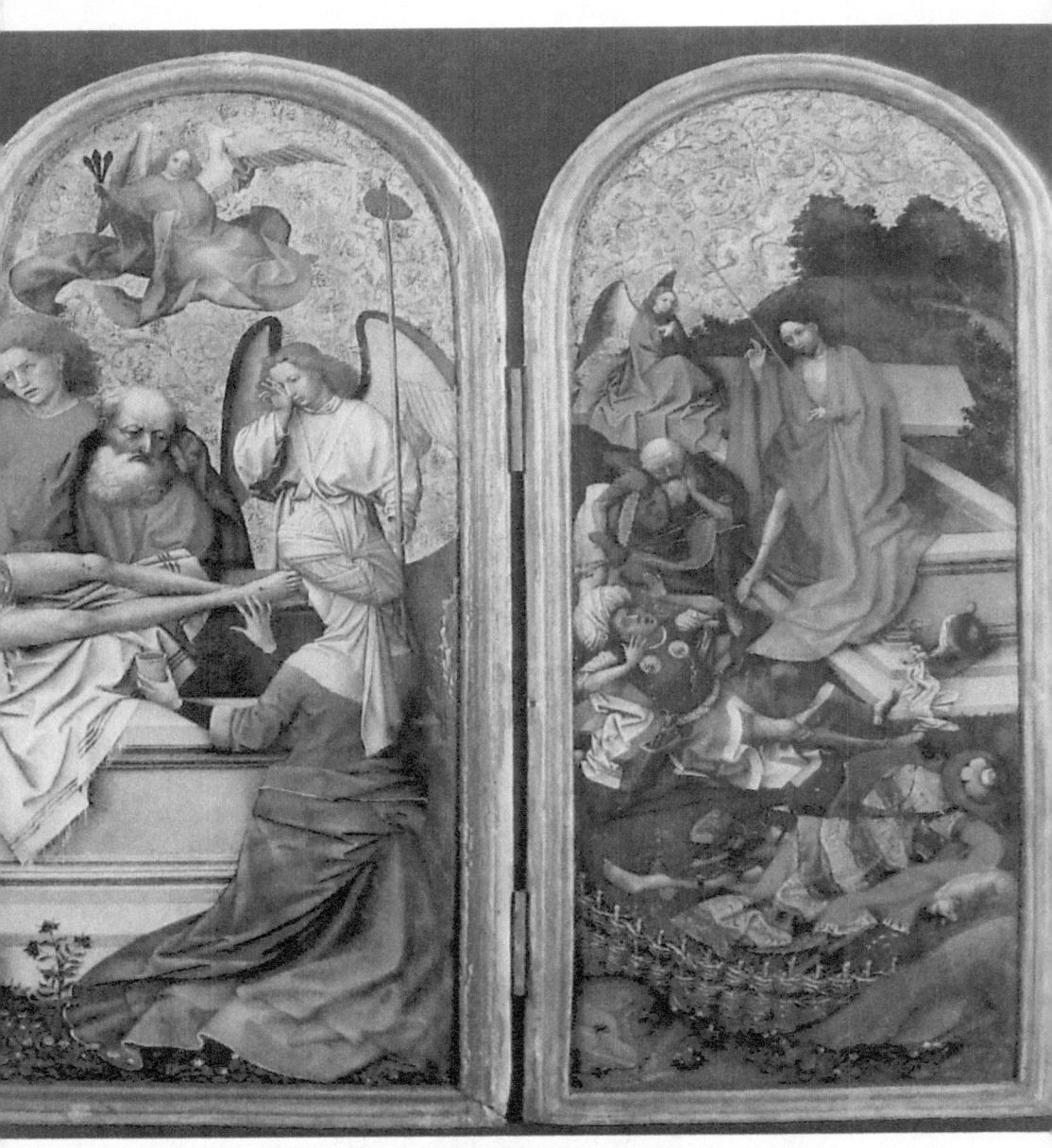

The Seilern Triptych by the Master of Flémalle, also known as Robert Campin, Courtauld Institute, London

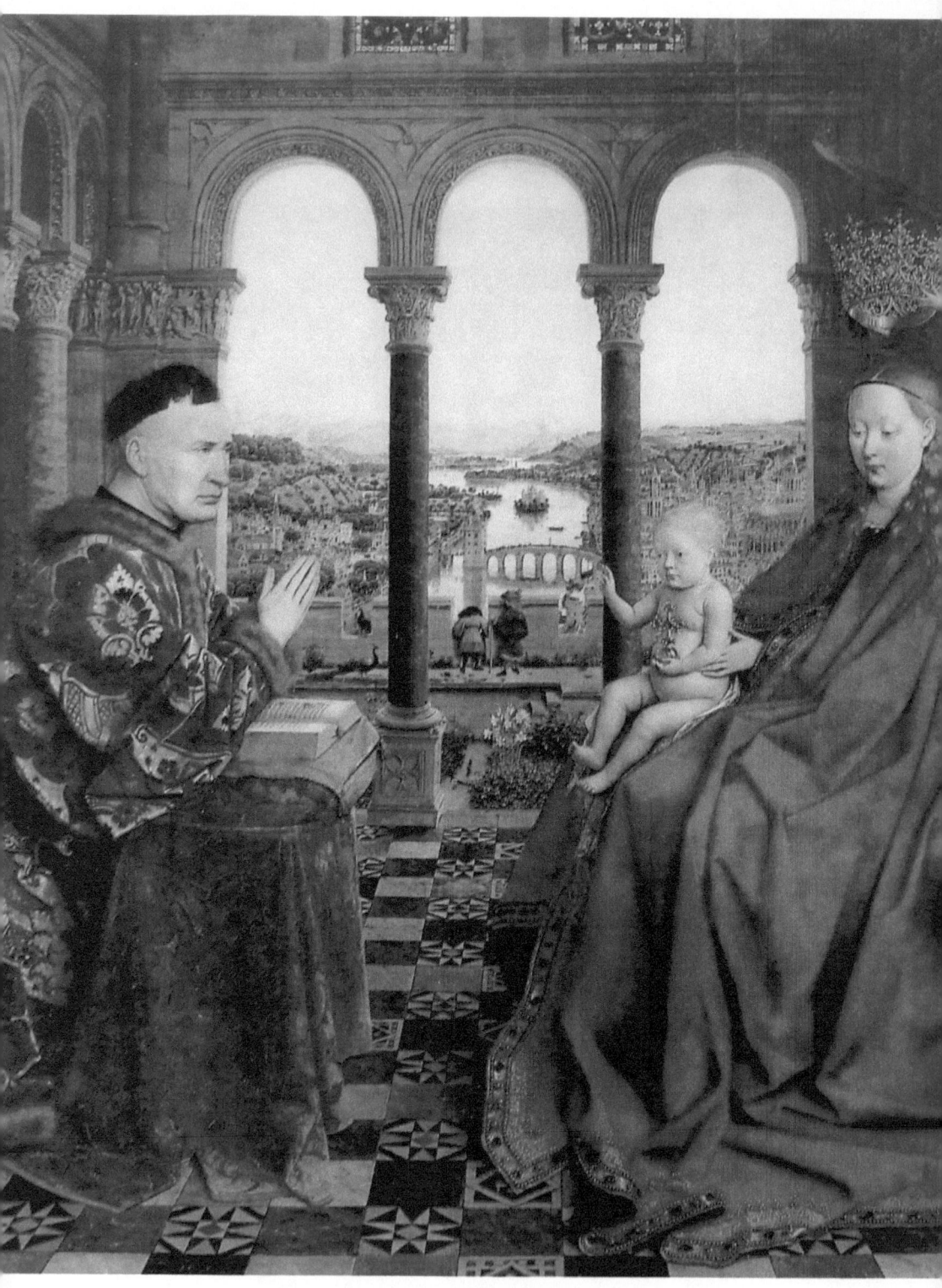
Jan van Eyck, The Rolin Madonna, Louvre, Paris

I
The Early Netherlandish World

Flemish painting will, generally speaking, please the devout better than any painting in Italy, which will never cause him to shed a tear, whereas that of Flanders will cause him to shed many...

Michelangelo Buonarroti[1]

EARLY NETHERLANDISH OR Flemish[2] painting is characterized by its figurative realism, its incredible sense of domestic interior and detail, its luminous light, its 'realist' faces, and its fusions of a micro- and macro-cosmic vision (C. Eisler, 1989, 14). We concentrate here on painters such as Rogier van der Weyden (1400-1464), Jan van Eyck (*c.* 1390-1441), commonly described as the founder of modern oil painting, Gerard David (*c.* 1460-1523), Hugo van der Goes (1440-1482), Hans Memling (1433-1494), Joos van Cleve (*c.* 1485-1540), Jan Gossaert, also called Mabuse (*c.* 1475/8-1532), Geertgen tot Sint Jans (*fl.* late 15th century-1485/95), Quentin Massys (*c.* 1465-1530), Joachim Patinir (*c.* 1485-1524), Dieric Bouts (*c.* 1415-1475), Petrus Christus (*fl.* 1442-1473) and Bernard van Orley (*c.* 1488-1541).

Hieronymous Bosch is not discussed here – he is amply studied in many books. His vision is so extraordinary and singular, he deserves a book of his own, while painters such as Petrus Christus and Dieric Bouts are still relatively unknown. Other Northern European painters, such as Dürer, Grünewald, Lochner and Baldung, long associated with the Early Netherlandish painters, are mentioned in passing only. These painters do not form a school or a group; they are individuals. They are simply the artists we will study in this book. From these artists one can move onto a study of artists such as the Brueghels, Hieronymous Bosch, Lucas Cranach, Hans Holbein, Albrecht Altdorfer, Hans Baldung and other Northern European artists.

*

One of the most celebrated aspects of Early Netherlandish or Flemish painting is its heartfelt, intense religious emotion. It is this aspect that interests us in this book. The new æsthetic vision of Early Netherlandish art was later applied to still life paintings, satires, landscapes, seascapes and portraits, but it is the religious works with which we are concerned here. Michelangelo's famous statement pinpoints the depth of devout feeling found in so much of Early Netherlandish art. Even art historians such as Bernhard Berenson, who should know better, denigrate, as Michelangelo did, Early Netherlandish painting. Astonishingly, after acknowledging the painterly technique of the Flemish painters, and how far in advance of anyone in Tuscany they were, Berenson states: 'yet the bulk, if not the whole, of Flemish painting, to the extent that it is not touched by Florentine influences, is important only as Imitation and Illustration.' (1960, 175) Early Netherlandish painting is not nor ever was mere 'illustration' or 'imitation'. It is in every way the equal, and often the superior art form, to Italian Renaissance painting. Bernhard Berenson's criticisms of Early Netherlandish art are not confined to that particular art historian – his reluctant, somewhat grudging acknowledgement of Early Netherlandish art can be discerned in other art critics. Berenson, though, does astonish with his generalized statements about Early Netherlandish painting, such as this: '[t]he trouble with Northern painting was that, with all its qualities, it was not founded upon any specifically artistic ideas.' (ib., 176)

Early Netherlandish Painting

*

The new vision of Northern European painting which flourished in the 15th century was a combination of a new æsthetic approach to reality and an intensifying of religious fervour. The new vision aimed at realism, sculptural accuracy, a naturalistic use of lighting, and three dimensionality. Mixed with the new use of oil paint, the new vision gave the art of Philip the Good's reign a special flavour and style well suited to the circumscription of devout religious truths. The new painting style inherited its jewel-like brilliancy partly because many painters were first trained as goldsmiths. This skilled handling of metalwork and miniature illustration shows in Early Netherlandish art (C. Eisler, 1989, 13f). All the Early Netherlandish paintings were made on wood panels (Whinney, 24) and painted from light to dark in thin glazes. It is partly this subtle glazing which gives Early Netherlandish painting its glorious luminescence. The Early Netherlandish artists exploited the effects of different hues and thicknesses of glazes of oil paint, controlling how the glazes reflected light.[3]

The artistic centres included Antwerp, Ghent, Bruges, Brussels, Utrecht, Delft and Tournai. The Early Netherlandish painters, like their Italian Renaissance counterparts, were working for wealthy patrons, merchants, ducal functionaries and bankers, the new bourgeoisie of Renaissance Europe. It was partly the increase in material wealth and secular power which encouraged the two great renascences in art in Flanders and Italy. The commissions for panel paintings grew as the new middle class of merchants increased in size and influence: panels, though, were not the only highly prized badges of status: gold and jewellry, illuminated manuscripts, and, most coveted of all, sets of tapestries were also cherished. All these luxury consumer goods are found in Early Netherlandish paintings: the paintings themselves glitter with depictions of expensive carpets, tapestries, costumes, jewels, books, windows, colonnaded interiors; the paintings as objects are also as showy as Italian Renaissance paintings.

The Early Netherlandish artists, however, lacked the Classical models of the Mediterranean countries, and the Early Netherlandish painters subsequently became introspective and subjective. The paintings were expensive, they were a form of conspicuous consumption. Many of them were small panels, diptychs and triptychs, made for private use, to be set in an alcove or niche, easily accessible for daily prayer. Some of the public sacred works were massive altarpieces, for churches.

II

Mysticism and Art in Mediæval Northern Europe

EARLY NETHERLANDISH PAINTINGS were created in a world of intense religious feeling. The 14th century, as Rufus Jones notes, saw 'the greatest wave of mystical religion that has ever appeared in any one period of Christian history'.[2] The mystics of the mediæval era include Meister Eckhart (*c.* 1260-1328), Jan van Ruysbroeck (1293-1381), Henry Suso (*c.* 1295-1366), Johann Tauler (*c.* 1300-1361), Nicholas of Cusa (1401-1464), Thomas à Kempis (1379-1471) and British mystics such as Richard Rolle (*c.* 1300-1349), Margarery Kempe (*c.* 1373-1440), Julian of Norwich (*c.* 1342-1420) and the author of *The Cloud of Unknowing*.

The two great mystics of mediæval times were Ruysbroeck and Eckhart: they expounded the *via negativa*, a devout approach to the Godhead through quiet interior lucubration. Meister Eckhart's austere form of God-intoxicated mysticism postulated a Godhead beyond the God of religion, with Whom the soul desires union. Eckhart's methodology of mysticism had much in common with Buddhism, even though the goal is different.[3] Eckhart spoke of the need to 'sink down eternally from nothingness to nothingness.'[4]

Jan van Ruysbroeck also spoke in negative terms of the way towards living a 'superessential life'. He wrote of emptying the self of images. Yet Ruysbroeck's greatest writing concerns love: the soul's love of God, and God's love for the human soul. It suffuses all his prose, most markedly in *The Adornment of the Spiritual Marriage*. Here, Ruysbroeck describes the soul's desire for a mystical union with God, which traditionally occurs during ecstasy.5 Ruysbroeck, though, is one of the most brilliant poets of mystical love: it is never cloying, but always authentic and serious:

> *These two spirits, that is, our own spirit and the Spirit of God, sparkle and shine one into the other, and each shows the other its face. This makes each of the spirits yearn for the other in love... This makes the lovers melt into each other.*6

This is the sort of intense faith and love that lies behind Northern European culture. It is the religious fervour that informs much of Early Netherlandish painting. It is a quiet, interiorized way of relating to the Divine. The emphasis is on silence, tranquillity and devotion seen through ever-darkening glazes of umbrageous oils. Northern European paintings have affinities with the great cathedrals of the era: Chartres, Rheims, Freiburg, Ely, Prague, Orvieto, Rouen and Canterbury.

※

There is a feminine discourse of Early Netherlandish art, which is apparent in the images of 'female' symbols (niches, vessels, bowls and other vulvic shapes). Churches and cathedrals are associated with wombs and motherhood (E. Male, 231-266). One speaks of 'Mother Church'. The Virgin Mary is sometimes shown as a 'Madonna della Misericordia', sheltering a flock of humanity under Her cloak. Often, in Early Netherlandish painting, the Madonna stands in the Church building itself, or in front of a portal or doorway. This type of Madonna painting occurs in the art of Rogier van der Weyden, Jan Gossaert, Gerard David, Jan van Eyck and Hans Memling.

In placing the Virgin Mary inside a Church the Early Netherlandish painters were combining many forms of symbolism, dealing with vessels, wombs, 'feminine mysteries', earth magic and the cosmic cycles of a fecund Goddess.⁷ The Goddess inside the Church is a female deity inside a female deity, a series of layers of 'feminine' divinity, like Chinese boxes or Russian dolls. The Madonna-in-a-Church pictures by Jan van Eyck, Rogier van der Weyden, Hans Memling *et al* recall the prehistoric mounds or tombs of Old Europe. In the mediæval cathedral or the megalithic monument a symbolic complex of earth-womb-tomb is explored. The mediæval cathedral is a key religious site, like the Bronze Age stone circle or the Egyptian Pyramids, where the fundamental experiences of life are ritualized and sacralized: birth, love, marriage, death. The Virgin Mary standing in the mediæval cathedral or church in Early Netherlandish paintings thus unites many symbolic and religious discourses.

III

Space, Light and Aesthetics in Early Netherlandish Art

AS COMPARISONS ARE made between Early Netherlandish painting and Italian Renaissance painting, some contrasts emerge which art critics refer to from time to time:

South	North
Catholic	Protestant
light	dark
ideal/ism	real/ism
Classical	personal
exterior scenes	interior scenes

Few Italian Renaissance painters were as dark, tonally, as the Early Netherlandish painters (Jan van Eyck, Rogier van der Weyden, Hans Memling, Quentin Massys, Gerard David). Even though they employ dark tones at times, the Quattrocento painters (Masaccio, Angelico, Masolino, Pisanello, Gentile, Sassetta, Domenico), are still all lightness and airiness. In Early Netherlandish painting (of 1400-1450) there is a darkness which produces rounded forms: in the Master of Flémalle/ Robert Campin's *Madonna* (London), or Rogier van der Weyden's *Madonna and Child*

Early Netherlandish Painting

Standing in a Niche (Vienna) or Jan van Eyck's *Madonna of Chancellor Rolin,* of *c.* 1435.

The space of Early Netherlandish painting is quite different from that of Early Italian Renaissance art. While painters such as Masaccio and Bellini strived for the sense of a painting being a visual extension of the interior of the church, with their elaborate simulations of church apses and niches, the Early Netherlandish painters seemed to be replicating the domestic interior. As with *trompe l'oeil* ceilings of the Baroque era, the aim of much of Renaissance art was to produce the illusion that the spectator was in the same space as the holy figures. Sacred and secular merge: the viewer is included in the same 'working space' of the painting, as Frank Stella suggests. The 'working space' of Early Netherlandish art was not so much the church as the house; not the bright, airy Classical landscape of Italian Renaissance painting, but the dark, enclosed space of Northern European interior and landscapes. John White, discussing the early Flemish sense of space, speaks of the

> *development and exploitation of the true interior as the most popular element in the new art. It is in the interior that the distortions that accompany any synthetic system are most acute and the pressure to use an 'artificial' method at its strongest. This is particularly so when, as is habitually the case with Jan van Eyck, the rectilinear frame itself is being incorporated in the design as an actual window, often of imitation marble.*
> (233)

The Early Netherlandish painters depict people as flesh and blood humans, with all the blemishes and idiosyncrasies that real people have. Italian Renaissance painting is much more idealized, smoothing over blemishes, making people look wonderful. The Early Netherlandish painters emphasized the individual personality of the figures. The faces in Early Netherlandish painting are so expressive, so full of emotion. Of course, Italian Renaissance artists painted real people, used real people as models for their images. Some, like Andrea del Sarto and Fra Filippo Lippi, used their wives and lovers as models for the Virgin Mary. Yet there is always a powerful idealization at work in Italian Renaissance painting. In Early Netherlandish art, the idealization is put into the emotions, into the spiritual feeling of the scenes depicted.

The 'realism' of Early Netherlandish painting creates a tension between realism and deism, between figurative, material depictions in oil paint, and the abstractions of divine presences. In Early Netherlandish art, divinity has a very 'real', palpable presence. The Madonnas and Christs of Early Netherlandish painting look like 'real people'. The Madonnas sit in real rooms, on real furniture. Early Netherlandish art purveys a realistic, domestic, even mundane vision of the divine. It is as if one could turn a corner in one of those cobbled Flemish streets and come across the Virgin Mary in some dimly lit interior. She really seems to be there, whereas in Italian Renaissance art, the Madonna is untouchable, distant, idealized, aloof.

It's the same with the enclosed gardens of Renaissance art, or the landscapes, or the cities. Each element has a symbolic component (the enclosed garden symbolizing the Virgin Mary's virginity) as well as a pictorial function. But the cities of Early Netherlandish art looked definitely lived in, distinctly realistic. They are not anonymous cities, not mere backdrops, they are actual places, lovingly painted (see the walled garden and town behind the *sacra conversazione* of Gerard David's London *The Virgin and Child with Saints and Donor*). The city in the background of so many Renaissance landscapes signifies culture, the presence of culture and humanity in Nature. Even in the countryside, seemingly uncontrolled by people, there are always people. So, the city is always there, in the background of the Renaissance painting. The Early Netherlandish painters explored the relation between inside and outside, between inner, psychological space and outer, public space. One of their trademarks is the domestic interior, which is treated in an anecdotal, personal fashion, which works against as well as with the regal, divine figures who inhabit them. It's one of the delights of Renaissance art to see holy personages such as the Virgin Mary and Jesus standing in distinctly 'everyday', 'realistic' Flemish and Florentine interiors, as they've just called round for a bag of sugar.

Early Netherlandish Painting

In Early Netherlandish art, we see the deities of Western religion appearing right in the midst of homely scenes. This mirror-like realism (the *vera icon*) may present problems for the modern day viewer. Here is a new vision of divinity, quite different from the traditional, received images of deities in Italian Renaissance art.

NATURE, FLOWERS, SYMBOLISM

The sense of landscape and Nature is very powerful in Early Netherlandish art. It is this love of landscape that would later emerge with the rise of landscape painting as a major art form, which was partly the expression of an increasing secularization. The Madonnas and Christs faded into the background of the pictures, and the landscape itself took over. Indeed, landscape painting itself grew out of the use of flowers in the foreground of Madonna paintings in Flanders. In Early Netherlandish art there is a wealth of symbolism in the landscapes, in motifs such as the *hortus conclusus* or enclosed garden, and especially in floral symbolism. The flowers of Early Netherlandish painting underline the meanings of the scene, modulating the action. Set in a Madonna painting, flowers suggest the ancient connections between women, female power, the Earth, Nature, the cycles of time and seasons, the realms of growth, love and death. Flowers appear in images of the Crucifixion, Nativity, Annunciation, Assumption, Pietà, and so on. In Madonna pictures, the Madonna becomes the Goddess of Flowers, who presides over vegetation, nourishment, growth and other 'feminine mysteries'. The Goddesses of ancient mythology expressed a *participation mystique* with Nature and the Earth. The Earth-Goddess is the ruler of life essentials such as food, sexuality, Nature, and the deepest 'feminine' mysteries are symbolized by the transformation of the Earth.[1] The Virgin Mary as in Her aspect as Mother

Earth is a symbolic continuation of the pre-Classic Corn Goddess.[2]

Flowers that are associated with the Virgin Mary include roses (the Occidental equivalent of the Eastern lotus), lilies, violets, carnations, irises, columbines, poppies and anemones. The symbolism of the rose is easily apprehended (She is the heavenly rose, the Mystic Rose, in eternal bloom; red = blood of Christ; petals as female genitals; the enclosed garden was called the Rose Garden, etc). The lily also suggests, like the rose, royalty and purity – and also peace and innocence. The lily is the symbol of all Virgin-Goddesses (J.C. Cooper, 68, 98), and makes an obligatory appearance in all *Annunciation* paintings (it also symbolized the Immaculate Conception). Some of Leonardo da Vinci's most elaborate drawings were studies of the *lilium candidum* or Madonna lily. The iris is sometimes confused with the lily (its other name is 'sword lily' [J. Hall, 162]). St Bridget said that the iris 'surpassed all other flowers… or the greatly blessed Queen of Heaven surpasses every creature in majesty and might.'[3] The violet is a symbol of humility, and is typically found in *Adoration of the Magi* paintings, while the carnation is a symbol of betrothal, and can be seen in the background of some Flemish *Annunciations* (J. Hall, 323, 57). The colours of flowers also have meanings. The blue flower, for instance, is a 'legendary symbol of the impossible' (J. Cirlot, 110). Some of the plants in Early Netherlandish paintings were medicinal herbs.

The Early Netherlandish painters made finely wrought floral symbolism their own: the flowers became one of the distinctive features of an Early Netherlandish painting. Hans Memling, Robert Campin, Gerard David, Rogier van der Weyden, Joos van Cleve and many others used flowers to symbolize aspects of the personages in their paintings. In Rogier van der Weyden's *Madonna Enthroned* (discussed below) we find columbines, carnations and irises. Bernard van Orley's *The Rest on the Flight to Egypt* (Thyssen-Bornemisza) offered a good opportunity, as usual, for floral symbolism. The painter places five red carnations in the landscape which perhaps allude to the five wounds of Christ.

The Madonna portrayed in an enclosed garden is a development of the symbolism of the *hortus conclusus* of mediæval mythology. The Rose Garden or 'Garden of Love' is associated mythopoeically with the troubadours, courtly love, Ovid, mediæval erotic art and Classical mythology.[1] Traditionally, the Garden of Love was presided over by the Goddess of Love, Venus. During the Early Renaissance, the Virgin Mary took Venus's place (P. Watson, 82f). The mediæval *hortus conclusus* was celebrated in vernacular poetry, associated with myths such as Diana turning Actaeon into a stag. In the Christian transformation of secular mediæval imagery, the sexual discourse of the Garden of Love was turned into something chaste and virginal. Mary's virginal body was associated with Paradise, which was a holy space untainted by earthly sins. One aspect of the vernacular or earthly Rose Garden was kept in Christian symbolism: Mary was not only the Mother but also the lover of Jesus. In the enclosed garden Mary waited with Her retinue of 'sisters' or virgins, like a bride waiting for her spouse. For Mary is also Christ's bride, as well as His Mother. In the *hortus conclusus*, then, the Virgin Mary retained some of the sexual connotations of the Goddess of Love, Venus.

The Garden of Love typically features a lawn, a fountain (Mary was the *fons signatus*, the sealed fountain, of the *Song of Songs*), trees, walls and a profusion of flowers and plants. Here the Lady tames the wild, milk-white unicorn, a scene of so many mediæval tapestries and illuminations (most famous perhaps are the exquisite *La Dame à la Licorne* tapestries in the Musée Cluny in Paris).[5] The Jan van Eyck *Adoration of the Mystic Lamb* in *The Ghent Altarpiece* is a form of the mediæval Rose Garden, as is the scene depicted in Sandro Botticelli's mysterious *Primavera* (P. Watson, 113, 129).

The tree is also a part of floral and plant symbolism, and in seemingly 'innocent', Paradisal *Madonna and Child* paintings the tree looks forward towards the Cross. The symbolic links between trees and Christ's Cross are well-known. Piero della Francesca's great fresco cycle in Arezzo celebrates the passages of the 'true Cross' from the days of Adam to Jesus. The deeper meaning of the symbolic identification of the Cross and the tree is feminine. The tree is Nature, and Christ is crucified on Nature, on

Mother Nature. The Cross is the maternal presence: Christ is crucified on the body of His Mother.⁶

Gerard David's *The Virgin and Child with Saints and Donor* in London's National Gallery (a painting as equally mysterious as Botticelli's *Primavera*) is set in a Flemish version of a mediæval Garden of Love, with Bruges behind the walled garden. On the far side of the throne are lilies and irises. The soft Flemish illumination picks out the minute detail of the plants.

Often the Madonna was shown sitting amongst virginal companions. This was called the *Virgo inter Virgines*, and was popular in Bruges around 1500. Early versions showed the virgins in an enclosed garden. In later pictures, the Madonna is enthroned and the virgins become participants in an Italian-type *sacra conversazione*. The saints included in the *Virgo inter Virgines* paintings are typically Mary Magdalene, St Catherine, St Barbara and St Elizabeth. The *Virgo inter Virgines* pictures depicted a sisterhood, a counter-balancing to the brotherhoods which dominate Western art. There is also a sexism at work here, these virginal (pre-sexual, pre-marital) women are assigned particular modes of existence, particular tasks, often of a domestic nature (sewing, for instance). While men in their brotherhoods are shown fighting, debating solemnly in councils, and so on, women are shown doing the mundane, everyday domestic tasks. The very name 'virgin' defines these women in (hetero)sexual terms. They are shown as incomplete vessels waiting to be filled by holy maleness. Mary Herself is the ultimate Virgin, never fulfilled until She is full of God's Holy Word or Seed, never complete until She has borne and nurtured the Holy Child. The virgins are allowed to be seen in a sisterly way in the same space because of their sexual abstinence. Their non-sexual involvement defines them as pure enough to be seen in the same enclosed garden as the Queen of virgins, the Madonna. It may seem odd, then, that the sacred prostitute, Mary Magdalene, is allowed to be in the *Virgo inter Virgines* pictures. Presumably she is there in a pre-sexual capacity, before she became a whore.

The women in the *Virgo inter Virgines* paintings are involved in slight but symbolic gestures: St Dorothea might be offering Christ a flower; St Catherine might be reading, or fingering a ring (alluding to her mystic marriage with Christ); the Magdalene will hold her jar of ointment.

Some paintings of the *Virgo inter Virgines* theme are more like *sacra conversazione* images than enclosed gardens (for example, paintings by the Master of the Lucia Legend and the Master of the Ursula Legend).[7] Their *Virgo inter Virgines* look like the *sacra conversaziones* of Giovanni Bellini, Andreas Mantegna or Gerard David. They are silent, hermetically sealed worlds. Nothing is said, and no one looks at the others. In the Master of the St Lucy Legend's *Madonna and Child with Female Saints* (Brussels) there are eleven virgins surrounding the Madonna. One might think there might be some words spoken by the fifteen people in the painting (eleven virgins, plus the Madonna and Christ plus two angels who hover behind the throne holding up the cloth of honour). But no, every mouth is shut.

Another painting of the Virgin Mary surrounded by saintly women, the Detroit Institute of Arts *Virgin and Child with Saints Catherine of Alexandria, Barbara, Ursula and Cecilia* shows the same silence and self-containment, the same series of quiet gestures (ring-giving, book-reading), in a Rose Garden. What the painter is really interested in, however, is not what the saints are saying to each other, but painting as well as s/he can the opulent setting. The costumes are extravagant. The dresses of the two saints in the foreground spill over and flow over the grass which is sprinkled with tiny flowers. The painting depicts natural and spiritual abundance: behind the Mother of God is a finely detailed hedge rich with red roses. Though the other women wear red (one has red trim on her white dress, another wears a red blouse under her dress, there is a red angel above and red flowers everywhere), the Virgin Mary's red costume is dominant.

IV

Robert Campin-the Master of Flémalle

IT IS TRADITIONAL to begin discussions of Early Netherlandish painting with Robert Campin or the Master of Flémalle, then to move on to the van Eycks, Rogier van der Weyden, Petrus Christus, Dieric Bouts, and so on, usually in that order.[1] We will not enter into the debate about the identity of Robert Campin, who is sometimes called the Master of Flémalle. We will refer to the Robert Campin-Master of Flémalle problem by referring to the painter as the Master of Flémalle. One of the Master of Flémalle's most powerful pictures is *The Entombment* triptych (London). What is striking about this picture is the new sense of expressiveness and space, a marked development from the works of the Limbourg Brothers, Melchior Broederlam, Jacques de Baerze, Master Francke and Konrad von Soest. The Master of Flémalle is traditionally seen in art istory as the pioneer of the international style, although painters such as Master Francke were highly accomplished. With the Master of Flémalle, though, we can see the Gothic style of the mediæval world being modernized into a Renaissance conception of space and spirituality.

Early Netherlandish Painting

THE ENTOMBMENT TRIPTYCH

The Entombment Triptych achieves this new sophistication. While the background is as flat as in Byzantine icon painting, the figures lowering Christ into the sepulchre possess a new roundedness and expressivity. In Tournai the Master of Flémalle seems to have effected a new direction in painting. While passages in his paintings can seem crude (such as in his *Nativity* of *c.* 1420, in Dijon, or that tilted perspective in the *Annunciation*, New York), there is no denying the emotional power of his work. Paintings such as *The Dying Thief* (see below) and *The Trinity* (Frankfurt) have a sculptural plasticity which would make Michelangelo jealous. These innovations occurred in the 1420s and 30s, some 60 or 70 years before the Renaissance painters of Italy achieved similar volumetric and spatial sophistication.

THE THIEF ON THE CROSS

The Master of Flémalle's *Thief on the Cross* (Staedel Institute, Frankfurt), a wing of a lost altarpiece, is one of those portrayals of anguished humanity that is a speciality in Early Netherlandish art. The painter does not let us forget for a moment that his subject is torture. The body of the near-naked man is cruelly twisted and deformed on the T-cross, the legs bound and bent to one side, the torso stretched and buckled, the arms thrown back, impossibly, over the bar of the cross, the face frowning in agony, eyes half shut. As so often in depictions of the Crucifixion, the opulence of the onlookers contrasts cruelly and ironically with the naked degradation of the men on the crosses. The bystanders are dressed comfortably and richly, while the thief is in rags, his body exposed to the elements.

Early Netherlandish Painting

THE MADONNA OF THE FIRESCREEN

The Master of Flémalle is well known for his statuesque Madonnas, such as in his London *Madonna* (known as *The Madonna of the Firescreen*). The fleshly delights of motherhood are celebrated here, the Virgin offers Her nipple to the Child Who is more concerned with turning to glance at the spectator. It is one of the more homely Madonna and Child paintings. The Virgin Mary dominates the painting: Her gown flows to the front edge of the painting, to the left and right, while Her head nears the top edge. Behind Her is a fire, just visible: the Madonna is seen here as the centrepiece of the home: She is the cornerstone, the hearthstone, the hearth itself, the foundation of natural energy upon which the edifice of the house of Christianity is built.

THE MÉRODE ALTARPIECE

Robert Campin-the Master of Flémalle's *Mérode Altarpiece* (c. 1426, New York) is full of Marian symbolism (the vase of lilies; the rosebush; the enclosed garden from the *Song of Songs*; symbolic flowers in front of the donors; the hearth; the clear water in the kettle; the Spring garden evoking March 25th, Lady Day; the windows (glass = purity/ virginity); the room as womb, and so on). The space and perspective of the triptych is not unified or continuous: beyond the Virgin's room's windows only sky is seen, as if the room were high up in a tower (another symbol of virginity, just as in the fairy story *Rapunzel* or the Danaë myth), while outside Joseph's window a busy Flemish town is shown.

The central room curves upwards, so that the floor and the bench beside the fire rear up at the viewer. This seemingly crude use of perspective, however, does not detract one jot from the sweetness and power of the painting, which is packed with beauty. Joseph, for example, is depicted in classic Biblical style in his narrow workshop, with the tools of his trade clustered around him. Here the rendering of a man at work seems wholly convincing, based on long and careful observation of people. The light, one of Campin-Flémalle's specialities, is superbly portrayed, fluid and open, conjuring exquisite shadows that far surpass any that occur in Italian art of the same era. In the hearth, for instance, there is a deep shadow, far darker than anything in Quattrocento painting. It's as if shadows had never really been depicted before the time of Robert Campin-the Master of Flémalle. After Campin-Flémalle's deep space and lyrical lighting art could never go back to the pale, rigid lighting of 15th century Italian art. After Campin-Flémalle, the lightness of Francesco di Stefano Pessellino, Sandro Botticelli, Andrea del Castagno and Sassetta seems insubstantial.

V

Jan van Eyck

THE GHENT ALTARPIECE

JAN VAN EYCK is perhaps the most celebrated of the Early Netherlandish painters. When art critics discuss the Early Netherlandish era, Jan van Eyck is often cited as being one of the best artists, as well the creator of some of the most typical Early Netherlandish paintings. With Hubert van Eyck he created the *Ghent Altarpiece*, not the most typical Renaissance painting, but certainly very influential. By any standards, van Eyck's *Ghent Altarpiece* is an exceptional work, one of the great altarpieces of the Renaissance, Italian or Northern. With the wings closed, the *Ghent Altarpiece* is a shadowy promise, a suggestion merely of the greatness inside. As in the exteriors of the Lugano *Annunciation Diptych* and the *Dresden Triptych*, the shadowy statues and *grisaille* figures are closed in upon themselves. They offer a marked contrast to the wonders within. The multi-panel exterior of the *Ghent Altarpiece* suggests a sombre and devout work within: indeed, the interior, with the wings opened, is sombre and devout, but it is also extraordinarily visionary. The figures of Adam and Eve frame the apocalyptic narrative of the upper half of the interior. These figures of Adam and Eve, in these poses, crop up in many subsequent Early Netherlandish paintings. Standing in their Gothic niches, the figures of

Early Netherlandish Painting

Adam and Eve offer a continuity with the exterior of *The Ghent Altarpiece*.

It is no wonder that many Early Netherlandish painters were inspired by the *Ghent Altarpiece*: in scale and conception (as well as its physical size – about twelve by fifteen feet), it is extremely impressive. The twelve panels of the interior, in two rows, present a bold and imaginative vision of the world. In the top row, with the parents of humanity on each side, are various angels flanking God, the Madonna and the Baptist. The facial expressions of the angels have oft been remarked upon, and rightly: for these angels really do look like they are singing, instead of, as is usual, an oval mouth painted on a face which does not connect with it.

The lower row depicts *The Adoration of the Lamb*, *The Ghent Altarpiece*'s meaning is debated strongly, but it is clear that Jan van Eyck drew upon the *Revelations*, upon the Last Judgement and apocalyptic visions of religion. The painting is associated too with All Saints' Day, where 'all nations and kindreds, and people, and tongues, stood before the throne and before the Lamb' (*Revelations*, 7: 2f). The figure of God resembles Christ in his Last Judgement pose, when read horizontally, but He is God when read vertically. The central axis of the whole *Ghent Altarpiece* is indeed the Holy Trinity: God the Father on His throne at the top, below Him, halfway between Heaven and Earth, the Holy Ghost, as a white dove, and below that, the Mystic Lamb. In importance the many-spouted Fountain of Life displaces the Lamb on the altar behind it. The fountain is an inspirational motif here, dominating the foreground of the mystic scene. The gathering of the nobles and saints are kneeling as much before the Fountain of Life as the Lamb of God, it seems. The mysteries and rites of blood and water are eloquently pointed up in van Eyck's altarpiece. Perhaps the only sound in this timeless hierophanic scene would be the trickle of the many spouts of water into the basin of the fountain: the throng, as so often in Renaissance altarpieces, would be respectfully silent.

The painting is packed with symbols: the lamb, the crown at God's feet, the hieratic gestures, the Fountain of Life, the greensward. It is the lower half that is most impressive. Jan van Eyck conceives of a gathering of

Early Netherlandish Painting

multitudes that really does feel 'epic' and of a truly monumental scale, like Albrecht Altdorfer's later battle scenes. The gathering of the dignitaries – the saints, hermits, apostles, prophets, martyrs, patriarchs, confessors and virgins – is highly accomplished, certainly more accomplished than anything seen in European painting before this date (1432). The group of virgins, for example, is an amazing vision of saintly women all bowing their heads before the Lamb. The depiction of the landscape in *The Ghent Altarpiece* is superb, with a wealth of foliage and flowers painted with a lyrical precision.

One thing has always bothered me about *The Ghent Altarpiece*, however, and that is the weakness of the lamb on the altar, as both a physical object and a symbol. It was Ursula Brangwen in *The Rainbow* who complained that Christ as a lamb was simply not a strong enough symbol – she preferred a tiger or a lion. As a symbol of sacrifice, of course, the lamb works fine, but as the centrepiece of Jan van Eyck's altarpiece, it seems a lamentably weedy being. The dribble of blood into the chalice on the altar out of the Lamb's side seems plain silly. After all, this is meant to be the *mystic* Lamb, but no amount of painterly skill on the part of Hubert or Jan van Eyck can make the lamb look spiritually powerful. We are so used to seeing a lamb at the heart of this famous painting, it would be odd to replace it with something like a lion. And anyway, one can wander away from the insipidity of the fluffy white lamb to survey the throng and the setting which is sprinkled with flowers. One great touch was to have the white dove of the Holy Ghost in the place of the sun, so that God becomes the source of all light, both divine and earthly. Acres of critical prose have sailed across the surface of van Eyck's *Arnolfini Marriage*, so we will not discuss it here. Besides, van Eyck's *Madonnas* are just as fine, just as worthy of discussion.

Early Netherlandish Painting

THE LUCCA MADONNA

Jan van Eyck produced a series of paintings of the Madonna which are among the most accomplished of the Early Renaissance. In paintings such as the *van der Paele Altarpiece* (in Bruges) and the *Madonna of the Fountain* (1439, Koninklijk Museum voor Schone Kunsten, Antwerp), van Eyck created that meticulous attention to detail that was so influential for painters working in the era after Robert Campin/ the Master of Flémalle. There are four paintings by van Eyck of the seated Virgin Mary – the *Dresden Triptych,* the *van der Paele Madonna, The Madonna of Chancellor Rolin* and *The Lucca Madonna.*

The Virgin and Child in an Interior, known as *The Lucca Madonna* (Städelsches Kunst-institut, Frankfurt) depicts an enclosed scene, a recess in a rich interior that is created especially for the Virgin and Her son. Jan van Eyck's sense of colour is what immediately attracts the eye: the red dress of the Madonna is particularly vivid, it takes up a good third of the painting, and is the dominant visual element. The red of the Madonnas' dresses of van Eyck's seated Madonnas is emblematic obviously of blood – though not only the sacrifical blood of Christ at the circumcision and Crucifixion, but also the blood of the Virgin Mary. For She is the centre of life, literally the heart (womb) of life. There are many dark folds and shadows in the crimson dress, and van Eyck has, as usual in his art, edged the dress ornately. The Virgin is shown in Her motherly function, offering Her breast to the Child. This primal scene is not the heart of the painting, however: van Eyck's painterly skills are so dazzling and luxurious they overshadow the narratives or themes of the painting. Behind the enormous crimson dress, as thick and bulked up as a huge curtain, is a wooden carved throne and a cloth of honour. Van Eyck proves to be a consumate colourist, and makes the cloth of honour a dark green, to offset the brilliance of the red dress. The drapes, the canopy and the carpet are extremely rich, in design and execution.

There are many passages of paintwork to marvel at in *The Lucca Madonna*: what strikes me each time I consider the painting is the recess on

Early Netherlandish Painting

the right which contains a crystal flagon half full of water and a wash bowl, also containing water. The symbolism of the vessel and the water is obvious, relating to the purity of the Virgin, and to Her function as mother and womb, the container of Christ. How skillfully van Eyck paints this simple brass bowl, the reflections of the window in it, the sheen of light, and contours of it and shadows beneath it. It is the most 'domestic' of van Eyck's religious works, with its incidents evoking a homely scene. The imagery of the water, the fruit on the window sill, the flowers in the drape and the milk and Virgin's breast seem to make this a painting about earthly, fleshly abundance, a meditation on the sensual delights of childhood and motherhood. In short, an evocation of a maternal Paradise. But no, this is a painting with a Christian narrative, like other Early Netherlandish works, so the water refers to the purity of the Virgin, the flowery tapestry to the Rose Garden (more purity and virginity), and the fruit refers of course to Eve and the Fall, to sin and redemption through Christ.

The abundant red of the dress continually reminds us in *The Lucca Virgin and Child* of the immense scale of the Mother of God. She is one of the most massive of Madonnas in the Renaissance, an epoch which specialized in gigantic female divinities. The social – and religious – status of the Virgin is emphasized in *The Lucca Madonna*; Jan van Eyck makes it clear that the Virgin's presence is the most prominent aspect of the painting. The details – of the fruit, the carved lion (referring to King Solomon), the carafe and bowl, the floral cloth of honour – are all subsumed to the Madonna and Her bulky, luxurious red dress. The Virgin is like a solid, ornate piece of architecture – that is, like a church building. She offers Her breast and nurtures Her Child just as the Christ child will later nurture his followers, and the Christian Church will nurture the faithful, just as religion comforts the child in all people. Here the milk of motherhood is celebrated, recalling the mythological phrase *a kid, I was born into milk*. Later, as the Madonna's bright red dress indicates, this milk will change into the blood of sacrifice at the Crucifixion.

Early Netherlandish Painting

THE VAN DER PAELE MADONNA

Jan van Eyck's *The Madonna and Child with George van der Pale* (1434-6, Groeningemuseum Bruges) is one of his most sophisticated and grand works. It is large – after *The Ghent Altarpiece,* it is the largest of his works, some seventy inches wide. The secular signs of social wealth are everywhere apparent in this painting. Not only in the costumes, which are always rich in van Eyck's art, but in the metalwork, the jewels and semi-precious stones, the fur, feathers, flowers, the inlaid tiles and the luxurious brocades. As with *The Lucca Madonna* and *The Dresden Triptych*, the spiritual focal point of the painting is made clear by the dramatic crimson of the Virgin's costume, which, as in *The Lucca Madonna,* overflow the throne and spills over the carpet before Her. This seated Virgin is a type no other painter of the Northern (or Southern) Renaissance could depict with quite the same grandeur and munificence as van Eyck. True, some of Giovanni Bellini's seated Madonnas are suitably regal and impressive, and High Renaissance painters such as Andrea del Sarto and Raphael produced large, noble altarpieces of the seated Madonna. In their works, though, the bravura of the painter's skills tends to over-shadow the significance of the Virgin Herself. In van Eyck's seated Madonnas, there is more humility at work. The painter's talents are still proudly on display (van Eyck knows he's good), but, unlike High Renaissance and Baroque painting, the sense of Early Netherlandish humility and decorum dissipates arrogance.

Some of the motifs of the *van der Paele Virgin* are similar to those of *The Lucca Madonna*: the carved throne, the canopy, cloth of honour and carpet. The space of the painting is one of Jan van Eyck's most beguiling: we become gradually aware of the space in front of the Virgin and Child: the soft carpet inviting the viewer to kneel before the deities as the secular canon does; the space behind the Virgin is all shadows, with the pillars, bull's-eye windows and little arches exquisitely depicted. But every interpretation of this carefully sculpted space, and of the painting itself, is modulated by the presence around the Virgin of three powerful men. The psychology of the gestures and interconnected glances points towards a different, political and social reading from the usual spiritual one. The donor himself threatens to displace the Virgin and Child as the object of attention: he wears a bright white surplice. As with the Chancellor Rolin, the Canon's apparent debasement before the Madonna and Child is a pose. Though appearing to be humble, he is also displaying himself as a powerful, influential societal personality. The corporate character of the painting is not the least of its functions, as with *The Madonna and Child with Chancellor Rolin*. The commissions for these Renaissance paintings, we have to remind ourselves, were not the selfless acts of patrons who wished to further the artistic and spiritual development of particular painters, or for the general edification of the public. They were commissions with specific social goals, and the painter had to work within these givens.

Even so, Jan van Eyck found much to be exploring while he satisfied the socio-political ambitions of this or that canon, patron or church. There is the tender touch of the saint (St George), for example, clad in his opulent, burnished armour: he raises his hat to the Virgin and Child. It is a touch of if not comedy, then certainly humour. The opulence of the soldier, in his full military regalia, symbolizes state power – but he is more than matched as a figure of might and wealth by Saint Donatian, emblematic of the influence of the church. St Donatian, patron of Canon van der Paele's church in Bruges, stands in a grim silence, the wealth of his blue robes, with its embroidered Apostles and gold-brocaded capes, more than matching St George's splendour. A painting such as *The Virgin and Child with Canon van der Paele* offers many pleasures for the viewer: not only the sensuality of the paintwork itself, but there are many religious, theological, historical, Biblical, social, political and ideological levels to the picture.

Early Netherlandish Painting

THE DRESDEN MADONNA

Jan van Eyck's *Dresden Triptych* (1437, Gemäldegalerie Alte Meister, Dresden) depicts the Virgin and Child seated in the interior of a church, flanked by the patron and St Michael on the left, and St Catherine on the right. It is a small painting, about thirteen inches high and twenty one inches wide. It is clearly a painting intended for private devotion. The relatively small physical size of the triptych, though, as so often with van Eyck's work, does not mean that what the painting depicts is small scale. In fact, the church or palace chapel interior, as with the later *Virgin and Child in a Church*, is huge. The usual symbolic equivalents are made – between the Virgin, the church building, and Christianity. Here the House of God is shown as an edifice that shelters humankind. The imagery of motherhood – not only of the Virgin and Child but also the carvings which show a pelican plucking her breast to feed her young – extends outwards from the Goddess to include all of the church, and by extension, all of life outside the church. The perspective of the Dresden *Madonna and Child* is the most dramatic of van Eyck's Madonna paintings: all lines appear to lead towards the Virgin and Child. She is seen in a space of Her own, not crowded in by patrons and other dignitaries, as in the *Virgin and Child with Canon van der Paele*. As with *The Virgin and Child in a Church*, the interior is spacious, with an abundance of light around the Virgin Mary. The Madonna and Child occupy the whole of the central panel: the patron and saints are kept to the side panels, although this is a continuous space, as in many Early Netherlandish triptychs.

The Virgin Mary is another large, heavily-built woman, Her dress is again a flood of red which piles onto the carpet below the throne. The Child is held up by the Virgin Mary for the viewer and the patron. The Child holds a scroll which reads *Discite a me quia mitis et humilis corde* ('Learn from me, for I am meek and humble in heart'), from the Gospel of *St Matthew* (a reference to the Sacred Heart of Jesus).

Early Netherlandish Painting

THE VIRGIN AND CHILD AND SAINTS

Jan van Eyck's *Virgin and Child with Saints and a Donor* (New York) developed the Master of Flémalle/ Robert Campin's structural form of the Madonna with Her Child standing before a richly embroidered cloth of honour in an elegant arched and tiled interior with distant views of garden or town. Some critics have seen a self-aware eroticism in van Eyck's Madonnas: for example, of the Virgin Mary in van Eyck's *Ghent Altarpiece*, a British critic sees a flesh and blood young woman who exudes 'worldly beauty' and unavoidable sexuality (E. Mullins, 28). I don't see that at all. I can't see why this particular Madonna of van Eyck's is any more erotic than any of his others. It's true there is a fleshy, 'realistic' sensuality about the Virgin Mary in van Eyck's *Ghent Altarpiece*, but does this automatically have to be sexual? Or is this a typical response from a male/ masculinist critic? Isn't the Madonna's rounded presence the result of van Eyck's project to depict the world in a full, rounded fashion? Van Eyck strived for a certain kind of realism, albeit idealized: for some critics, however, the attractiveness of the Virgin Mary becomes a problem, because She is meant to be worshipped in a wholly non-sexual way, from afar.

THE CHANCELLOR ROLIN MADONNA

Jan van Eyck's *The Madonna of the Chancellor Rolin* is one of his most successful paintings.[1] Like paintings which depict St Luke painting the Virgin, one adult man confronts the Mother of God in an ornate interior. Like many Early Netherlandish paintings, *The Madonna of the Chancellor Rolin* includes a patterned tiled floor, many carefully observed and recreated architectural details, a soft overall illumination, silent and sombre figures, and a distant view of a Flemish town. The interior is elegant and speaks of great wealth: the elegantly carved capitals on the pillars, the stained glass, the large filigree crown an angel holds over the Virgin's head, the tiled floor, the bull's eye glass windows. The Virgin's robes are royal red, taking up a good third of the picture.

Nicolas Rolin, one of Philip the Good's chief administrators, was a wealthy man, all the signs in the painting are of wealth. A large purse was included in the painting; but was later painted over.[2] The Chancellor is shown in a kneeling position, as is usual with donors. His body mirrors that of the Virgin, visually, although his eyes are not much lower down the picture than the Virgin's – the Chancellor is almost the social equal of the Virgin. After all, donor paintings show men bowing and scraping before a woman. No matter how highly elevated or royal the woman is (whether she be Queens such as Cleopatra or Elizabeth I or Russian Empresses), there must always be a certain amount of resentment. And anyway, it is not so much the Virgin Mary the wealthy donors of the Renaissance bow and kneel before, it is the Christ Child, whose maleness is usually prominently displayed.

In van Eyck's *The Madonna of the Chancellor Rolin* the Child is presented to Chancellor Rolin on the Virgin's knee. She holds him forward, as if realizing this is the boy, not Her, that the donor has come to worship. Yet the infant Christ does not look at the donor: He looks off to one side. The Madonna looks down at the Child, or past Him, to the floor. Chancellor Rolin, too, has his sightlines mixed up: he stares grimly past the Virgin Mary into some remote space.

The painting, as usual in Renaissance art which depicts divinity, is full of symbolic and psychological contrasts. For example, though a hieratic and holy scene is occurring in the foreground, in the background we see 'ordinary life' going on. There is the river, the bridge and the buildings of the Northern European town. There are two people, the gardener and his chum, perhaps, peering over the crenellations beyond the garden. Beyond the pillars is an enclosed garden, symbol of virginity and purity. The Rose Garden, though, is halfway between the divine and the secular. It's halfway to Paradise but it is also a garden, firmly planted on Earth.

The Madonna of the Chancellor Rolin, then, depicts an interconnected series of spaces which run from the sacred to the profane, from spiritual to material, moving back from the picture plane. First there is the Virgin and Christ, then, beyond them, the garden, an in between zone that connects the ordinary, outside world and the highly select, wealthy, holy world of the domestic interior. For the garden it is still within the bounds of the building in which the Virgin Mary appears. But the gardeners or everyday folk look outwards, away from the Virgin and Chancellor, to the city beyond. Perhaps the two figures look away because it is indecorous to stare at the Chancellor kneeling before the Madonna and Christ Child, or perhaps the city simply offers more interesting sights. Perhaps the city is, after all, going to provide more diversions to while away the day than a mother and baby and a worshipping politician.

In Jan van Eyck's *The Madonna of the Chancellor Rolin* Nicolas Rolin appears pious but is in fact powerful and wealthy; he is, as a mere mortal, far lower down the spiritual chain of being than the Virgin Mary, but he is shown as just about Her social equal; as spiritual richness is contrasted with material richness, Chancellor Rolin shows he is not going to give up the latter in his feigned pursuit of the former. Rolin's debasement before the Virgin is a social pose, an act of obeisance that's much more act than obeisance.

Early Netherlandish Painting

THE VIRGIN IN A CHURCH & THE VIRGIN OF THE FOUNTAIN

Two late works, the small panels of *The Madonna and Child By a Fountain* and *The Virgin and Child in a Church* are worth considering in detail. Jan van Eyck's *Virgin in a Church* (c. 1435, in Berlin) is the classic example of the Mother of God set in a Northern European cathedral. She stands, between twenty and thirty feet tall, in an ornate Gothic interior, crowned as the Queen of Heaven. The body of the building and the body of the Mother of God become identical. For Erwin Panofsky, Mary here *is* the Church, there is a direct correlation between the Virgin Mary and the Church (also E. Mullins, 156). It is a visual, physical, painterly identification, as well as a psychological, religious identification. *The Virgin and Child in a Church* is one of the largest small pictures in existence, whether Renaissance or otherwise (it is about twelve inches high). Some art historians blether about the possibility of van Eyck creating a church in which the sunlight comes from the wrong direction: what is clear is that the *The Virgin and Child in a Church* is one of the most accomplished of Early Netherlandish paintings, and unsurpassed in its evocation of the interior of a major Gothic church or cathedral. Seldom have the sculpted stone windows, the vaulting, the balconies, the triforium arcades, the apses and naves of church architecture been so lyrically depicted. 'Its brushwork is so light-filled, the effects so evocative and various, that it seems the ultimate expression of his art' writes a critic of the painting (C. Harbison, 1991, 172).

The light dapples the floor near the Virgin, and is seen, beyond the sturdy pillars of the nave, pouring into the building. In *The Virgin and Child in a Church* there is the pleasure, as in other Jan van Eyck works (*The Chancellor Rolin Madonna*, or the *van der Paele Madonna*), of looking beyond the main action or foreground into corners and alcoves, recesses and other rooms. In the Washington *Annunciation* and *The Virgin and Child in a Church*, for example, one can obtain glimpses of the alluring spaces beyond the nave. These shadowy corners are just as enticing as the space of the main narrative of the paintings. Few painters have such a

Early Netherlandish Painting

mastery of light and shadow, the way light falls on objects and reveals their contours. Van Eyck is the master of light. While Impressionists such as Claude Monet and Pierre Renoir seem to be full of light, often a Mediterranean light, van Eyck's Northern luminescence seems so much more convincing. There is a view that the Impressionists were not light-filled so much as opaque and drab: their broken colour disguised a spiritual flatness in their light. The light of Early Netherlandish art, however, is made all the more radiant by its darks and shadows. The deeper the shadows, the more luminous the lights appear. Van Eyck, Rogier van der Weyden, Petrus Christus, Hans Memling *et al* understands this quality very well: their paintings shine like jewels. Thus, although large portions of van Eyck's *The Virgin and Child in a Church* are cloaked in darkness – from the Virgin's robe to the church floor to the shadows under the arches – it is one of the lightest and airiest of paintings.

The poetic evocations of light and space in this Gothic interior would be enough to satisfy, but Jan van Eyck includes a monumental Madonna, one of the largest, in terms of scale, in Renaissance art, Southern or Northern. The sheer scale of the Madonna, though, is not overpowering: Her size is modulated by Her humble, tender gestures and expression. The richly bejewelled crown, which must weigh Her down considerably, is worn lightly; She holds the Child delicately; Her head is tilted to Her left and Her facial expression is wistful, thoughtful, full of repose, even happiness. She is resplendent as the crowned Queen of Heaven, yet Her self-possession and pride never slip into hubris. *The Virgin and Child in a Church* smoothly transcends the theological and formal problems it creates: the majesty of the conception and execution flies above the symbolic and doctrinal confusions.

*

The Madonna of the Fountain is a small panel, one of Jan van Eyck's small but beautiful paintings. It is an image designed to be, above all, beautiful and contemplative, an object of veneration, which the viewer is invited to adore as sensual in itself: but that is but the first stage of contemplation: always in van Eyck's work, as in most Early

Early Netherlandish Painting

Netherlandish art, one moves beyond the sensuality of the painting, to the mystical experiences or divine figures beyond. The paintwork is not as crisp and as full of luminescence as in van Eyck's earlier *Madonna of the Chancellor Rolin* or the *van der Paele Madonna*, but *The Madonna and Child By a Fountain* has its own power and magnetism. It is an image clothed in softness – the softness of the mother-child relation, depicted here with tender gestures such as the little hands of the Child caressing the Madonna's neck. And also the softness of the objects themselves, which seem to be diffusing into the air around them. The colours are muted, quite different from the spectral brightness of *The Ghent Altarpiece*. Even without the fountain playing quietly on the right this would be a magical picture. Van Eyck depicts another of his glorious landscapes. Here it is a small-scale rendering of a Rose Garden: behind the Madonna and the cloth of honour held up by the angels is a row of roses, and other flowers, such as irises.

The symbolism is of the courtly love garden, where lovers would tryst in the mediæval *hortus conclusus* where fountains quietly played. The erotic, heterosexual courtship of lovers is displaced in Jan van Eyck's *Madonna of the Fountain* by an enshrinement of maternity. The troubadours, *Minnesängers* and *stilnovisti* (Dante Alighieri, Guido Guinicelli, Guido Cavalcanti) sang of the prolongation of an adolescent form of love in some utopian Rose Garden, hidden from the spying eyes of husbands, parents, watchmen and the clergy. In van Eyck's *Madonna and Child By a Fountain*, the exaltation is not of a love that stops short of marriage and child-rearing, but another moment of bonding and softness that pre-dates the late adolescent lurch into erotic love. As the waters of life gently play in the fountain of life in van Eyck's painting, the connections are made quite explicitly between Nature, the 'feminine', and the source of life itself, indicated by the water, fountain, rose, landscape and Child. Even in this small, unassuming panel the primacy of motherhood is forcefully affirmed.

Early Netherlandish Painting

THE ANNUNCIATION

Jan van Eyck's *Annunciation* of 1435 (Washington, DC) has the angelic salutation occurring in the nave of a Gothic church. The dove enters the church (and by implication, the Madonna's body) via the clerestory windows. On the floor are the signs of the zodiac and *Old Testament* scenes, which back up the symbolic import of the painting (E. Panofsky, 1953, 145). The architecture of the setting is as flamboyantly and painstakingly portrayed as in van Eyck's other church and palatial interiors.

One of the oddest smiles in Early Netherlandish art occurs in Jan van Eyck's *Annunciation*. Gabriel's smile is distinctly ambiguous: what for him is an ecstatic occasion (he flies from God's side through all of Heaven and Earth, to appear at the Virgin's side), is for the Virgin a deeply disquieting experience. While he smiles and greets Her with the immortal words *Ave Maria*, She lifts Her hands in the air, in as much uncertainty as wonderment. Max Friedlander said that van Eyck's colour sense was

> *moved alike by hieratic monumentality and charm, by a sense of the abstract and the petrified, as well as the corporeal, the holy and the lively, both idealized and individualized.*[3]

ST BARBARA

One of Jan van Eyck's most famous drawings is his *St Barbara* in Antwerp. Here the identification of woman/ Nature/ Church/ Christianity/ life is made explicit, as in the paintings of the Madonna in a church (*The Annunciation, The Virgin and Child in a Church*). The brush drawing displays van Eyck's unsurpassed ability to render architecture, as well as his talent for evoking a mass of symbolism and symbolic landscape. At the centre of the artistic bravado, as so often in van Eyck's art, is the tranquil face of the figure, who humbly deflects the viewer's attention from herself by looking down and to one side.

THE CRUCIFIXION

Jan van Eyck's *Crucifixion* (in the Metropolitan Museum, New York) depicts the crisis point of Western theology as a horror show. Like Hieronymous Bosch's treatment of the Passion, there are some ugly people gathered at the Crucifixion. Van Eyck's painting is thronged with people. The violence of the act of crucifying the one who came to save humanity is emphasized by the fact that many people are not looking at or considering the three crucified figures. The crosses tower above the mob, but the mob concerns itself with shouting, talking, jeering, grinning. Merchants, soldiers and noblemen ride on horses amidst the crowd and louts. The *indifference* of the herd to the Crucifixion is as striking and brutal as the act itself. Like Bosch and others, van Eyck depicts a mob that doesn't care at all about salvation. They are more concerned with their worldly affairs.

In the foreground, in an exaggerated perspective, however, are the weeping, grieving figures of the three Marys, the Madonna and Mary Magdalene. The social aspects of Jan van Eyck's *Crucifixion* are split into three distinct groups: the women, the male mob, and the dying thieves and Christ. The sharp points of the crowd's weapons (lances and swords) offer a disturbing contrast with the exposed flesh of the dying men. The sorrow and tenderness of the women in the foreground contrasts with the laughter and toughness of the men in the crowd. While the soldiers and thugs laugh and banter, many of them deliberately ignoring Christ's suffering, the women in attendance weep and moan. The Magdalene, as in so many *Crucifixions* and *Pietàs*, wrings her hands together in desperation. At this point in the Christian story, with Christ expiring on the Cross with the spear being jabbed into His side, it seems as if humanity won't be saved because it doesn't *want* to be saved.

VI

Rogier van der Weyden

ROGIER VAN DER WEYDEN is one of the great talents of Renaissance art, Northern or Southern. Like Jan van Eyck, Sandro Botticelli, Michelangelo Buonarroti and Leonardo da Vinci, Rogier towers over other Renaissance artists. Rogier's paintings do everything you ask for from art. They are beautiful, deeply moving, immaculately executed, sensually powerful and full of as much religious fervour and abstruse symbolism as one could wish for. The more one considers Rogier van der Weyden's art, the more one sees in him one of those few artists who are truly monumental, lyrical and poignant. One can return to his works repeatedly and find much that is enriching in them. He is among the highest ranking of artists. One thinks of Leonardo da Vinci, Hokusai, Rembrandt van Rijn, Vincent van Gogh and Henri Matisse in the same way. If one had to pick just one Early Netherlandish painter out of the whole group, it might well be Rogier van der Weyden. True, Jan van Eyck may have achieved greater things, technically, while Dieric Bouts is viscerally dramatic. But the sheer plangency of the emotions in Rogier's paintings, the subtlety and lyricism, the softness and beauty of his space and light, the tenderness of his characters' gestures, the precision of his geometry and proportion, all these elements and more conspire to make Rogier van der Weyden the most beguiling and significant of Early Netherlandish painters.

Early Netherlandish Painting

Rogier van der Weyden stands out also as one of the most religiously fervent artists of the Renaissance.[2] His paintings are the lyrical equivalent of the writings of mystics such as Meister Eckhart and Jan van Ruysbroeck. Indeed, some art historians have seen Rogier as a mystic in himself. Among painters, few made works so clearly devout and humble. One thinks of Fra Angelico, whose works display passionate religiosity, and Giotto, and later painters such as Matthias Grünewald.

THE MADONNA IN A NICHE

Some of Rogier van der Weyden's early works are tiny panels only inches across. One of these really minute paintings shows the Mother of God standing in a niche or doorway. The Thyssen *Madonna Enthroned* (c. 1433, in Vienna) displays the crowned Virgin suckling the red-robed infant Jesus in an oak panel only 5.5 by 4 inches. The work is a fusion of sculpture (*grisaille*) and painting in which 'Divinity is stressed because it has transcended media definition.' (S. Blum, 103) It is indeed a triumph of Rogier's that he can compress as much emotion and spirituality into a little block of wood 5.5 by 4 inches as there is in endless acres of canvas by Jacopo Tintoretto or Giovanni Battista Tiepolo. There is an astonishing amount of information in such a small physical space in Rogier's *Madonna Enthroned in a Niche*. It is a technical *tour-de-force*, in its way no less breathtaking than the traditionally 'heroic' artist's creations, such as Michelangelo's Sistine Chapel. Above the Madonna, over the arch, are painted versions of sculptural reliefs. Each of these is only half an inch high. The reliefs depict scenes from the life of the Virgin Mary, from the Annunciation to the Coronation. Here you have one of the wonders of Early Netherlandish painting, whole worlds in a few square inches of pigment.

Rogier van der Weyden's art has this sense of monumentality and cosmic suffering even on the smallest of scales. W. Vogelsang writes:

> Van der Weyden's art is always monumental. It is aloof rather than intimate, significant rather than pleasing... He knows exactly how to subordinate everything to a fixed rhythm. This is his greatness; none of his many followers has been able to approach him in this. (p.14)

Rogier van der Weyden absorbed the lessons of Robert Campin and Jan van Eyck, and developed their pictorial motifs. In other *Madonna in a Niche* paintings, the architecture has been extended to form a frame around the figure, as in the Prado *Virgin and Child* (c. 1438) or *The Madonna and Child Standing in a Niche* in Vienna (c. 1435). In these Virgin Mary paintings, the Madonna stands at the entrance to the body of Church, whose portals are themselves shaped like vaginas (P. Fingesten, 93-4). Of Rogier's *Madonna in the Niche* (Prado), W. Vogelsang wrote:

> The Madonna is thus seated as though on a balcony in front of the niche containing her own image. In front of her own picture! That moment when the art of painting succeeded in carrying the vision into the depths of the picture and in creating space behind the framework, must always excite wonder and admiration. (10)

The *Virgin and Child* in the Prado is indeed a wondrous sight. Again, as in Jan van Eyck's *The Madonna of Chancellor Rolin* or Rogier van der Weyden's *Pietà*, or the Master of the Embroidered Leaf's *Virgin and Child*, the Madonna wears a voluminous crimson dress and headdress. In Rogier's Prado *Madonna*, the red is all-consuming, overwhelming the painting. The red dress is what first arrests you about the picture, and, after taking in the many delights of the work, you can't help admiring the red costume again.

On this small scale Rogier van der Weyden achieves a sense of regal magnificence few painters of any age could match. Yet, as with Fra Angelico's or Fra Filippo Lippi's Madonna paintings, it is a quiet, unassuming, humble magnificence. The Madonna is sitting quietly, circumspectly. In Rogier's Prado painting the Virgin seems to be deflecting the spectator's attention away from herself and towards the Christ child.

Early Netherlandish Painting

He sits on Her lap, rifling through the pages of some expensive leatherbound book. He ruffles up the pages, treating them in a manner that would make an art restorer wither. Yet, delightful as the boy child is, with his white tunic and cute fat fingers and toes, it is the Virgin's presence which is the foundation and *raison d'être* of the painting. She defers to Jesus – She might claim that any aura She has comes via Christ's divinity. But She does govern this painting, and so many Renaissance images. Such is Her power – the power of the maternal – that She commands every pictorial device in the painting: Her red dress sings louder than the black behind Her or the yellow/ gold of the stonework and arch; She sits centre frame; She is the axis of the picture's lines of perspective, its proportions; the composition conspires to lead the spectator's eyes always back to Her face. Such is Her divine power, the scarlet dress floods out from her body to fill up the alcove, until it is spilling over the sides, like a flood of maternity. The portal cannot contain Her power – as in so many Renaissance *Madonna and Child* images, the Virgin Mary's costumes flows outwards on all sides. The costumes of the Renaissance, and most obviously in Madonna paintings, have an uncontainable *jouissance*, a life of their own, outside and beyond their wearers. Sometimes Renaissance art looks like a sumptuous fashion show, as each painter tries to outdo the others in displaying their gifts for extraordinary, flowing, tasteful clothes.

She looks down, head tilted to one side, watching the boy crease the book's pages. She neither smiles or looks sad. She is not at all a wistful Madonna like those of Botticelli, Lippi or Angelico. There is none of that idealized, wistful sentimentality that one finds in Italian Renaissance art in the work of Rogier, or Jan van Eyck, or Petrus Christus. The emotions of Early Netherlandish painting are of a different order from the painters South of the Alps.

The emotion in the art of Rogier van der Weyden is never trite or silly or misplaced or banal. Somehow, Rogier and other Early Netherlandish painters managed to create wholly believable emotional discourses. The faces and gestures of their figures look believable, exact, authentic.[3] They might not always look like 'real' people (though more so than in Italian

Early Netherlandish Painting

Renaissance art), but the people in Early Netherlandish art look convincing. They are always firmly planted in the painting. They always look like they belong. Early Netherlandish painters developed a series of faces and characters that seemed 'right'. In Rogier's art the faces are especially powerful, especially poignant and realistic. Of course, Rogier van der Weyden has his facial type that he paints many times. In Rogier's women, for instance, there is a narrow, 'weak' chin, and protuberant, heavily-lidded eyes. And often Rogier's faces look wan, white, a little haggard. All Renaissance painters, though, painted 'types' in their Madonnas and Christs (think of Leonardo's early, smiling Virgins, or Raphael's highly idealized Christs). And all Renaissance painters too showed that they could paint real, individual people when they made portraits.

THE BLADELIN ALTARPIECE

In Rogier van der Weyden's *Nativity* (c. 1445, Berlin, the full title is *The Virgin and Child Appearing to the Emperor Augustus and the Tiburtine Sibyl; The Nativity with the Donor Peeter Bladelin; The Star of Bethlehem Appearing to the Kings*), the Child assumes a visionary role as the symbol of new life, a spiritual renascence: He is literally and religiously the coming of new life in the world. The visionary status of the Child is emphasized by His appearance in the sky to the Magi: he is literally a Star of Light: at this level, the painting is both literal and symbolic, emphasizing both the physical and the metaphoric aspects of life. The Child floating in the sky as a star is not such a strange image: it finds its way into 20th century discourse as the child-like aliens of movies such as *Close Encounters of the Third Kind,* and of course the final image of the 1968 film *2,001: A Space Odyssey* is of a huge new-born child floating above the

Earth. The Child is related to ancient deities such as the Star-son of Aegean religion. The floating child, like the flying angels, signifies the inrush of the sacred into the secular world in Renaissance art. The two metaphors – flying and light – are the ones most often employed by Renaissance artists. When they wish to signify holiness, they have rays of light issuing from a head (as lines of light spread out of the Virgin Mary's in Rogier's *Nativity*). Or they have a halo. Divinity is forever expressed in terms of light in Renaissance (Western) art. The other mode of sacrality, flying, speaks for itself. You place a human above the ground and instantly there is strangeness.

Rogier van der Weyden's *Bladelin Altarpiece* depicts the moment of revelation of divinity in three situations. The central epiphany of the *Nativity* is a standard moment of revelation in Renaissance art. Leonardo's Uffizi *Adoration of the Magic* (1481) is perhaps the most commanding depiction of this moment. Rogier van der Weyden's *Nativity*, as with most other *Nativities*, Early Netherlandish or Italian, is a quiet, sombre affair: Leonardo's image is definitely the exception rather than the rule. Rogier ensures that the humility of the protagonists remains uppermost in his *Bladelin Triptych*: every glance and gesture bespeaks humility before the vision of divinity. While the Child floating in the sky as the Star of Bethlehem does not present many problems in the right-hand panel, the left wing features the Virgin and Child floating outside the Emperor Augustus's palace. The Virgin and Child are the point of origin – of life itself – all the lines of perspective in the room converge on them. There is more than a tinge of the ridiculous to this section of the altarpiece, which should be sublime not silly. When the Virgin is seen hovering without the framing devices of a window or a curtain, it is accepted by the viewer as a normal practice. The viewer is quite used to seeing the Virgin Mary flying upwards – most often in the depictions of Her death and coronation. The Virgin and Child gliding about in a *mandorla* is also accepted. But seen through the window of this Flemish interior in Rogier van der Weyden's *Bladelin Altarpiece*, it can look more than a little odd.

Early Netherlandish Painting

THE COLUMBA ALTARPIECE

Rogier van der Weyden's *Columba Altarpiece* (*The Annunciation, The Adoration of the Magi, The Presentation in the Temple*, Munich) is seen by some as 'far more splendid' than the *Bladelin Altarpiece* (M. Whinney, 65), but there is much to commend both altarpieces. True, *The Columba Altarpiece* is a much grander conception than *The Bladelin Altarpiece*: the continuity between the central and right-hand panels is particularly impressive: the central image depicts the outside of a Romanesque church, and the right wing the interior. The arrangement of the figures is proficient, as always in Rogier van der Weyden's work (though not in many Early Netherlandish painters). Of the many *Adorations of the Magi* in Early Netherlandish art, Rogier's Munich altarpiece is one of the most spiritually moving. No glance or gesture is allowed to go astray, as every participant concentrates on the solemn worship of the Christ Child. While other painters allowed some of the participants in an Adoration picture to express joy, or at least to smile, even a little, Rogier keeps every face sombre.

THE SEVEN SACRAMENTS

Set in a huge Northern European church, Rogier van der Weyden's *The Seven Sacraments* (c. 1448, Musée Royal des Beaux-Arts, Antwerp) is a triptych displaying a welter of details and incidents. It was painted for Jean Chevrot, Bishop of Antwerp from 1437-60. The central panel depicts the Crucifixion, but as if it were taking place in the midst of a service in the cathedral (Rogier's church has been identified as Ste-Gudule in Brussels). The theological paradoxes of the Crucifixion occurring in a mediæval European cathedral are ignored. Instead, Rogier creates a view of life that

Early Netherlandish Painting

is rich in human and tender observations. In the foreground of *The Seven Sacraments Triptych* we see the usual retinue of regular Crucifixion participants: the Virgin Mary slumped back onto Joseph, and the three weeping Marys. The Cross itself is huge, but this is not, finally, what dominates the painting. It is the light streaming in through the upper windows of the cathedral that is so striking in *The Seven Sacraments*. Rogier has really caught the sense of light flooding a cathedral, and this beautiful illumination works against the pain of the Crucifixion scene. The implication is that, however awful the Crucifixion is, natural energies such as light will ultimately overcome them. If God is symbolized by Light, then it is definitely Light which is triumphant in *The Seven Sacraments*. The cool light of the painting suffuses every object in it, harmonizing the elements. The light softens the strife and sorrow of the Crucifixion, and modulates the many incidents depicted. However terrible the Crucifixion is (or was) its suffering will lead on, the painting says, to what is happening all around it in the church. People continue to live, and thrive. We see a baby being baptized, boys being confirmed, people ritiualize the sacraments, while others look on, and behind the Crucifixion the priest is shown raising the Host during Mass (M. Levey, 1967, 135).

The Seven Sacraments, like Rogier van der Weyden's *Last Judgement* or Jan van Eyck's *Ghent Altarpiece*, is a vision of a panoply of human life, portraying or suggesting the range of passions from ecstasy to grief, from pleasure to pain. We see baptism, confirmation, confession, marriage, ordination, death, crucifixion and extreme unction. Over there is a new life, a baby, being baptized, while over there a woman marries a man. On the bed, a man dies. Over every act are fluttering, praying, singing angels, flying around the interior of the cathedral with banners. Each of the rituals or acts taking place in the church has its own angel to guard over it.

What strikes one also about Rogier van der Weyden's *Seven Sacraments* is the ritualization of power it depicts (in this case, patriarchal power). We see people kneeling before other people, people being blessed, joined in matrimony, given last rites, etc. The people doing the annointing and blessing and so on are all male, of course. The actions in the painting are controlled by middle-aged men; the women are distinctly adjuncts, not essentials. They help with the baptism at the font, but do not do the actual blessing – the priest does that. They help with the dying man, but, again the male clergy deal with that, and so on.

THE LAST JUDGEMENT

The most 'visionary' of Rogier van der Weyden's major paintings (and also one of his largest) is his *Last Judgment Altarpiece* (c. 1444-8) in the Musée de l'Hôtel-Dieu, Beaune. Rogier's *Last Judgment* is one of the most accomplished depictions in the Renaissance, South or North. The composition is based on that strongest of forms, the pyramid, with Christ in glory at its apex. Christ sits clothed in a lush crimson garment atop a rainbow. The rainbow of the Apocalypse is solid; Christ's robe hangs off it as if it were made of wood. Behind Christ is the boiling cauldron of heavenly light, the gold of the sun and the outer edges of red and brown as the clouds part to reveal Christ in Majesty. As is usual in *Last Judgement* paintings, this is no sweet and endearing Christ of *Madonna and Child* images, or the pain-wracked Christ of the Crucifixion. Here, Christ is revealed as a God, Lord of all He surveys. His emissary on Earth is St Michael, who strides towards the viewer with highly elongated legs. Clothed in white, with enormous red wings, St Michael is about 30 feet high, towering over the humans who inhabit the lower levels of the painting. St Michael holds the scales and is in the process of weighing a soul. What lets St Michael's presence down is the usual elliptical-shaped Rogier van der Weyden face. Simply, St Michael does not look severe and potent enough for the chief of the archangels.

There is no space here for romantic, earthly love, and the Virgin Mary is no equal of Christ's: She is shown kneeling at one end of the rainbow, with John the Baptist on the other side. Unlike *Assumptions* and *Coronations*, which show the Madonna as Jesus's spiritual companion, indeed, as His spouse or lover, *The Last Judgement* is the time when patriarchal power is wielded at its most violent. It is not a 'feminine' moment, a moment in which women play an important part as an intercessor. God, Christ and St Michael are a trio of presences expressing masculine power. Christ is shown as the controller of *everything* in Heaven and Earth and Hell. To ascend to Heaven, one must beg, one must pray, one must prostrate oneself before the Lord. This is what not only the humans on Earth are shown doing, but also the attendant saints and apostles on either side of Christ. No one, it seems, is exempt from Christ's potential wrath. Nothing will stand in His way: He will judge *everybody*, regardless of their former status.

In Rogier van der Weyden's *Last Judgement*, everyone is shown cowering from the Lord in one way or another. The groups of saints on each side are seen looking up at Christ with expressions of awe and fear. Saints Peter and Paul are here, and a king, a bishop, a monk, Jean Chevrot, Chancellor Rolin, a virgin, a princess, a married woman, and the twelve apostles. The conception of the painting makes the possible trajectories of each soul very clear. On one side Heaven, on the other side, Hell and eternal damnation. On the left (Christ's right) the golden Gothic portal to Heaven, on the Lord's left, the rocks and fires of Hell, into which the souls tumble in agony. It is a noisy, tumultuous painting: around St Michael fly four dark red angels, blasting away on trumpets, drowning the cries of the damned. The naked humans are seen kneeling and praying; holding up their hands in grief or supplication; weeping; clambering out of graves; creased in pain; howling. They are reduced to the emotional level of children and madmen by the power of Christ. At the entrance to Hell the sinners crumble together, pulling at each other's hair, scratching and tearing at each other, lips pulled back to bare their teeth, eyes wide in horror, arms flung back behind their heads. It certainly is a horrific portrayal of damnation and pain – only Hieronymous Bosch or Matthias

Grünewald went further in the depiction of hellish suffering. The painting is so boldly designed and skillfully executed, it reveals Rogier van der Weyden at the height of his powers as a painter. *The Last Judgement* has as much religious weight and significance as any other *Last Judgements* - whether by Michelangelo or Fra Bartolommeo. The spiritual force of the work surpasses van Eyck's *Ghent Altarpiece*. The mystic vision of the painting shows the will of God at work in a dramatic manner. Nothing can stop the implementation of divine power. *The Last Judgement* depicts the inevitability of the Christian story.

VII

The Passion According to Rogier van der Weyden: The Descent From the Cross and Other Crucifixions

ONE PAINTING ENABLES Rogier van der Weyden to soar above all other Early Netherlandish painters, and above most other Renaissance painters: *The Descent From the Cross* (1439-43).[1] The painting, in tempera, is housed in the Prado, Madrid, where it is undoubtedly one of the highlights of the museum (no mean feat in amongst the Prado's extraordinary collection of works by Titian, Diego Velásquez, Peter Rubens and El Greco, among many others). *The Descent From the Cross* is not especially large either (220 x 262 centimetres) but it packs a lot into that area. *The Descent From the Cross*, in short, is one of the greatest religious paintings there is. Why? Here are a few reasons.

The painting is immaculately conceived. The composition employs a complex geometry which involves the pentagon, rebatement of the rectangle, forceful diagonals, and a draughtsmanship second to none. The fusion of colour and geometry, restless line and curve, gesture and facial expression is dazzling. The depth of spiritual suffering is focused by the triad of pentagons, and the use of the carefully controlled geometrical structure which has a sublime sense of harmony (C. Bouleau, 66f). Every aspect of the composition is necessary and adds to the central tragedy. Nothing is wasted, and nothing is left out either. *The Descent From the Cross* is one of those paintings that is simply *full*, simply full with the requisite colour, geometry, gesture, tone, architecture and form. It is one of those few paintings that require nothing else to make it a success: you couldn't add anything to improve it.

The composition hinges on the twin figures of Mary and Jesus, as so often in paintings depicting the moments after the Crucifixion. Both Christ and the Virgin Mary are slumped to one side. The Madonna is clearly linked to Her Son visually and emotionally. Rogier van der Weyden takes as his departure point in the composition the legend that the Virgin Mary suffered the same feelings as Jesus. In some *Pietàs* and *Depositions From the Cross* the Virgin's body lies next to Christ's, echoing His slumped posture. Here, in Rogier's *The Descent From the Cross* the Virgin is shown in the act of collapsing, so that Her body mirrors very closely Her Son's. The spectator is invited to make comparisons between Mother and Son, and to conclude that though Christ suffered terribly, so did the Virgin Mary. That the Madonna suffered as much as Christ Himself might seem blasphemous to those faithful who see Christ as *The One*, and everyone else in secondary role. Only the heartless, though, would not acknowledge the terrible effect that Her Son's death would have had on the Mother.

Around the infinitely suffering central duo nine followers move through emotions of anguish and despair. Rogier's masterful composition leads us on a journey, a meditation on pain, moving slowly from figure to figure, outwards from the slain God, then spiralling back to Him. However much the eye travels around the figures, all equally powerful and piquant, it keeps returning to the collapsed shapes of the Mother and Son. Finally, our eyes rest on the face of the Virgin Mary. It is one of the most moving faces in art: noble, exhausted, Her face is streaming with tears.

The critics have acknowledged Rogier's accomplishment in *The Descent From the Cross*, though not enough critics, perhaps, have written of the painting, which deserves as much critical coverage as Leonardo da

Early Netherlandish Painting

Vinci's *Virgin of the Rocks*, Michelangelo Buonarroti's *Last Judgement* or Raphael Sanzio's *Transfiguration*. Kenneth Clark wrote, rightly, that Rogier's *The Descent From the Cross* is 'perhaps the most self-possessed and serious picture ever painted north of the Alps.' (1972, 47) Always with critics there is this notion that however great the Early Netherlandish painters were, they can never, finally, make it into the big league with the big boys of the Italian Renaissance. I think this is wrong: for me, Rogier van der Weyden or Jan van Eyck are easily as rich and passionate and valuable as Leonardo da Vinci, Michelangelo Buonarroti, Titian, Giovanni Bellini, Sandro Botticelli, Michelangelo da Caravaggio, any painter you care to name. Italian Renaissance artists, for example, rarely achieved the level of tragedy and poignancy that Rogier van der Weyden's attained in *The Descent From the Cross*. One thinks of Italian Renaissance works such as Giotto's *Lamentation*, with its weeping angels circling the dead god. Or Botticelli's two *Pietàs* (in Munich and Milan), where the Magdalene and the Madonna clasp Christ so passionately.

Rogier van der Weyden's *The Descent From the Cross* confronts the viewer with a Passion play that is both theatrical and 'realistic', both highly artificial and highly serious. The spectator is invited into a picture with a shallow depth: the participants are just a few feet away from the viewer. One could reach into the painting and touch the cool back wall. Rogier portrays the event as happening in a shallow architectural recess, not, as usual with *Depositions From the Cross*, on some hilltop. As Walter Ueberwasser writes: 'The Descent from the Cross is actually happening, there at the altar, among the beholders.' (W. Ueberwasser, 1947, 7) Rogier orchestrates the architectonics of the painting so that the events have an emotional immediacy. The theatrical artifice of the recess, with its traceries and sculpted devices, might be expected to subvert the trajectory of the spiritual feeling, but it doesn't.

*

Julia Kristeva's reading of the crucifixion is pertinent to this discussion of Rogier van der Weyden's *Descent From the Cross*. For her, the moment of agony in the Crucifixion and its immediate aftermath is usefully regarded in terms of a psychoanalytic feminism:

> *Since resurrection there is, and, as Mother of God, she must know this, nothing justifies Mary's outburst of pain at the foot of the cross, unless it be the desire to experience within her own body the death of a human being, which her feminine fate of being the source of life spares her. Could it be that love, as puzzling as it is ancient, of mourners for corpses relates to the same longing of a woman whom nothing fulfills – the longing to experience the wholly masculine pain of a man who expires at every moment on account of jouissance due to obsession with his own death? And yet, Marian pain is in no way connected with tragic outburst: joy and even a kind of triumph follow upon tears, as if the conviction that death does not exist were an irrational but unshakable maternal certainty, on which the principle of resurrection had to rest.*[2]

CHRIST ON THE CROSS

Rogier van der Weyden's *Christ on the Cross with the Virgin and St John* (c. 1455-59, Philadelphia Museum of Art) is tremendous. So simple, so powerful. The Mother of God weeps before the crucified Christ. She wears a large white gown. Rogier has painted every crevice and fold so carefully, as he always did: crisp, sharply folded cloth, with the creases so precisely delineated. Mary is collapsing, just as she does in the Escorial *Descent from the Cross*. As Her body slumps, it forms a tortured curve, modulating the rigid, straight angles of Christ's equally tortured body. John, behind Her, supports Her as She slumps backwards. She is, rather than Christ, the focus of the painting. There are visual connections made between Christ and the Virgin, in their suffering. For instance, Christ wears a white loincloth, with the folds so clearly shown, which's wind-blown, as in *The Calvary Triptych*. These folds are echoed, but multiplied, in the Virgin's opulent costume. Behind both the Madonna and the dead Christ is a large bright red cloth, a 'cloth of honour', which is slung over a high grey wall.

This diptych, *Christ on the Cross with the Virgin and St John*, is so powerful because it is so simple. Rogier van der Weyden has left out the usual retinue of people and witnesses. Instead, he has organized a portrayal of suffering which reduces the viewer's attention to three people. St John is definitely secondary here, though. His main function is to support the collapsed Virgin. Rather, this diptych is a confrontation between two sorts of pain, two sorts of people. On the right, Christ expires in that heroic sacrifice. On the left, the Mother of God too expires, but in an agony of empathy, of shared suffering. Here the myth that the Virgin suffered as much as Her Son at the Crucifixion is made explicit. Rogier makes it plain that the Virgin's suffering was as radical and as passionate that of Her son. For, set against the pale bodies clad in their pale cloth, are those two large brilliant crimson hangings. These red hangings do the job of screaming pain. There is a little blood shown, running down from Christ's wound in His side, but the hangings do the job of expressing blood and pain so brilliantly.

THE CALVARY TRIPTYCH

In the *Crucifixion* in Vienna (c. 1438-40), known as *The Calvary Triptych*, the Mother of God clasps the foot of the Cross in Her grief. This is a gesture of heightened feeling usually associated with Mary Magdalene (J. Hall, 1984, 84). The crucifixion is lit by a limpid light, an overall illumination that is one of the hallmarks of Rogier van der Weyden's art. Forms are meticulously modelled, their contours are lovingly circumscribed. The triptych portrays a continuous space in which six human figures, four women and two men, stand in a tight, steeply tilted foreground space. This is a painting where 'female' or 'feminine' presences are very much to the fore. Female saints, Veronica and Magdalene, flank the central group in each of the wings. These two saints stand and bow their heads, both of them weeping. The facial expression of St Veronica is especially tender: Rogier manages to capture a certain tilt of the head, a certain sorrowful mood, combined with the subtle manifestation of a youthful woman. The folds and voluminous costumes of the women offer a visual anchor to the emotional interplay of the painting. The four darkened, grieving angels echo these many-shadowed dresses and cloaks. The angels flick up the ends of their costumes like mermaids' tails. They hold their hands to their faces, or throw them upwards in horror. All of this kinetically expressed emotion is taken up finally by the cloth around Christ's waist, which magically unfurls and spreads out into the air on each side. These floating clothes – which include not only the angels' and Christ's clothes, but also Joseph of Arimethea's cloak – give an immensely expressive dimension to the scene. It is as if a terrible wind is suddenly blowing up around the figures – the wind that presages the thunderstorm and earthquake that occurred when Christ gave up the ghost. Indeed, Rogier paints in a crack in the earth just to the right of the base of the Cross.

Always at the centre of *The Calvary Triptych*, however, and set along the vertical axis, is the dialogue between mother and son. Rogier van der Weyden's Jesus is an elongated figure, His arms painfully stretched outwards on the T-shaped Cross. Experiencing the same as His suffering, the Virgin Mary's pose is expressive of intense sorrow. Her hands clasp around the base of the Cross, Her fingers just an inch or two from Her son's feet. Here the spiritual and symbolic meaning of the Cross as the Mother is acutely manifested. Rarely has the mother-son relation been portrayed with such poignancy.

Early Netherlandish Painting

PIETÀ

Rogier van der Weyden's *Pietà* (c. 1450) in the Prado, Madrid, is related to the National Gallery, London, picture (both use colours derived from heraldry and chivalry). It has a cloudy blue sky, a sky with clouds tugged up into cumulus like candy floss. It is a tightly packed picture, with four figures squashed into a small foreground space. Here, Mary's cloak spills out over the grass, flowing under Christ's stiff body. Again, as in Rogier van der Weyden's other *Pietàs*, Mary clasps Jesus very closely, her face pressed against His. Mary's cloak is a mass of folds and shadows, while Christ is a pale, green-grey mass of bones.

The London *Pietà*, perhaps a studio work, depicts the Virgin Mary clutching Her dead son in an embrace that is very much like that of a lover. Her gigantic red costume envelops the dead Christ; it flows abundantly to the left and right of the painting, flowing under Christ's body. The Madonna clasps him round the waist, and blood from the wound in His side trickles over Her fingers. The Madonna dominates this small (35.5 x 45 cm) oak panel. This is very much *Her* picture, not Christ's, nor the three men surrounding Her. It is She who tends to the ravaged God: the men are auxiliaries. The donor prays, a Dominican saint reads a book, and St Jerome stands, his hand propping up Christ's head. But the agony of Rogier van der Weyden's *Pietà* is all the Madonna's: Her sorrowful face is the focus of the painting. As in Sandro Botticelli's *Pietàs*, the face of the Virgin is pressed up against Christ's face, as if their faces at this point were literally merging into one. The identification between Mother and Son is complete. No wonder the rest of the participants in so many *Pietà* paintings look uncomfortable: they are very definitely on the edges of the tragedy. The central relationship, between Mother and Her offspring, is so powerful, it excludes the others.

VIII

Petrus Christus

PETRUS CHRISTUS WAS the major painter in Bruges in the years between the death of Jan van Eyck and the rise in popularity of Hans Memling. Though little is known about his life, Petrus Christus was a highly accomplished artist, the creator of some of the most exquisite Early Netherlandish art. He (helpfully) signed his works, usually like this:

+ PETRVS · XPI = ME · FECIT or
PETRVS · XPI · ME · FECIT · A° · D¹ · 1449

THE LAMENTATION

Petrus Christus painted a beautiful *Lamentation* (c. 1455 in the Metropolitan Museum, New York) which echoes Rogier van der Weyden's *Descent From the Cross*. As in Rogier's work, the Virgin slumps to our left, Her right, the slumped curve of Her body reflecting that of Christ, who lies dead on the ground, about to be covered in a white cloth. The faces are those of Christus' and no one else: softly rounded faces and awkward postures. The heavily-lidded and protuberant eyes recall Rogier van der Weyden (a typical criticism of Christus' figures is that they look 'doll-like' [M. Friedlander, 1969, 14]). Once you get past the 'doll-like' faces and the sometimes stodgy treatment of figures, there is much to admire in Christus' work. The bodies in Christus' *Lamentation* do look as if they are actually there, carrying out various actions: holding up the Virgin, picking up the winding sheet, and so on. The light is beautiful, and the forms are exquisitely illuminated, as in all Early Netherlandish painting. But there is an unreality about the picture, brought on by the inadequacy of the figures. Petrus Christus has made better figures elsewhere, in other paintings. In the New York *Lamentation*, there is an awkwardness about the modelling which the colours and light cannot erase.

The Brussels *Lamentation* (c. 1448) is a more open, extended composition.[1] The central figures remain essentially the same: Christ is laid onto the linen shroud, while the Madonna swoons behind him. The painting directly recalls Rogier van der Weyden's *Descent From the Cross*. What is startling about the Brussels *Lamentation*, however, is not the various attributions it has had, but the figures Christus has added to the sacred central group. The man and the woman on the right of *The Lamentation* look strangely detached from the Passion occurring right in front of them. The man looks sidelong at the dead Christ and swooning Virgin, as if he wants no part in the painful affair. The Magdalene, meanwhile, is placed on the extreme left of the composition, kneeling near the foot of the Cross. She has her hands together, elbows raised, in prayer. This much is as usual in Flemish art, but what's odd about the Magdalene is her detachment from all the other figures, who visually overlap or are connected in gesture or deed. The Magdalene, though, is on her own, and her face is looking outwards, away from the *Pietà* group.

Early Netherlandish Painting

THE LAST JUDGEMENT

Petrus Christus' *Last Judgement* (1452, Staatliche Museen Preussischer Kultur-besitz, Gemäldegalerie, Berlin) clearly derives from the revelatory example of Jan van Eyck, and via van Eyck, from Rogier van der Weyden's *Last Judgement*. Christus' version, though, contains elements which mark it out from other interpretations of the subject. For example, Christus creates suitably macabre monsters to devour the sinners. Although Christus' vision of Hell is orthodox, he still manages to stamp it out as his own. The most startling thing about *The Last Judgement* is the grinning skeleton which straddles the cusp between Earth and Hell. The sinners are literally thrown down to Hell between the outstretched limbs of the skeleton – the journey to Hell is literally through the mouth-womb of Hell, either into the gaping mouth of the toothy monster on the left, or between the legs of Death.

PORTRAIT OF A MAN

Petrus Christus proved his painting skills could match those of the van Eycks, from whom he derived much of his technique. The evocation of detail in Christus' paintings is remarkable, at times exquisitely beautiful. In the London *Portrait of a Man*, on an oak panel, there is much to delight the eye. For a start, the costume the man sports is flamboyant, a rich red garment exuding confidence and wealth. Despite the 'ordinary' domestic interiors, the Early Netherlandish painters made sure they flattered their patrons' vanity by dressing them in rich clothes. No expense was spared in cladding the merchants and bankers of Northern Europe. In Christus' painting all the signs are of wealth: the private chapel, with its lovingly painted architectural details, the man's ring, his ornate black purse, his expensive hat and tunic, and the elegantly bound book he holds delicately in well-manicured fingers.

PORTRAIT OF A LADY

Another portrait, *The Portrait of a Lady in Fine Attire* (Gemäldegalerie der Staatlichen Museen, Berlin), shows that Petrus Christus could transcend his basic 'type' of face. Many of the Flemish painters could do this; produce 'types' for the history and religious paintings, but individuals for the portraits. *The Portrait of a Lady in Fine Attire* is a haunting picture. It has some of that mesmeric quality that Leonardo da Vinci could conjure up so powerfully. The rounded eyes and rounded faces of Christus' usual facial type have been replaced by elegant, modelled cheekbones and elongated eyes. The sitter's look is slightly Slavic, slightly Oriental. The tall headdress occupies a third of the height of the picture, and acts as a dark-toned counterpoint to the brightly-lit face. The hair is pulled back carefully under the brim of the hat, and clipped around the ears, producing stylish, clean lines to the skull. The simple cut of the dress and the simplicity of the necklace accentuates the clarity of the portrait. The dress is ornate but full of simple lines: the dark blue material is edged with a white fur collar. Underneath the dress is a plain black tunic, with a gold pin that holds in place a gauze which is only palely visible. There are only the faintest traces of eyebrows and eye lashes. Only a small glimmer of light in the eyes indicates the reflection of a window in the pupils.

Petrus Christus' painting recalls Rogier van der Weyden's *Portrait of a Lady* in London, and the *Portrait of a Lady* in Washington. Rogier's portrait shows a similar pose; a similar closed mouth, perhaps expressionless facial expression; a similar emphasis on clear, stylish drawing and lines; a similar severity in mood.

Early Netherlandish Painting

Like Piero's *Madonna della Misericordia*, Petrus Christus' *Portrait of a Lady* has a timelessness about it, some of the statuesque grandeur of Egyptian sculpture. The colours Christus has chosen add to the mystery and power of the painting. The background is all in shadow, the pale cream of the plaster on the wall and the brown of the wood are mixed with black. The sitter's face is turned to the source of light, the window, but her eyes slide to the left, to stare at the viewer. The face is softly illuminated, with the shadow only a tone or two darker than the bright skin. The high key lighting concentrates the attention on two natural forms: the lady's face and shoulders, and the white fur collar. All the other parts of the painting are dark. The skin of the woman glows, with an eroticism that is not as chilly as in the Walter Pater reading of Leonardo's *Mona Lisa*.

The sensuality of *Portrait of a Lady* is undeniable: one of the chief pleasures of the painting is the simultaneous sensualism of the painting itself and the subject it depicts. It is the age-old simultaneity of the beauty of skin and of painted skin, the art object as object and flesh and blood. The haughty look of the lady neither entices nor repels: she remains intact, aloof, proud. Her beauty is exquisite – the painter makes sure of that. For that reason, art critics such as John Ruskin or Walter Pater or Mario Praz might praise Petrus Christus for being such a talented painter that he could 'capture' a woman's beauty so dexterously. But this is not at all a painting offered up as a gift of sensuality, like Francisco de Goya's *Maja*, or a Venus by Titian. *Portrait of a Lady* works in quite a different way from the traditional 'high art' nude. The allure is of a different order. And Christus ensures that the sitter's body is not particularly eroticized in the conventional manner: she has a pubescent body, as far from the fleshy bodies of Peter Rubens as is possible. The breasts are small, attention is not drawn to them, as in portraits by, say, Rembrandt van Rijn or Jacopo Tintoretto. Instead, Christus flattens the sexuality of the woman, making her self-containment complete. The woman, who has not been definitively identified, retains her self-composure: the exchange she offers the viewer is not of the conventional model, who offers herself up to the viewer. The woman preserves her sanctity as a person, an object to be looked at. Petrus Christus cleverly maintains a balance between the viewer's desire to look without really wanting to look, and the sitter's desire to be looked at while remaining self-possessed. Certainly Christus' *Portrait of a Lady* is one of the most effective and enchanting of the Renaissance, North or South.

PETRUS CHRISTUS' *MADONNAS*

Petrus Christus' Madonnas are very sweet, gentle beings, like those of Fra Angelico and Sandro Botticelli. Clearly deriving much from Jan van Eyck's compositions, Christus' Madonnas sit in unified, enclosed spaces, their clothes spreading out towards the viewer to form statuesque, pyramidal figures: *The Madonna and Child Seated in a Hall* (Madrid), *The Virgin and Child in a Gothic Interior* and *Virgin and Child* (Budapest). The Budapest *Madonna and Child in an Archway* derives obviously from paintings such as van Eyck's *Virgin at the Fountain* or Rogier van der Weyden's *Virgin and Child in a Niche.* Christus' *Madonna* is a small-scale panel intended for private devotional use. The centre of the image is the orb, symbol of Salvator Mundi, which the child holds. As so often in the devotional images of the Virgin Mary and Christ, Adam and Eve also appear, indicating the theme of Redemption through Christ's Incarnation. Here, the Madonna and Jesus stand between two golden statues of Adam and Eve, and are related to them on each side (Christ as the Second Adam, the Madonna as the Second Eve). The presence of Adam and Eve reminds the spectator that humankind is already 'fallen', has already eaten of the fruit of the Tree of Knowledge. We see the serpent and Adam and Eve guiltily covering their genitals. However, Redemption is at hand: Adam and Eve are statues, lifeless, lost in the mists of time: between them, under the archway, stands the Madonna and Child, two flesh and blood beings who offer renewed hope and salvation.

The Madrid *Virgin and Child Enthroned in a Porch* (c. 1460-65) is related thematically to the Budapest *Madonna and Child in an Archway*. Petrus Christus shows Christ as Salvator Mundi, Saviour of the world, and balances this with the Virgin being crowned as Queen of Heaven. The centre of the Virgin's head is the visual centre of the painting, all the lines of perspective converge on Her nose. As with Jan van Eyck's and Rogier van der Weyden's Madonnas, the Virgin is an image of nurturance and opulence: Her huge red robe spills outwards, enfolding the child and spreading onto the tiled floor. Other aspects of the Prado picture connote opulence: the jasper and porphyry columns, the tapestry on the bench, the marble-panelled throne.

The Exeter Madonna (also called *Virgin and Child, St Barbara and Carthusian Donor*) depicts the figures in an expanded version of the Eyckian interior. Petrus Christus allows much more space around his figures than Jan van Eyck does – Christus' *Exeter Madonna* has a lightness and spaciousness that recalls Piero della Francesca (in *The Flagellation of Christ* perhaps). Christus never achieved the monumentality in his figures of Jan van Eyck or Piero della Francesca. His figures never have that sense of the strenuously serious, weighty presence of Piero, Rogier van der Weyden or van Eyck. In Madonna paintings which rework van Eyckian compositions, such as *The Madonna and Child with Saints Jerome and Francis* (1457, in Frankfurt), which develops van Eyck's *van der Paele Madonna* or *The Lucca Madonna*,[2] Christus uses van Eyck's major motifs and techniques, but puts his personal stamp on the proceedings as well. No Madonna in van Eyck's art, for instance, stares down and to one side in the same strange way as Christus' Virgin Mary. Although the Eyckian cloth of honour is there in the Frankfurt *Madonna Enthroned*, as well as the steps leading up to the throne, the view through the doorway and the saints flanking the holy family, Christus' space is much more relaxed and open.

A more open and light-filled sense of interior occurs in Petrus Christus'

Nativity in Washington. The focus of the painting is not so much the Child on the ground, as it's meant to be, but the complex architectonics of the shelter with its intricate carved arch, which contains figures such as Adam and Eve, Cain and Abel, and scenes from the *Book of Genesis*. As with images of the *Annunciation*, the symbolism of the Redemption is made explicit. In Christus' *Nativity*, Joseph is, unusually, given equal prominence to the Virgin Mary. He is shown next to the Virgin, the same size as Her, and not skulking in the background, as so often in *Nativities*. The appearance of the domestic, everyday, anecdotal aspects of the stable setting are enhanced by the pair of shoes, lower right. They are actually as large as the little Child lying on the golden disc.

In the Berlin *Nativity*, the scene is not at all wintry or Christmassy – behind the figures and the shed is a landscape in full bloom. As so often in Petrus Christus' art, and in miniature and manuscript illumination, the landscape looks like a toy world, a storybook landcape. There are trees dotted about, neatly-cut grass, perfectly-edged dust roads, a fairy tale castle. The landcape speaks of perfection and self-containment, like the enclosed gardens which allude to the purity and innocence of the Virgin Mary.

The two Berlin paintings, *The Nativity* and *The Annunciation*, depict quiet, calm, self-enclosed scenes. Petrus Christus' Berlin *Annunciation* is an image of spiritual perfection.[3] Already, in Christus' image, even before the spark of Christ was ignited in Her womb, the Virgin Mary was a holy and near-perfect being. The room She sits in is swept clean, with neat furnishings, spotless windows, everything in its place and in order. When the Archangel Gabriel appears on the left, he too fits into a specially-made place, the folds of his white robe respectfully echoing the creases in the Madonna's red dress. As with the Bruges *Annunciation*, Christus' Berlin *Annunciation* demonstrates what a mastery of interior spaces and lighting he had. Only the very best of Early Netherlandish painters had this sort of lyrical facility for portraying plastic, tactile space and light. In the Bruges *Annunciation* the eye moves from the two central figure in the foreground, with the vase of lillies at the front (as in the Berlin *Annunciation*), and across the smooth tiled floor, to the open doorway that leads out onto another of Christus' idealized townscapes. Painters in the North Countries would be painting such transitions from interior to exterior for centuries after Christus (Pieter de Hooch, Jan Vermeer).

THE VIRGIN AND CHILD IN A GOTHIC INTERIOR

Petrus Christus' *The Virgin and Child in a Gothic Interior* (*c.* 1457-60, in Kansas City) depicts one of those now familiar Early Netherlandish interiors, all subdued colours and dim lighting.[4] The space of *The Virgin and Child in a Domestic Interior* is one of Christus' most successful depictions. It is a unified space, no section of it looks out of place.[5] The details of *The Virgin and Child in a Gothic Interior* are very pleasing to the eye: the soft browns and ochres of the wooden window frames and doorways, the large hearth in shadow, the elegant hanging candle holder, the mid-green bed clothes and furnishings, the splayed pages of the book the Child gestures towards, the view to the town beyond. What makes Christus' paintings look uncluttered is the generalized treatment of large surfaces. Walls are left smooth and plain, without the attention to blemishes and marks that one finds in the really detailed and highly polished artists like van Eyck or Leonardo. Joseph lurks in the background, as if he's walked in from another painting. He looks a bit lost. The Madonna predominates here, She is the image of quietness and placidity as She holds the Child on Her lap. The red of Her cloak is the primary hue, outshining every other colour. Jesus is one of the few depictions of a child who doesn't look awkward. The distant, smiling expression of Jesus accords well with how real young children will stare and smile.

Petrus Christus' *The Death of the Virgin* (*c.* 1460-65, Timken Art

Gallery, San Diego) is one of his busiest pictures, and one of his most populous interiors.[6] The imagery of European death (Extreme Unction, holy water, a censer, Holy Scriptures, an aspergillum, a candle) are all here. Christus, though, has not just depicted the Virgin Mary's death or Dormition, but also Her Assumption and the reception of Her girdle by St Thomas. We see the prone Virgin on the bed, with the apostles around Her, and this is as expected. Above the bed, though, is another group of figures: on a smaller scale, the Virgin Mary is shown flying upwards, borne up by angels, towards God, Who wait to receive Her.

The conflation of two or more separate incidents is not uncommon in manuscript illumination of the time.[7] What is striking about *The Death of the Virgin* is the lack of female participants. While depictions of the Birth of the Virgin usually have the childbed surrounded by women performing all sorts of domestic and medical tasks, the Madonna in Petrus Christus' Timken *Death of the Virgin* is surrounded entirely by men. If birth is a largely female mystery, even in the severely patriarchal religion of Christianity, death is seen here as very much a masculine mystery, one presided over by men. While women are allowed to supervise and partially ritualize birth and early motherhood and childhood, death is very distinctly a male preserve. No way could a *female* priest supervise a death or a funeral in any Western or Renaissance painting.

Early Netherlandish Painting

OUR LADY OF THE DRY TREE

One of Petrus Christus' strangest and most haunting paintings is the tiny panel *Our Lady of the Dry Tree*. The painting depicts the Virgin Mary standing in a leafless tree, in between the curves of two branches (Christ appeared in trees or in between a stag's antlers). The Virgin wears a blue dress and a scarlet outer robe. Hanging on the tree, like Christmas decorations, are fifteen golden letter A's, suspended on thin chains. The A's perhaps stand for *Ave*, as in *Ave Maria*, the fifteen 'Hail Marys'. The Virgin Mary and Child are brightly lit: the background is deep night, but the gold letter A's reflect the light falling on the Madonna like candles.

Like Rogier van der Weyden's *Madonna Throned*, Petrus Christus' *Our Lady of the Dry Tree* displays the extraordinary control of the brush in painting details that is so characteristic of Early Netherlandish art. As in Jan van Eyck's work, there is a luminescence at the heart of the painting, as if the painting is giving out light as well as reflecting it. Many of the best paintings have this sense of self-illumination (and many unsuccessful paintings fail to deal with light).

Petrus Christus' painting is associated with the Bruges confraternity who worshipped 'Our Blessed Lady of the Dry Tree' ('Onse Lieve Vrauwe ten Drooghen Boome'). Christus joined the confraternity before 1463. The confraternity celebrated two Masses each year, the Virgin's birth and the Trinity. The fifteen gold letters refer perhaps to the Virgin as the source of new life which is expressed through Jesus. The number fifteen is one of the Virgin's occult numbers. Christus was also a member of the Confraternity of Our Lady of the Snow ('Onze Lieve Vrouwe-ter-Sneeuw'). The origin of the name of the Confraternity of Our Lady of the Snow referred to the miraculous snowfall that occurred before the founding of Santa Maria Maggiore in Rome. The records for the Confraternity feature Christus and other Bruges artists such as Hans Memling, Pierre Coustain and Willem Vrelant.

The twin branches form a *mandorla* or *mirroa piscis* (the Latin term for 'fish bladder'). The symbolism is obvious: it speaks of a unity being made out of a duality, and of feminine mysteries again, of the vulva and cosmic womb. The *vesica piscis* is a rebirth symbol, and Christ is portrayed inside a *vesica piscis* during the Transfiguration. He is born through the labial shapes of the *vesica piscis*. Often the Virgin Mary appears in a *mandorla* in paintings of the Assumption. The *vesica piscis* is 'the central diagram of Sacred Geometry for the Christian mysticism of the Middle Ages.' (R. Lawlor, 31) The geometric figure of the *vesica piscis* as constructed by intersecting two equal circles. It was an important element in the architecture of the Gothic cathedral (R. Lawlor, 35). Typically in our Age of Pisces, the *vesica piscis* was winged by angels, as in Andreas Mantegna's extraordinary *Madonna and Child with Singing Cherubim* (*c.* 1485, Brera, Milan) or Carpaccio's *Death of the Virgin* (in Ferrera).

But beyond the symbolism and the occult resonances of the composition, the painting remains mysterious. The spectator takes in details such as the thorns on the tree which are prominent and sharp, and obviously look forward to the Crown of Thorns. Or the golden A's, rotating in and out of the shadows. Or the Virgin Mary's facial expression, so calm and downcast while She stands in a thorny tree at nighttime. And always there is the blackness beyond the painting, an effect that always gives a figure an enhanced, ghostly aura.

OTHER PETRUS CHRISTUS PAINTINGS

Saint Anthony and a Donor (*c.* 1450, Copenhagen) contains some lyrical Rogier-like passages, in the shadows behind the kneeling donor, in the clasp of the bag the donor wears, of the castle in the background. Petrus Christus' panel is small (23.3 x 12.8 in) and has a self-assurance equal to that of Jan van Eyck or Rogier van der Weyden or the Master of Flémalle. One of Christus' most famous paintings is of another exquisitely

Early Netherlandish Painting

described interior, in *Saint Eligius* (1449, New York). The goldsmith's stall, with the goldsmith weighing a ring for the bridal couple, the objects on the shelf (coral, crystal, porphyry, seed pearls, precious stones, beads, rings, brooches, buckles), is one of Christus' most accomplished works. The composition is all Christus' own – that is, it is not derivable to any particular van Eyck or other Early Netherlandish work. There are Eyckian touched, such as the mirror in the foreground on the right, which reflects two onlookers standing outside in the street, but these Eyckian motifs work quite differently from the mirror in, say, Eyck's *Arnolfini Portrait*.

The Man of Sorrows (c. 1450, Birmingham Museum and Art Gallery) ought to be mentioned too, for it is another of Petrus Christus' more well-known works, if not his most representative or accomplished. It shows Christ displaying His wounds and staring directly at the viewer. Behind Him stand two angels, one in yellow-white, holding a lily stem, the other in pink-white, sternly wielding a sword. Here Jesus is the Lord of the Last Judgement; the aim of the work is to incite the viewer to meditate with pity on Christ's suffering, as found in devotional texts of the time (such as Thomas à Kempis's *Imitatio Christi*). *The Man of Sorrows* is also linked to Holy Communion and salvation – the blood flowing from Christ's wound emphasizes the sacrament of the Mass. The composition highlights Christ's wounds, the eye is constantly led back to the scar and blood. Christ is not speaking, but the picture is clearly saying 'I did this for you,' that is, 'I suffered these wounds for you'.

IX

Dieric Bouts

SOME CRITICS DO not rate Dieric Bouts highly. He is regarded as markedly inferior to Rogier van der Weyden or Jan van Eyck. Some critics have unfairly called his figures 'stiff and unemotional.' (P. Murray, 65) True, when you've absorbed the passion of Rogier van der Weyden or the splendours of Jan van Eyck, Dieric Bouts can seem weak and insubstantial. Yet Bouts has created some of the minor wonders of Early Netherlandish art. His figures are not in fact 'unemotional', but, because they derive (partly) from Rogier van der Weyden, they are full of feeling. The awkwardness and lack of finesse in Bouts' figures does detract from the impact his art makes (in the early work, *The Last Super Altarpiece*, in Louvain); at the same time, the 'primitive' drawing and colouration allows a certain rawness of emotion to come through. While Bouts' paintings do lack the accepted high standards of technical, composition and drawing skills, they make up for that lack with the force of their emotional content.

Early Netherlandish Painting

MATER DOLOROSA

One of Dieric Bouts' most emotional paintings is a tearful *Mater Dolorosa* (Art Institute of Chicago – there is a copy in the National Gallery, London). The painting is clearly intended to be an object of private contemplation. The *Mater Dolorosa* image is a vehicle for spiritual meditation. True, it plucks at the heartstrings with its weeping face of the Madonna. There is some bad religious art around today which shows the Madonna or Christ weeping in garish, plastic colours. Typically one sees this kind of art in stalls in churches, often in devoutly Catholic and Orthodox countries (Spain, Greece, Russia, Brazil). There are also framed sentimental pictures of young girls and boys, looking directly at the viewer, tears rolling down their cherub cheeks. The faces exude a tacky, idiotic melancholy. They sell for a dollar or two in main street stores.

Dieric Bouts' painting of the Madonna crying manages to step out of the garish, artificial sentimental images by its 'high art' æsthetics and the force of its execution. Even when Bouts produces mediocre work, as with Rogier van der Weyden or Hans Memling, the results are much better than most other works anyway. Even when they were coasting or churning out hack work, the Early Netherlandish painters were powerful.

LAMENTATION

Dieric Bouts worked in the religious atmosphere of the Brotherhood of the Common Life, a Dutch confraternity which Jan van Ruysbroeck championed in the 14th century. The religiosity of Bouts' is very apparent in his work, as with Rogier van der Weyden. In his Louvre *Lamentation* or *Pietà*, the pathetic sight of the Mother comforting Her dead Son is made even more moving by the artist pushing the figures up to the picture frame, pushing them right into the spectator's space. The Magdalene, again wringing her hands in despair, looks directly at the viewer. This direct stare is unsettling: a sense of complicity and connection is created between viewer and participants in the painting. The viewer becomes directly involved in the painting.

THE MADONNA AND CHILD ON A WALL

One of Dieric Bouts' followers produced *The Madonna and Child on a Wall* (private collection) which displays a 'crude' interpretation of Bouts' 'primitive' style. The perspective and scale is all over the place, and the figures are ungainly – the infant Christ, for example, stretches out His arms awkwardly, looking as if His arms are in plaster. The feeling is there in the painting: the intentions are honourable (though, alas, this is never enough in art). The Madonna sits on a grassy wall in an enclosed garden, with Her attendant ladies strolling behind her. It is an idyllic scene: the garden, the peacock, the swans, the lake and the distant hills. Yet, oddly in a *Madonna and Child* painting, God appears, bright red and gold in a chasm forged out of the great clouds.

Early Netherlandish Painting

THE MARTYRDOM OF ST ERASMUS

Not for the faint-hearted are Dieric Bouts' altarpieces of *The Martyrdom of St Erasmus* (Louvain) and *The Justice of Emperor Otto III* (Brussels). In these paintings torture is carried out with a philosophic detachment that is positively gruesome. Saint Erasmus lies on the torture machine, and nothing seems untoward about that, until you notice that his entrails are being winched out through a slit in his stomach. Nice. The *Justice of Emperor Otto III* depicts a story of infidelity and retribution, with a healthy dose of decapitation, ordeal by fire and the guilty woman being burnt at the stake.

THE INFANCY CYCLE

One of the Dieric Bouts' most successful and satisfying paintings is his *Infancy Cycle*. The four vertical format panels, in the Prado, Madrid, depict *The Annunciation, The Visitation, The Nativity* and *The Adoration of the Magi*. Each painting is framed by an ornate archway with Biblical figures cared into them, à la Rogier van der Weyden and Petrus Christus. The influence of Jan van Eyck, Christus and Rogier is apparent in these four paintings, but Bouts went off into his own exploration of the themes. His conception of space is not as sophisticated as van Eyck or Rogier van der Weyden, and there are startling idiosyncracies of scale – such as that tiny baby in the immediate foreground of the *Nativity*.

The four paintings offer up many continuities of narrative and theme, however, which're aided by the framing device of the doorway. Seen thus, the *Nativity Altarpiece* can seen as a large format *Book of Hours of the Virgin*, depicting those key moments from the Madonna's extraordinary life. The paintings become steadily more populous, as the Virgin's

Early Netherlandish Painting

fortunes change from a life of solitude (before the Annunciation), through the Visitation to the Birth and the Adoration of the Three Kings.

In the first panel, the Virgin Mary is living a chaste, quiet, solitary life. All this is disturbed in the most spectacular fashion by the arrival of the Archangel with his divine message. From that point onwards (and there is no turning back), the Madonna's life escalates in significance, until, in the fourth painting, She is being fêted by royalty from the Near East. Dieric Bouts keeps the essential elements of the narrative to the fore, quite literally, by having each figure take up a prominent place in the area framed by the sculpted archway.

As with Robert Campin/ the Master of Flémalle, one of the aspects of Dieric Bouts' art that keeps it buoyant is his vivacious sense of line and modelling: or, in a word, his humanity. This is true of most of the Flemish and Early Netherlandish painters. In Bouts' London *Madonna and Child*, or in his *Pearl of Brabant Altarpiece* (Alte Pinakothek, Munich), there is a tremendous sense, as with the Master of Flémalle/ Robert Campin, of life being lived, of the pleasures as well as the pains of humanity.

THE LAST JUDGEMENT

Dieric Bouts did have an eye for the epic statement, as his *Last Judgement* (Lille) shows: in the left-hand volet the blessed are seen being led towards Heaven and the Fountain of Life in a post-Eyckian image. Bouts demonstrated that he could depict tiny, detailed plants in the foreground, supple, believable figures, opulent angels, and the broad views of a hilly landscape and a brooding sky. *The Last Judgement* is, of course, not as accomplished or as dramatic as the apocalyptic visions of Jan van Eyck.

Illustrations

By the Early Netherlandish painters, followed by some of their Italian Renaissance contemporaries.

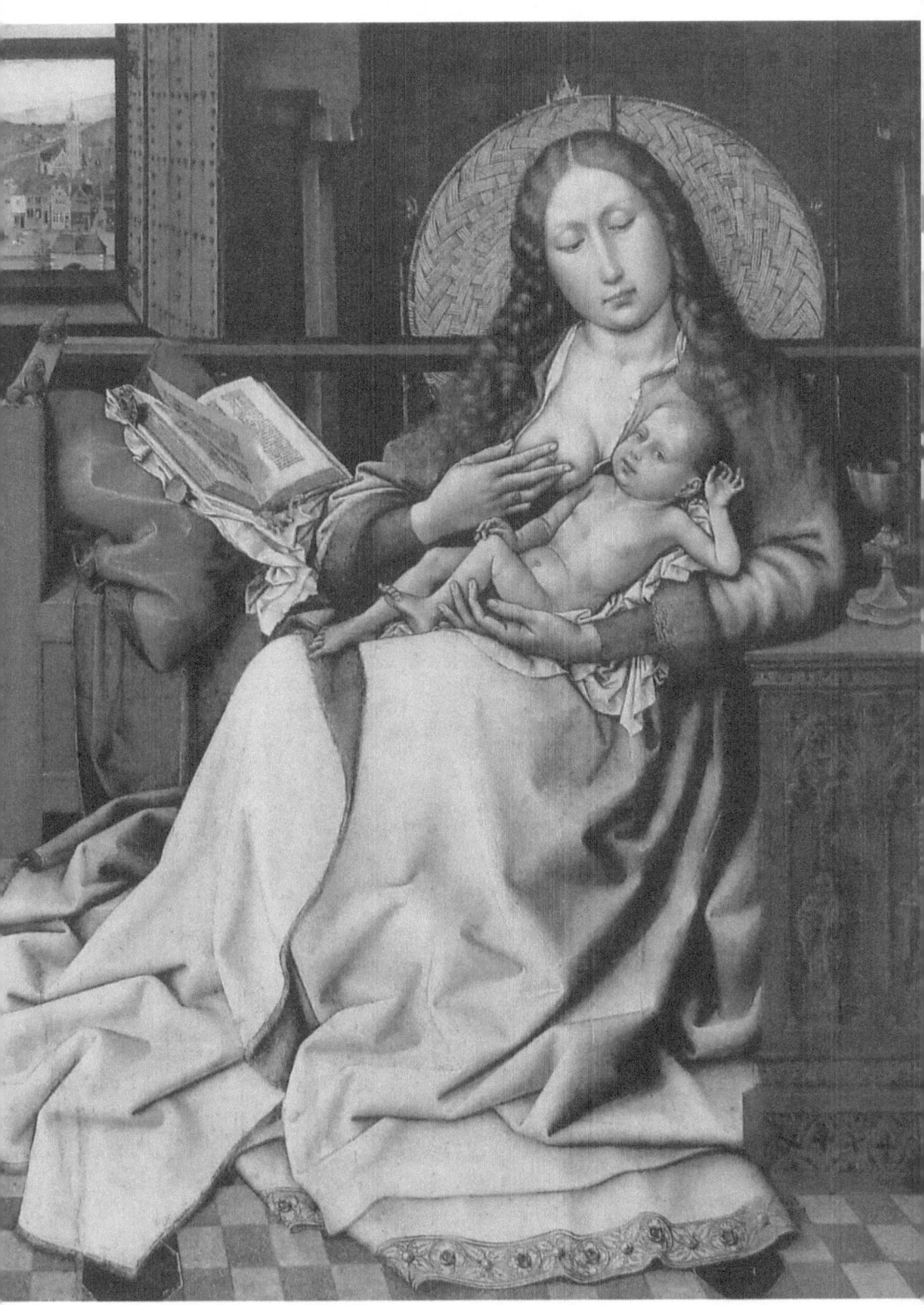
Robert Campin, Madonna With the Firescreen, National Gallery, London

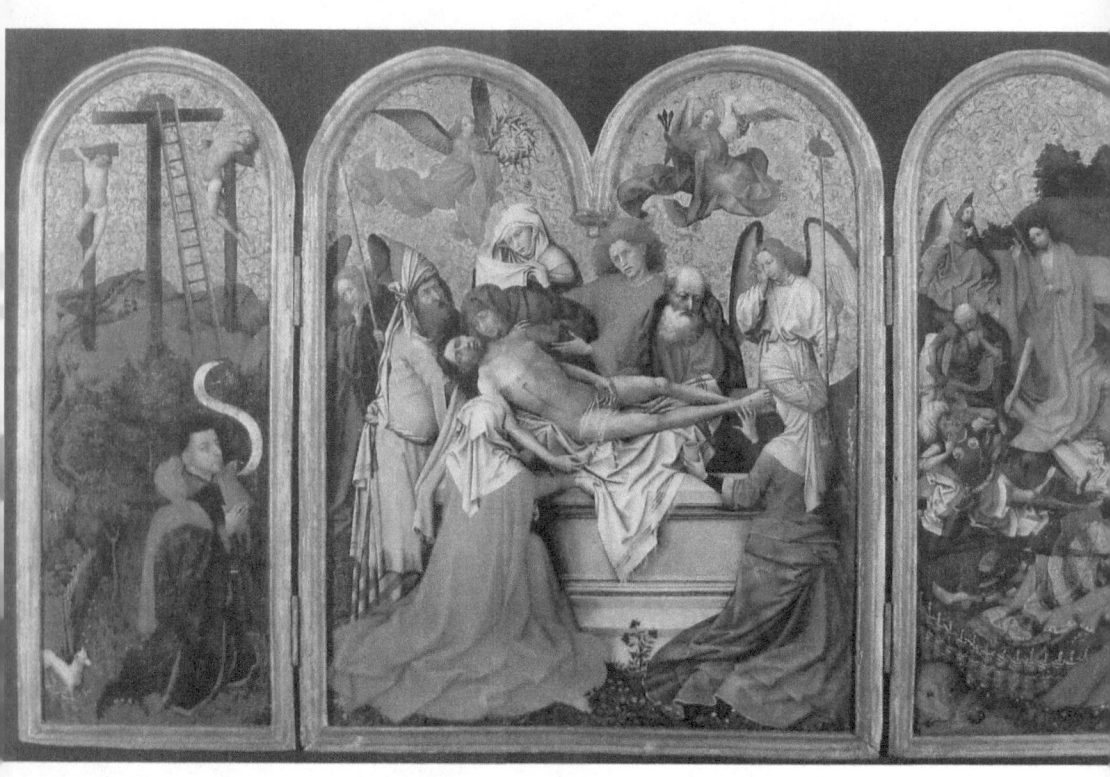

Robert Campin, Seilern Triptych, Courtlauld Institute, London

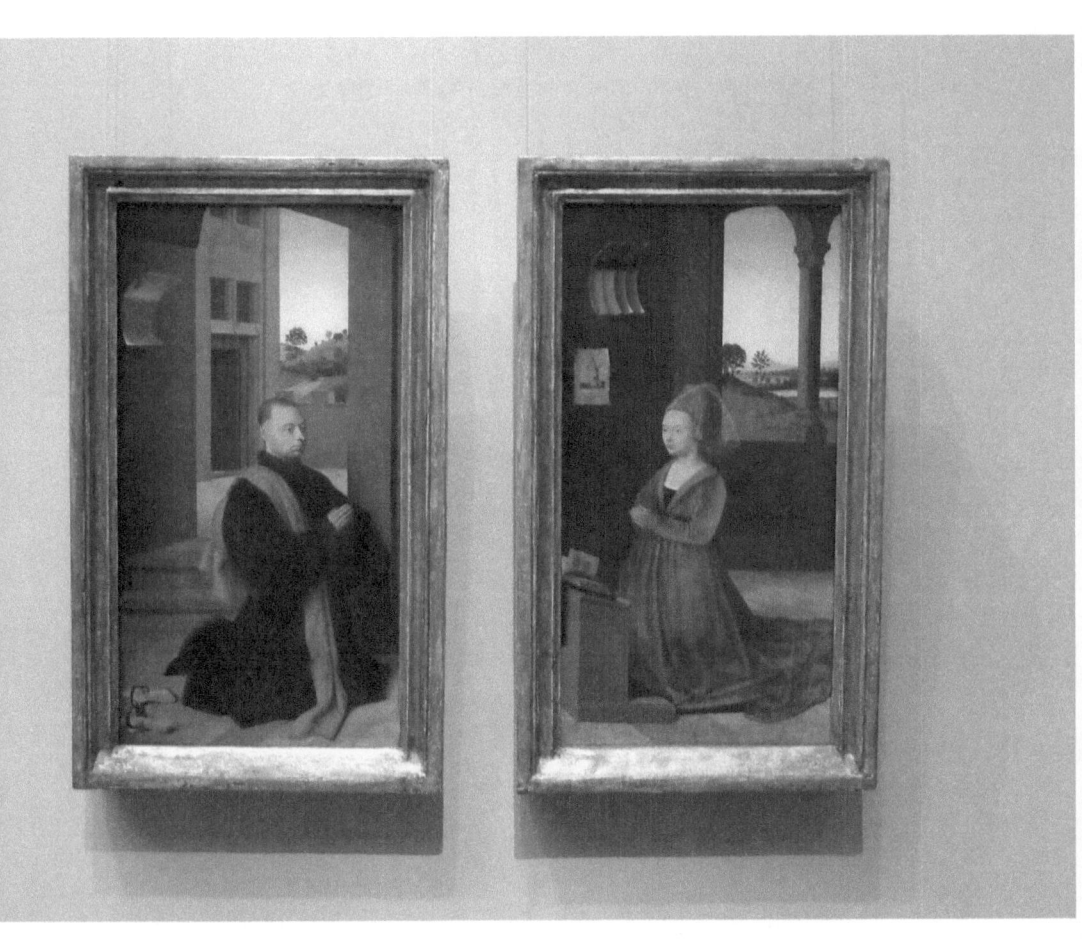

Petrus Christus, National Gallery of Art. Washington, DC

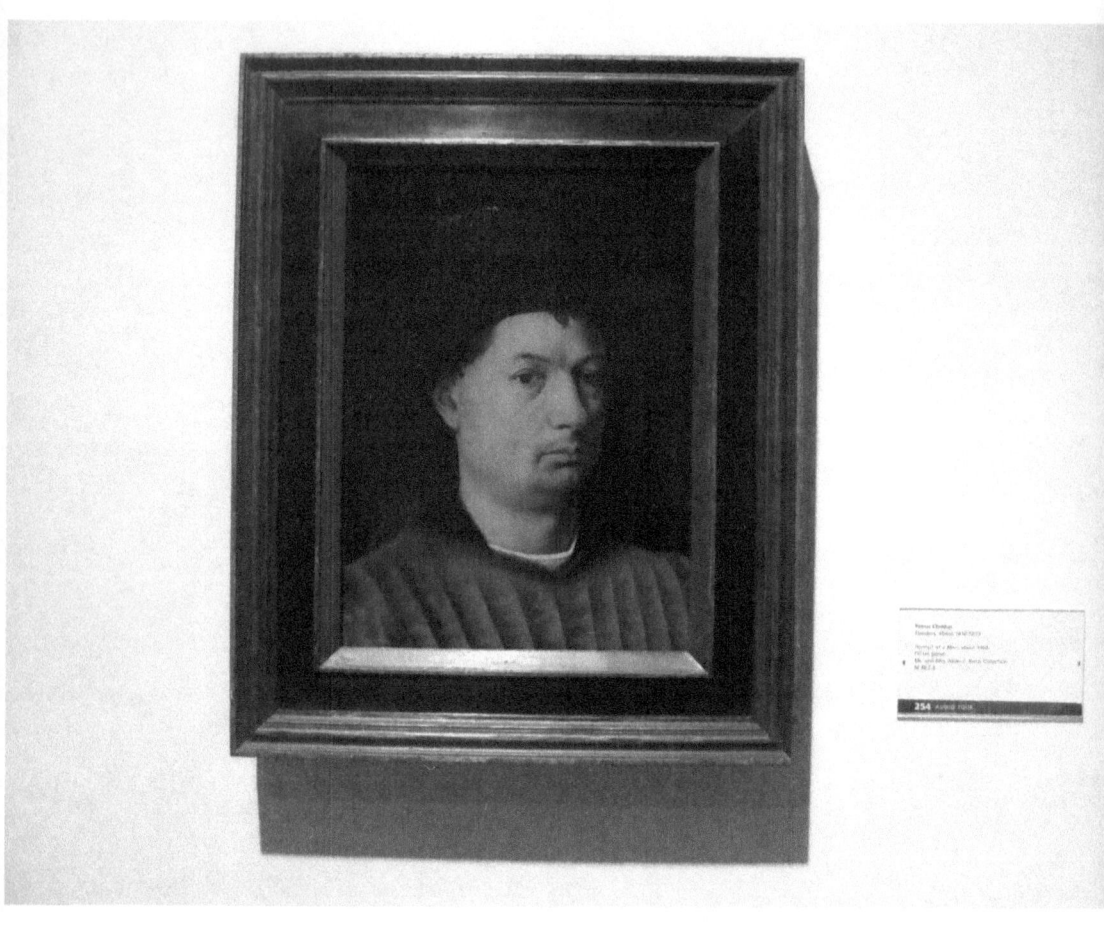

Petrus Christus, Portrait of a Man, Metropolitan Museum of Art

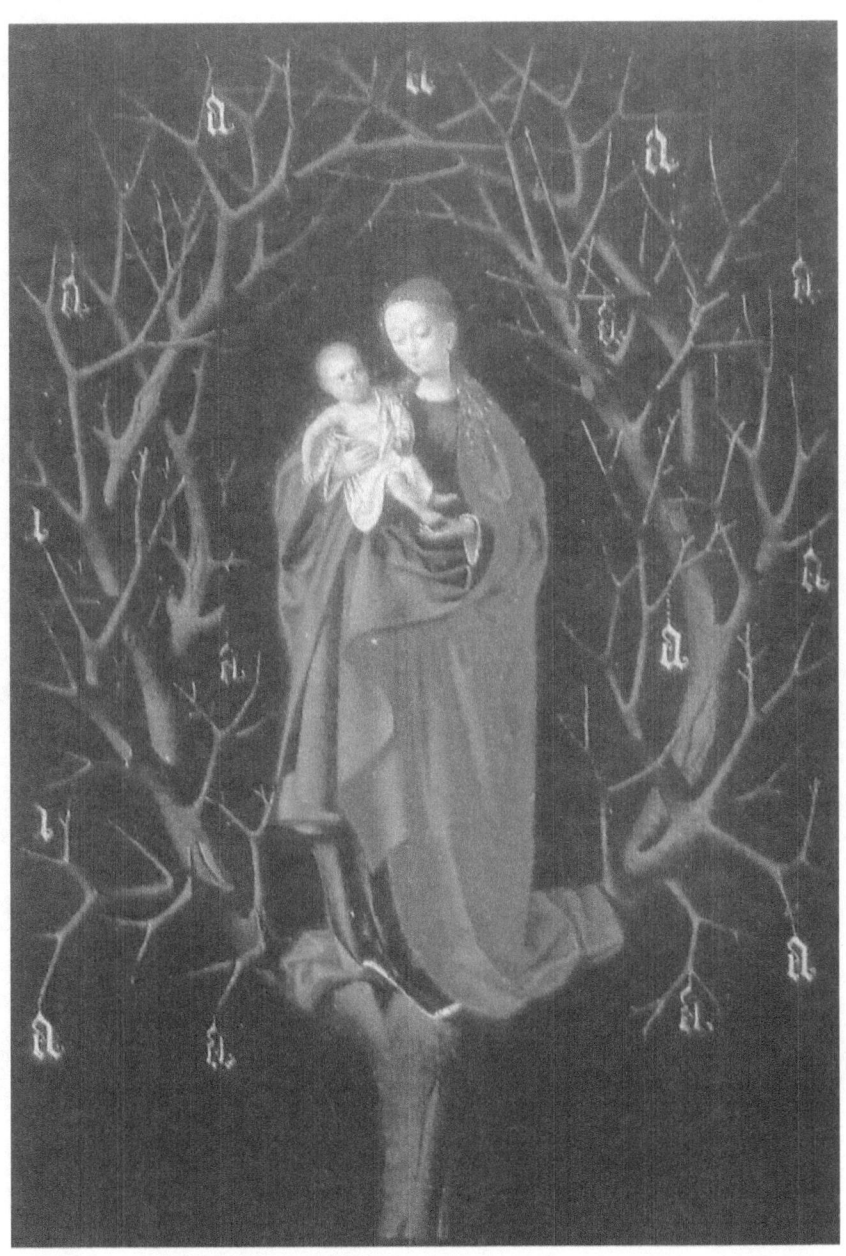

Petrus Christus, Madonna In a Barren Tree, 1450,
Prado, Madrid

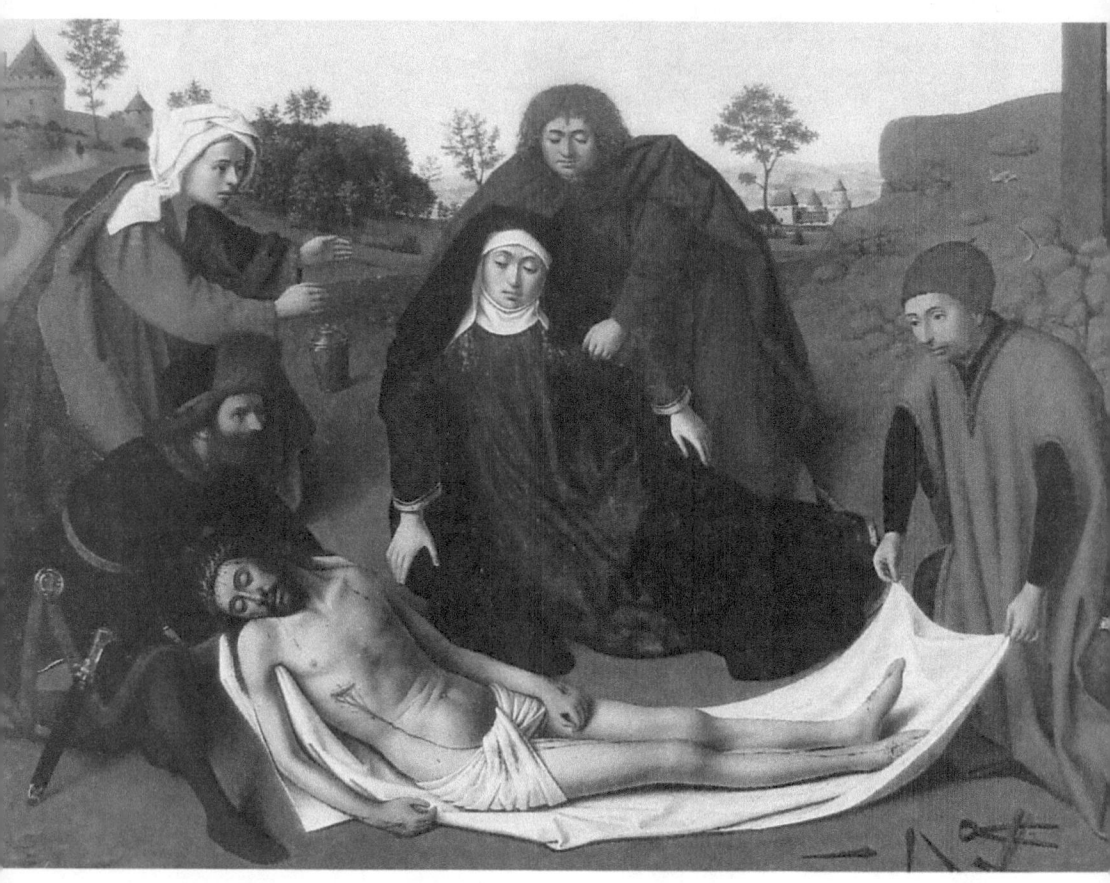

Petrus Christus, The Lamentation, Metropolitan Museum, New York City

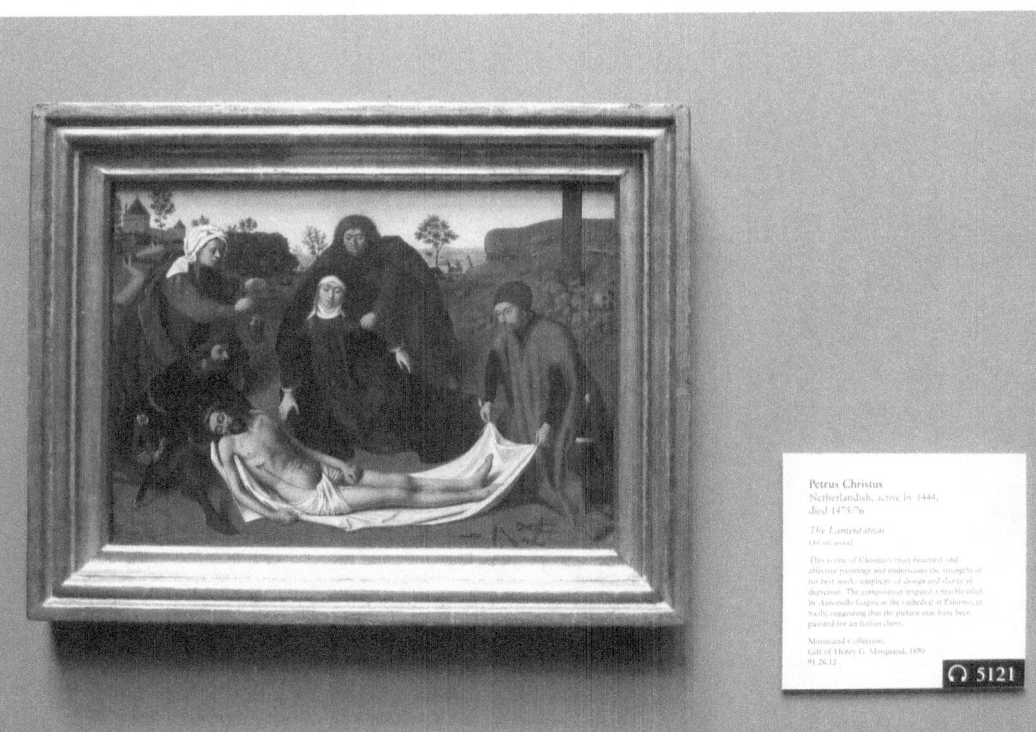

Petrus Christus, The Lamentation, Metropolitan Museum of Art

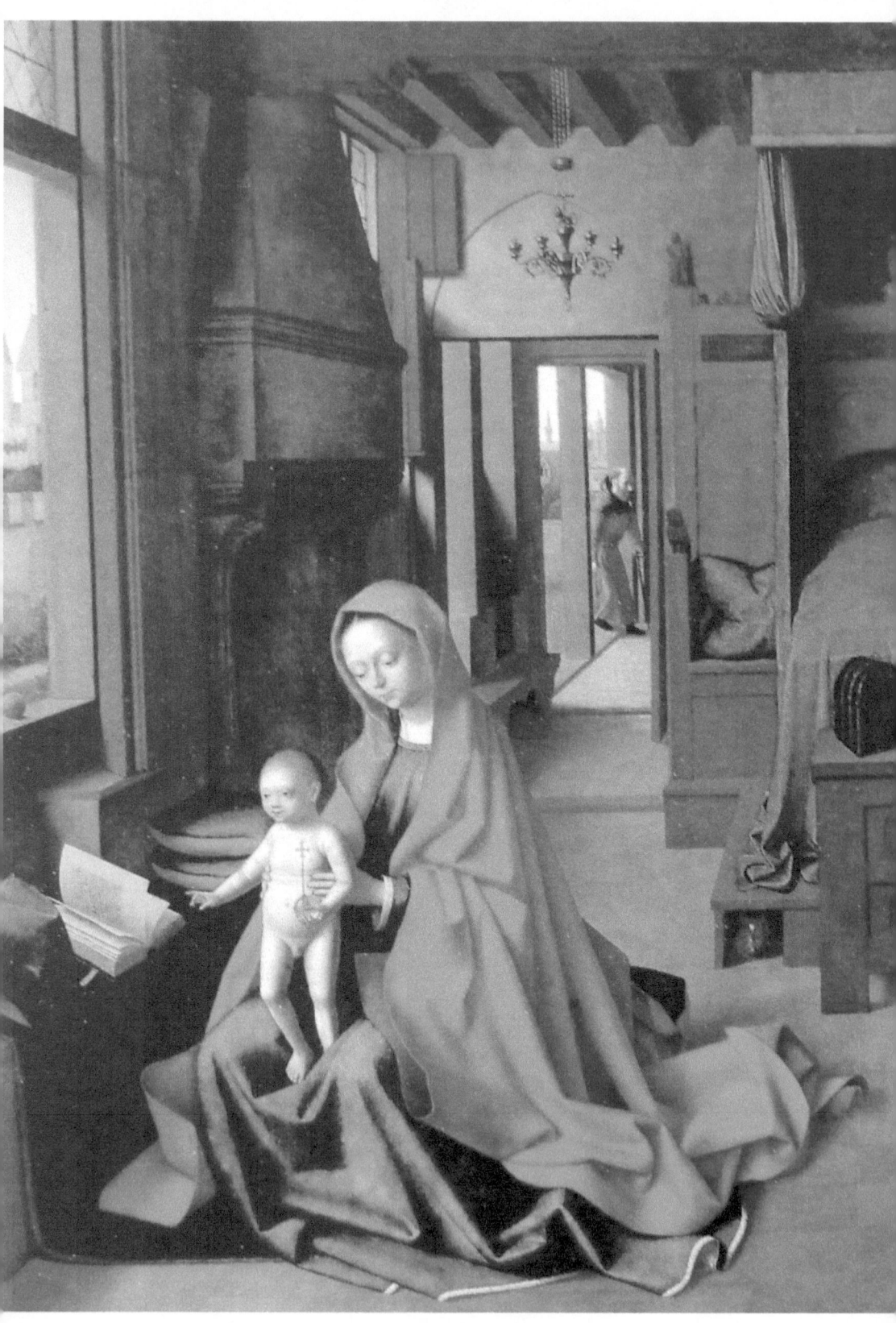

Petrus Christus, Virgin and Child In a Gothic Interior, Nelson-Atkins Museum of Art

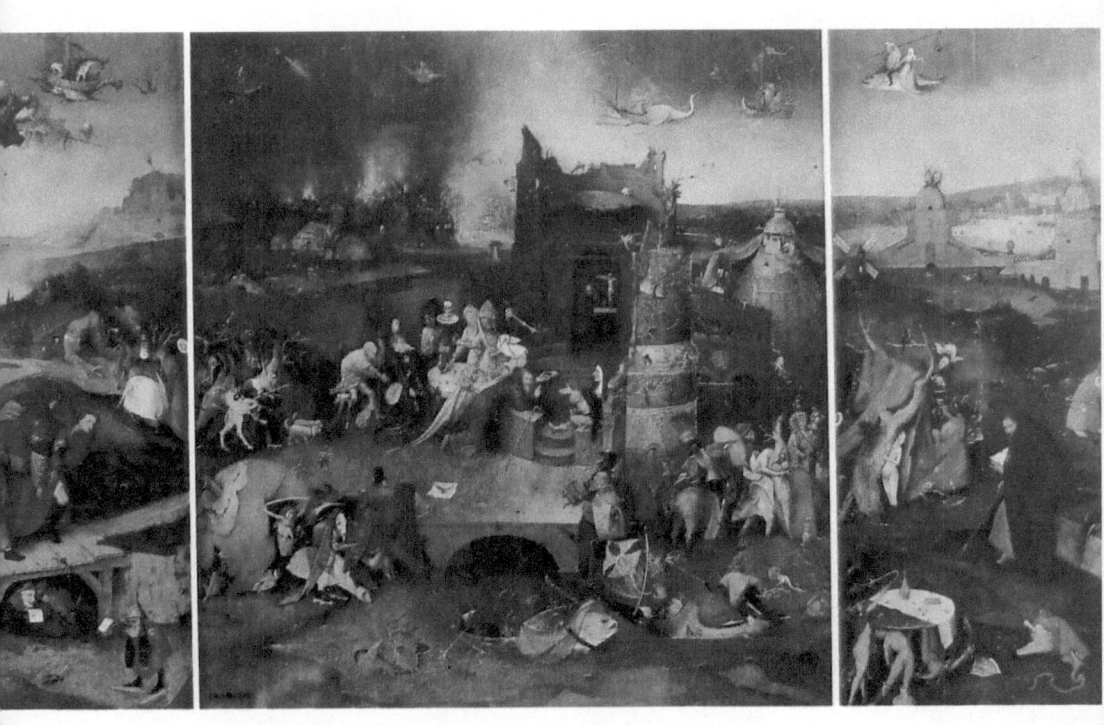

Hieronymous Bosch, The Temptations of St Anthony

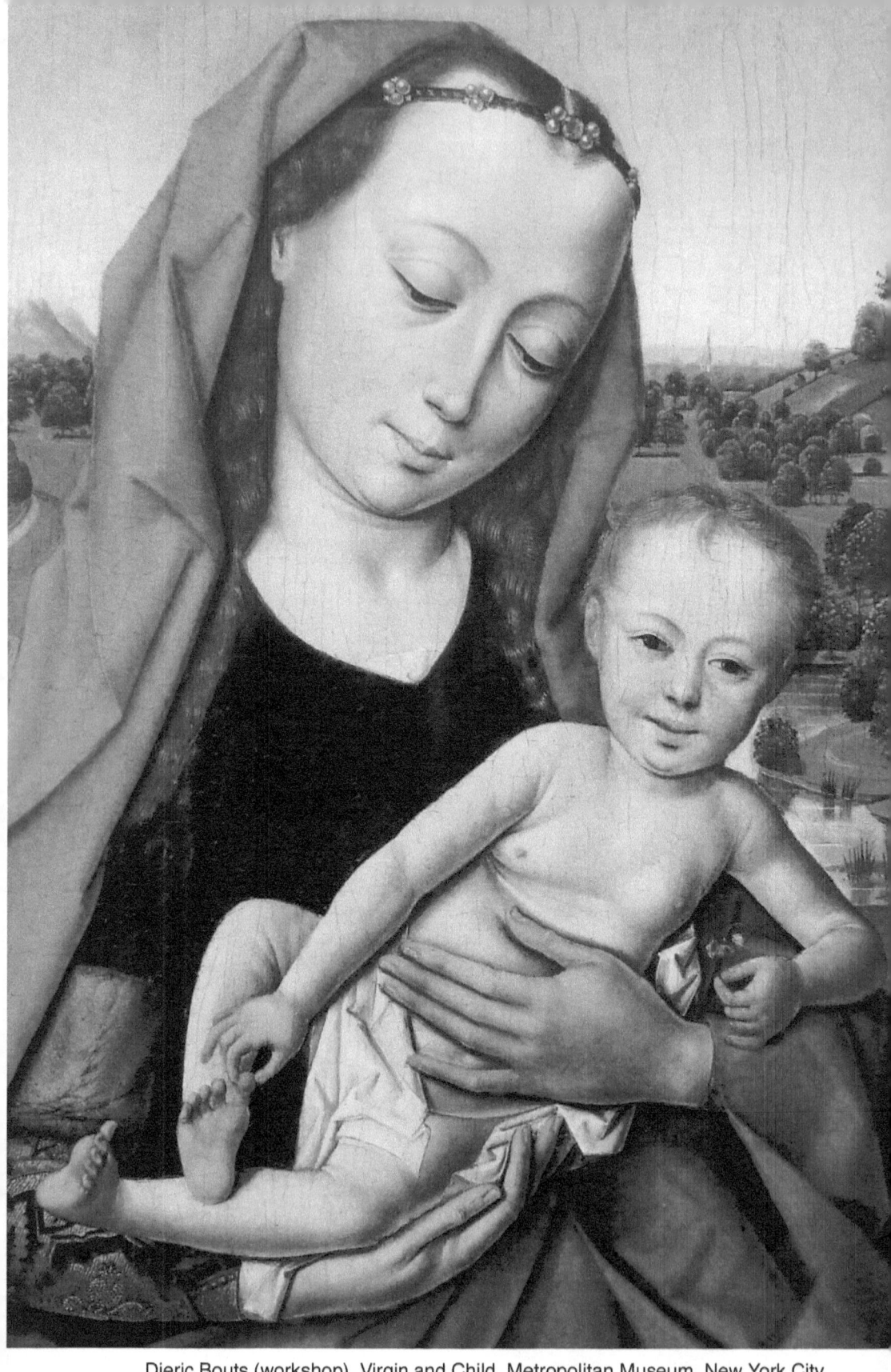
Dieric Bouts (workshop), Virgin and Child, Metropolitan Museum, New York City

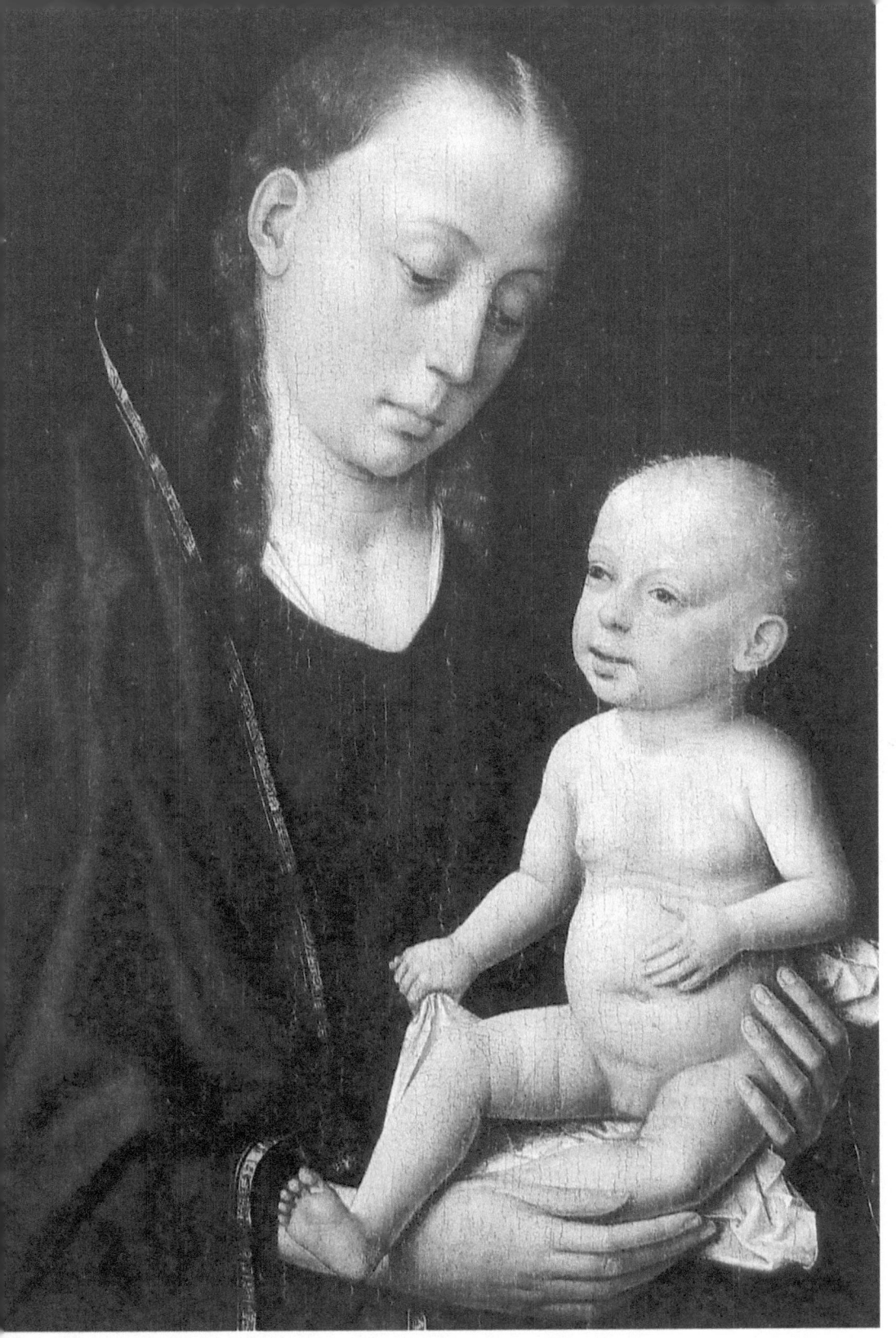

Dieric Bouts, Virgin and Child, National Gallery of Art, Washington, DC

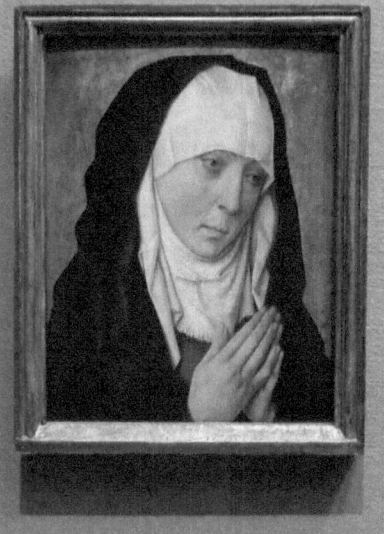

Deiric Bouts, workshop, Mater Dolorosa, Metropolitan Museum of Art

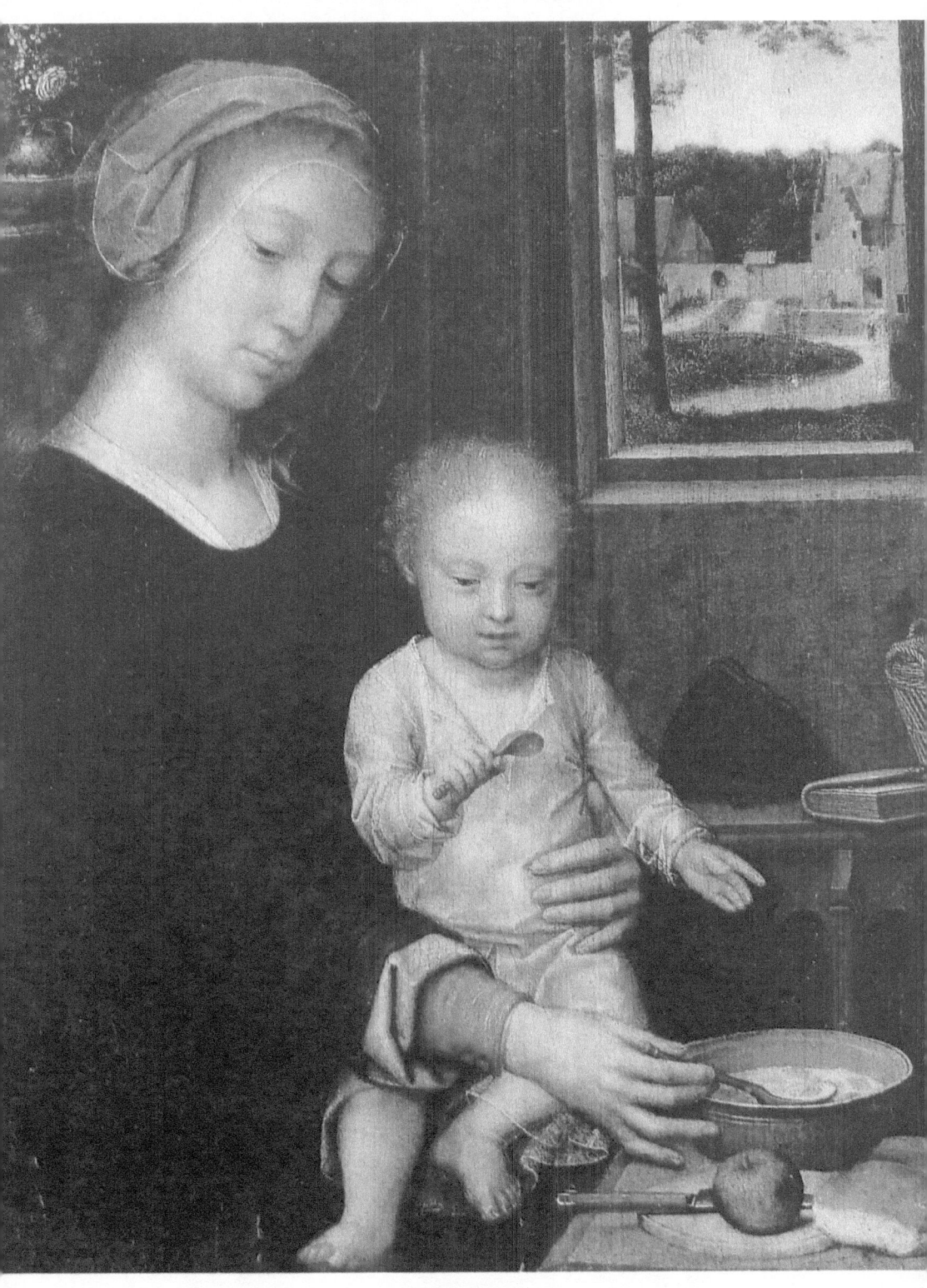

Gerard David, Virgin and Child, Brussels

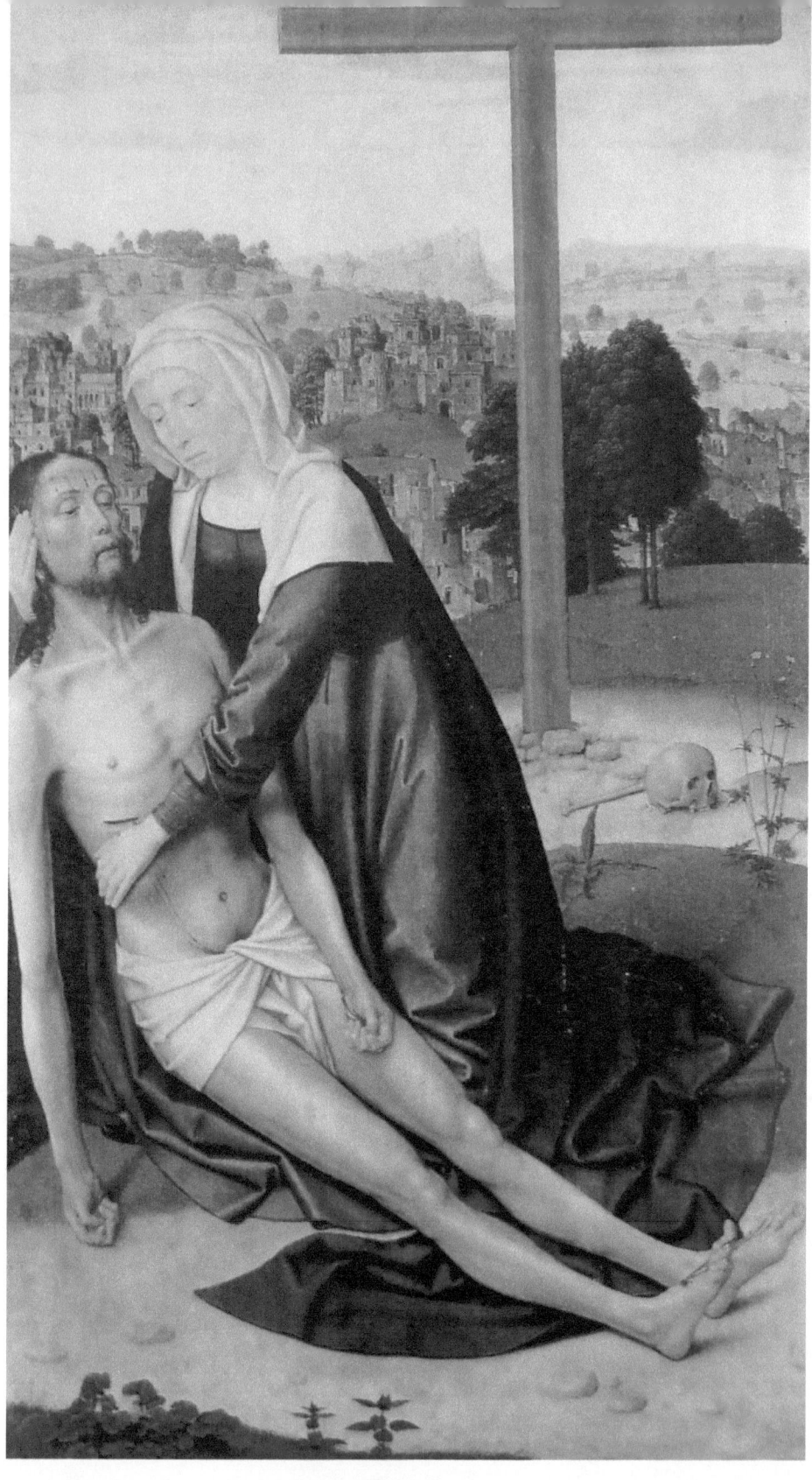

Gerard David, Pietà, Winterhur

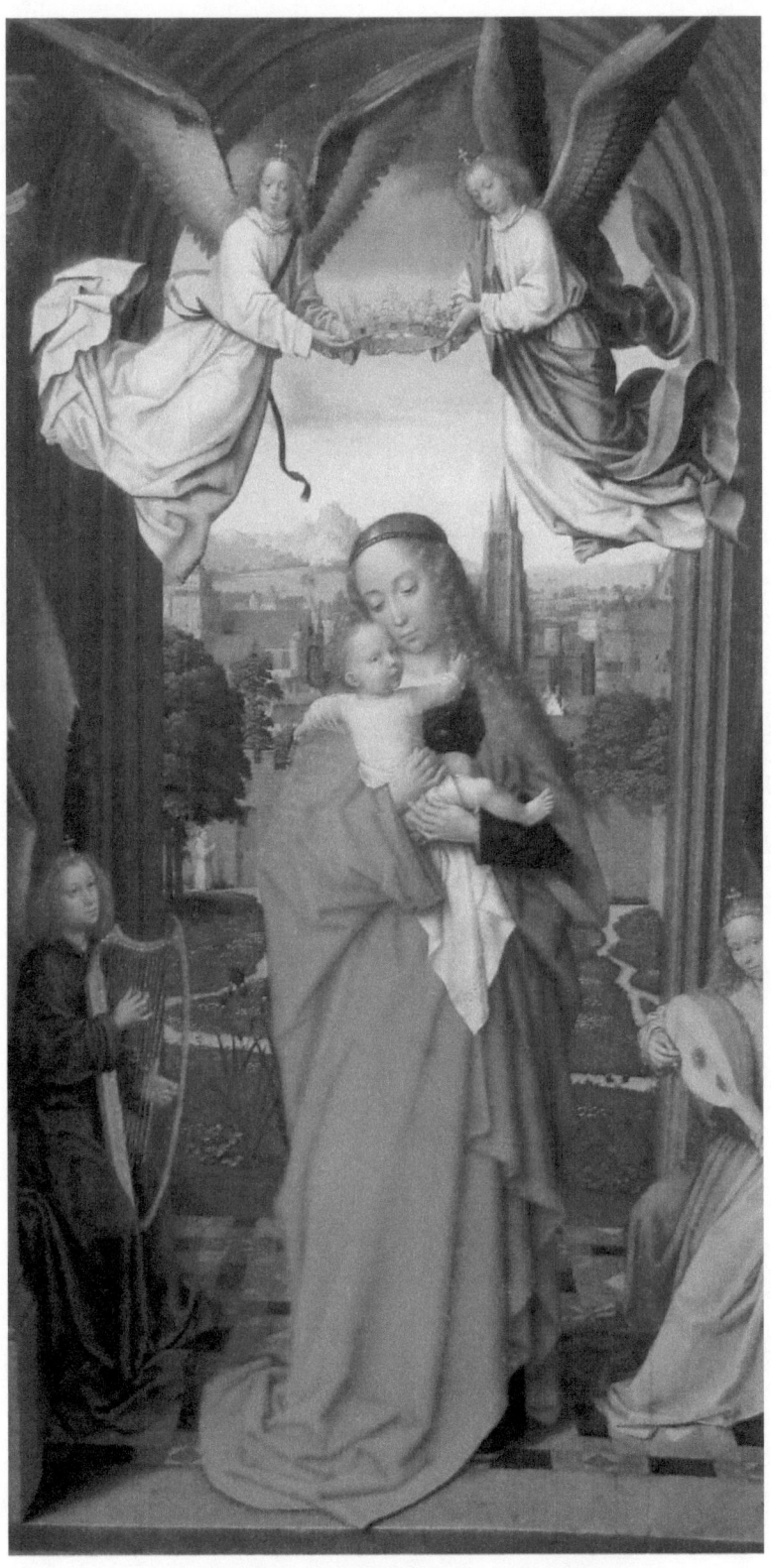

Gerard David, Virgin and Child With Angels,
Metropolitan Museum, New York City

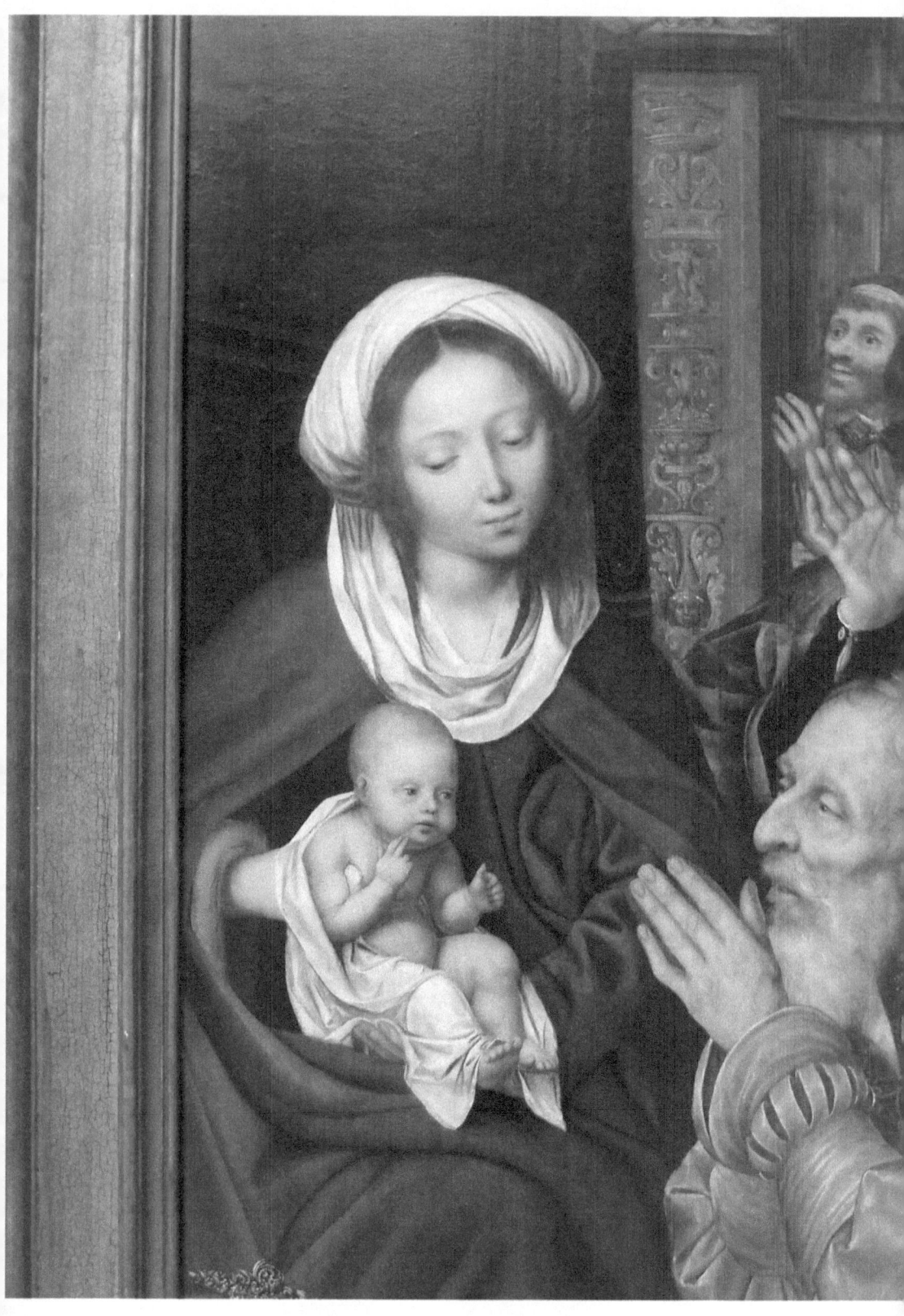

Gerard David, Adoration of the Magi, detail, Metropolitan Museum of Art

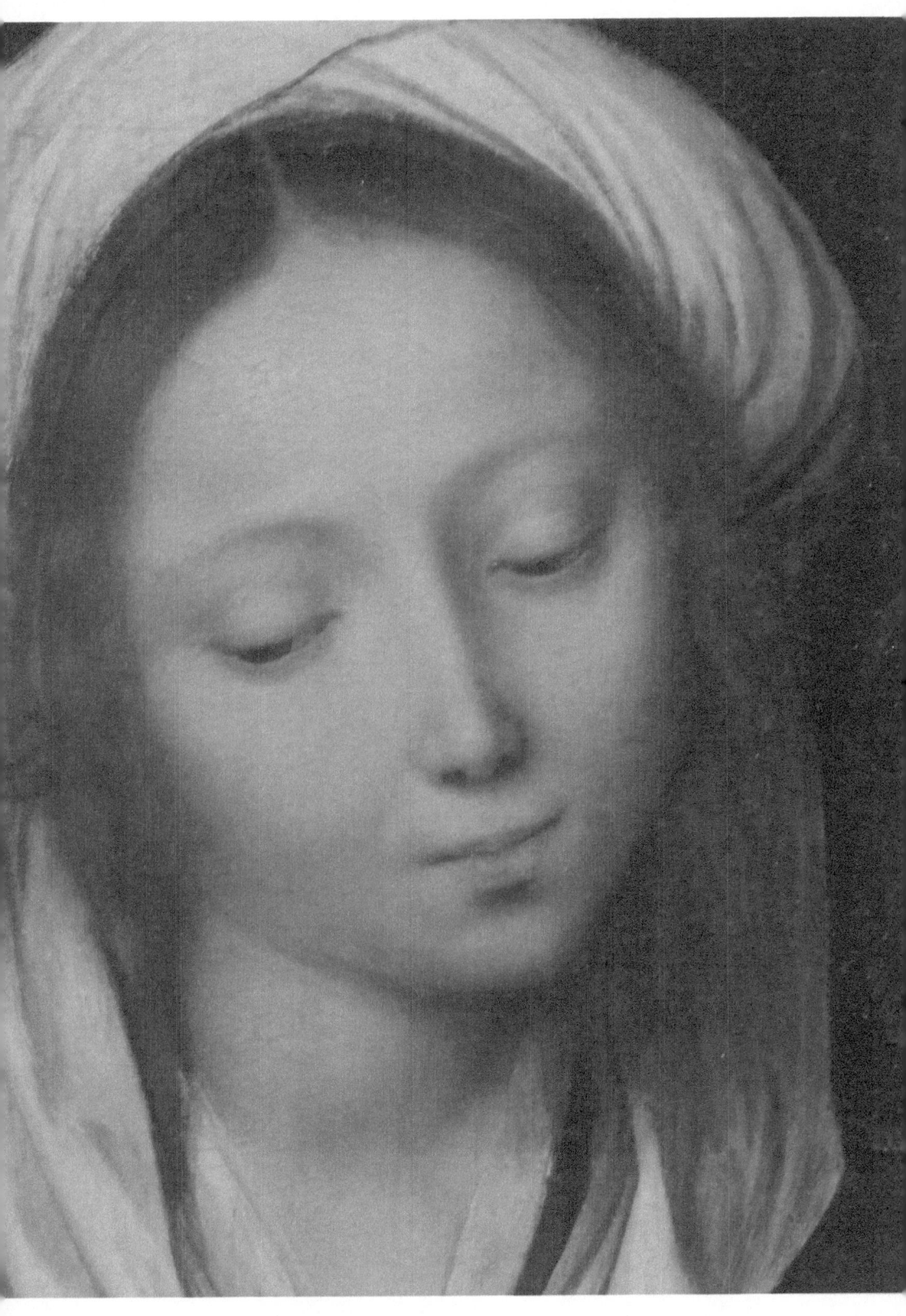

Gerard David, detail of the Adoration, Metropolitan Museum of Art

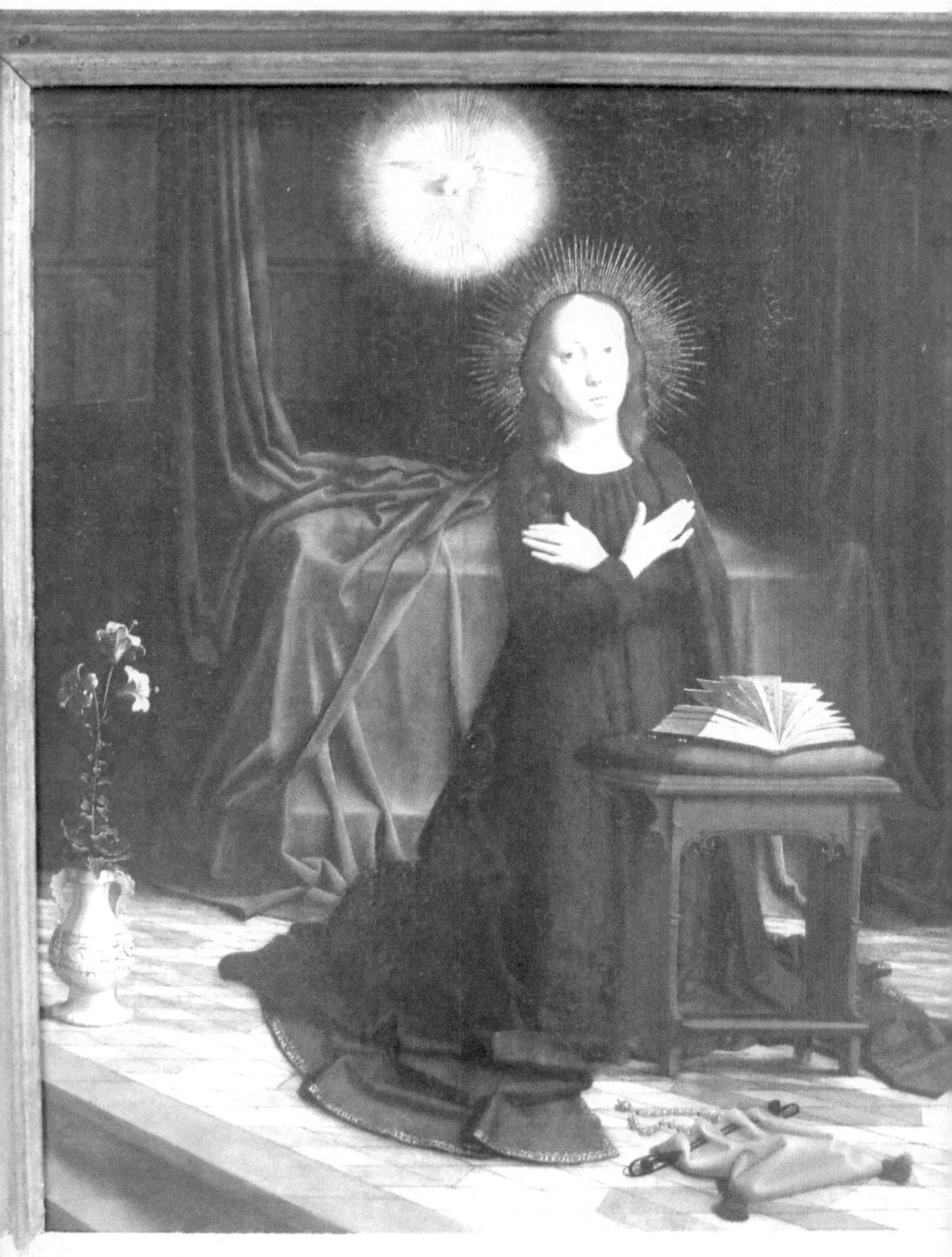

Gerard David, The Virgin, Metropolitan Museum of Art

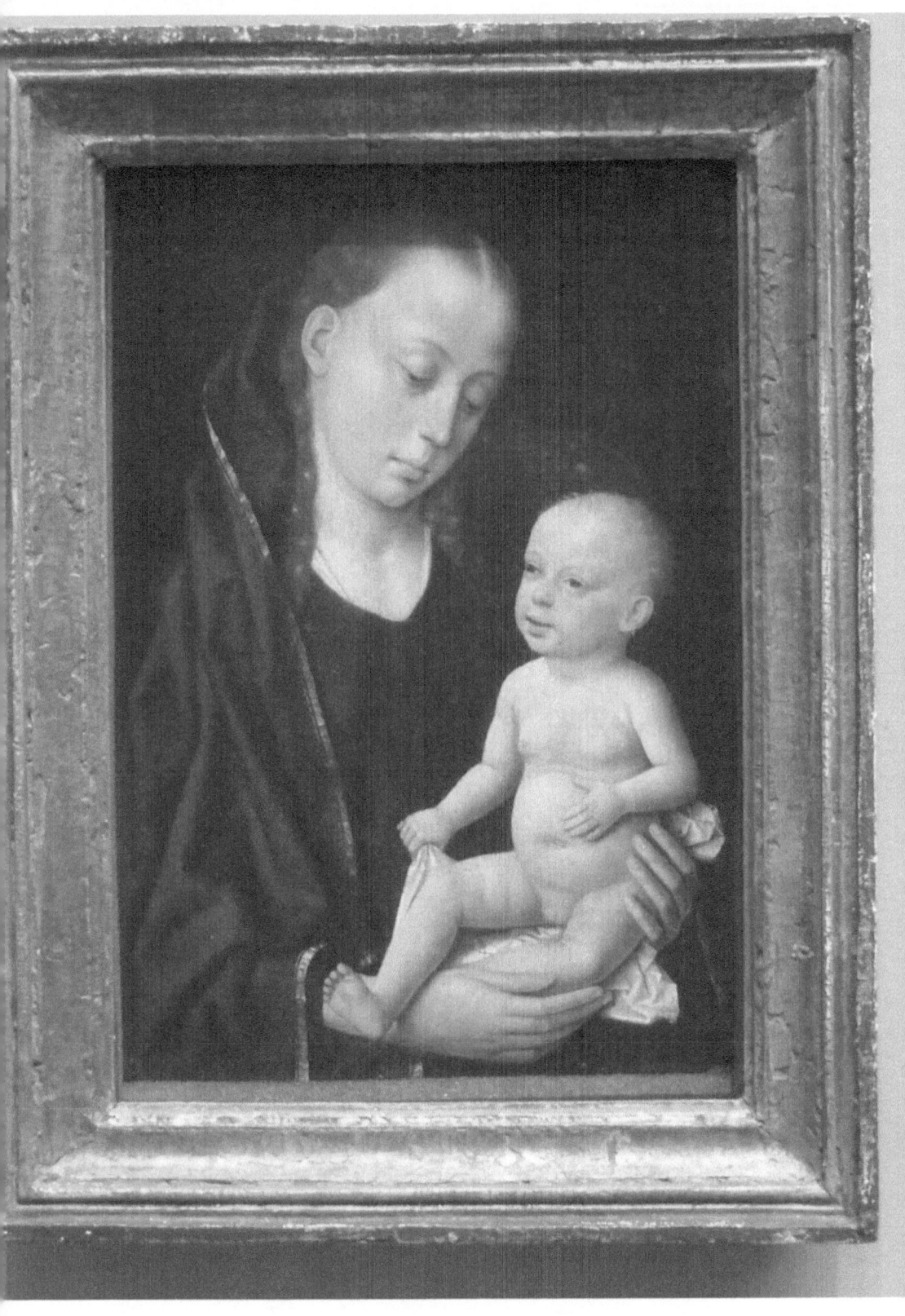

Gerard David, Madonna and Child, Metropolitan Museum of Art

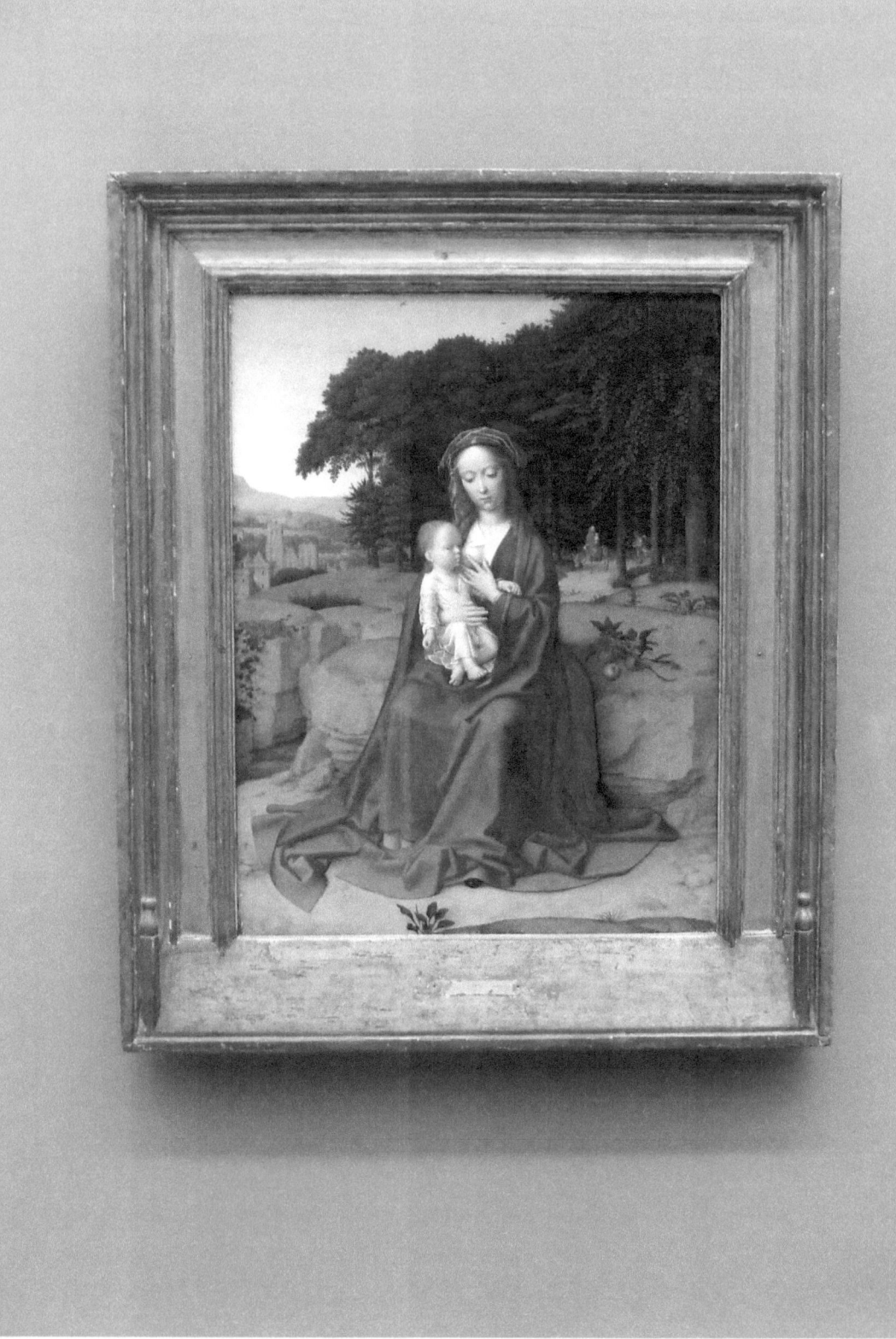

Gerard David, Rest On the Flight To Egypt, Metropolitan Museum of Art

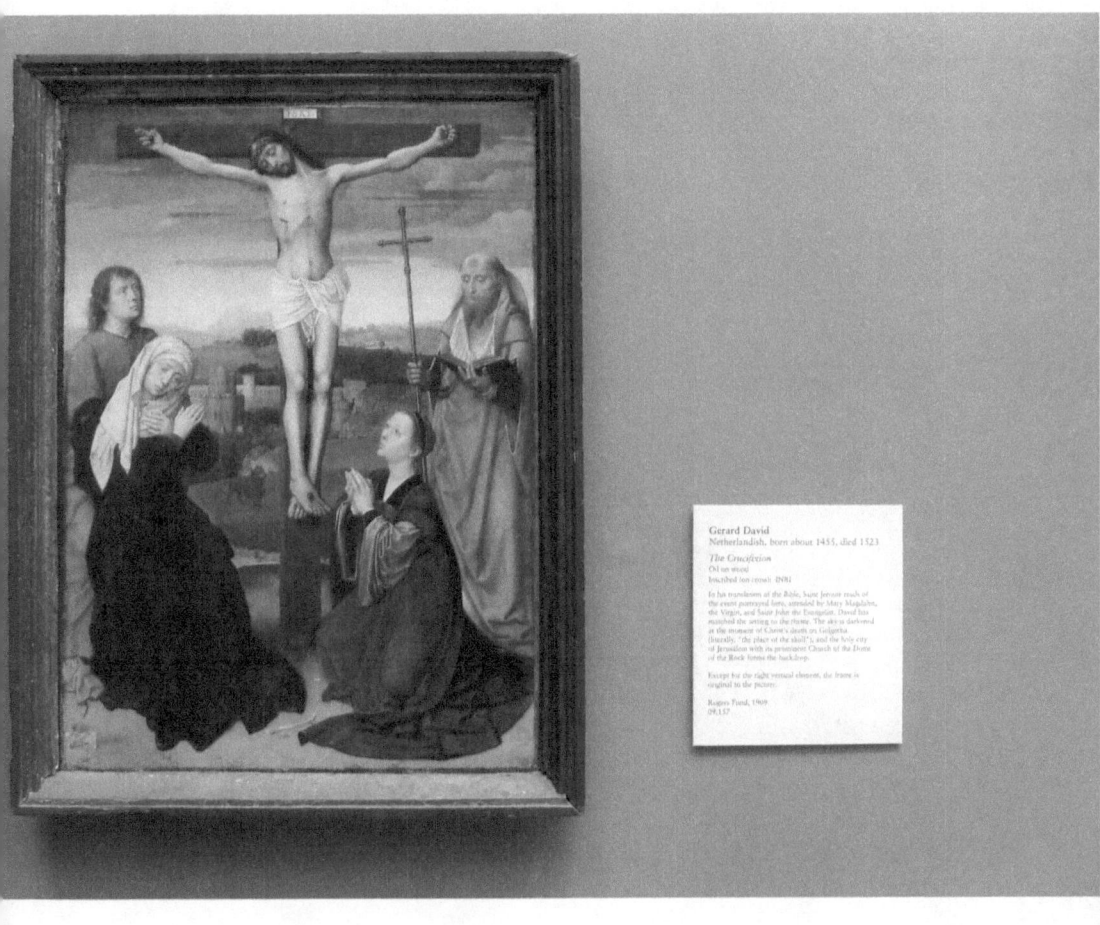

Gerard David, Crucifixion, Metropolitan Museum of Art

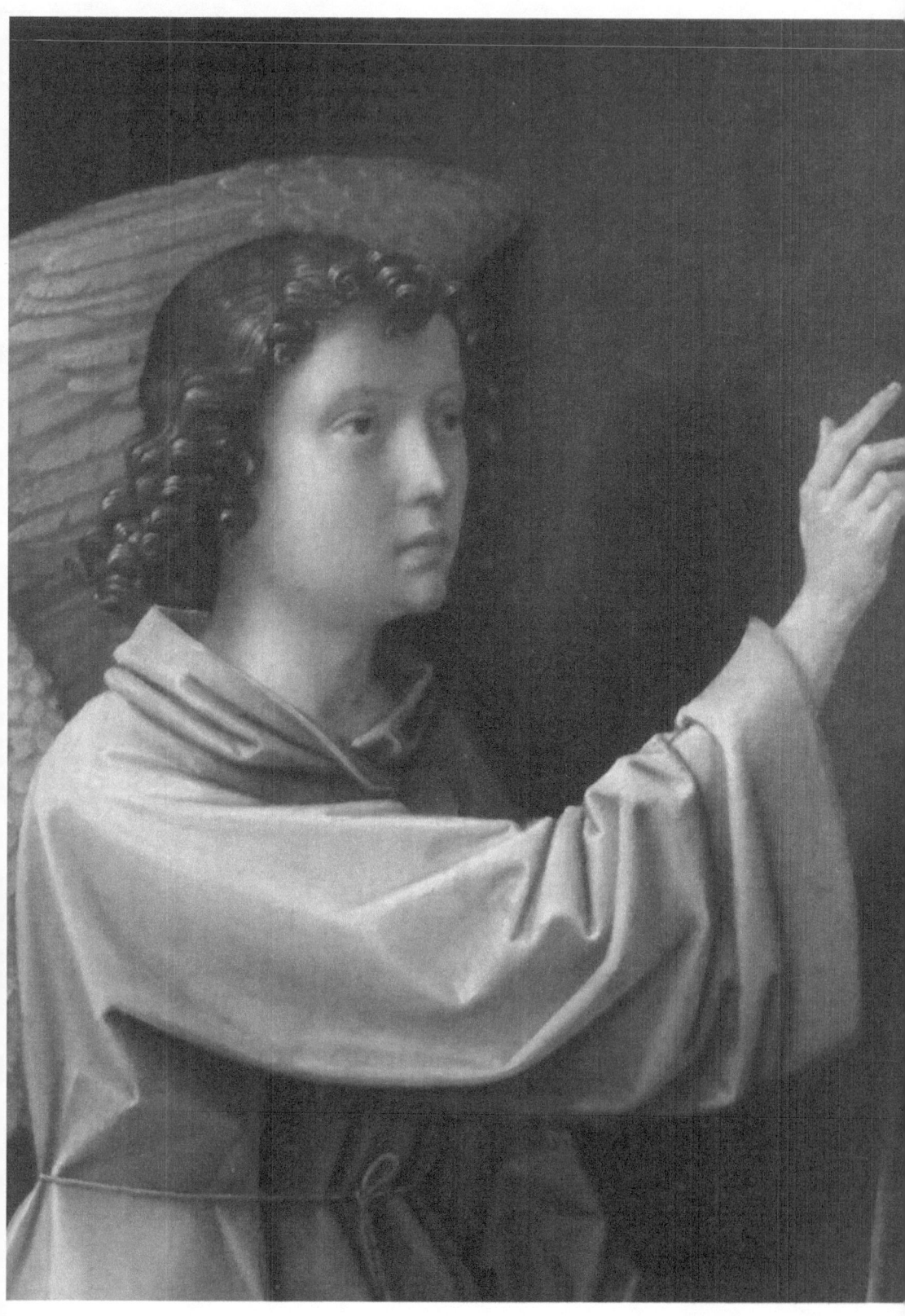

Gerard David in the Metropolitan Museum of Art

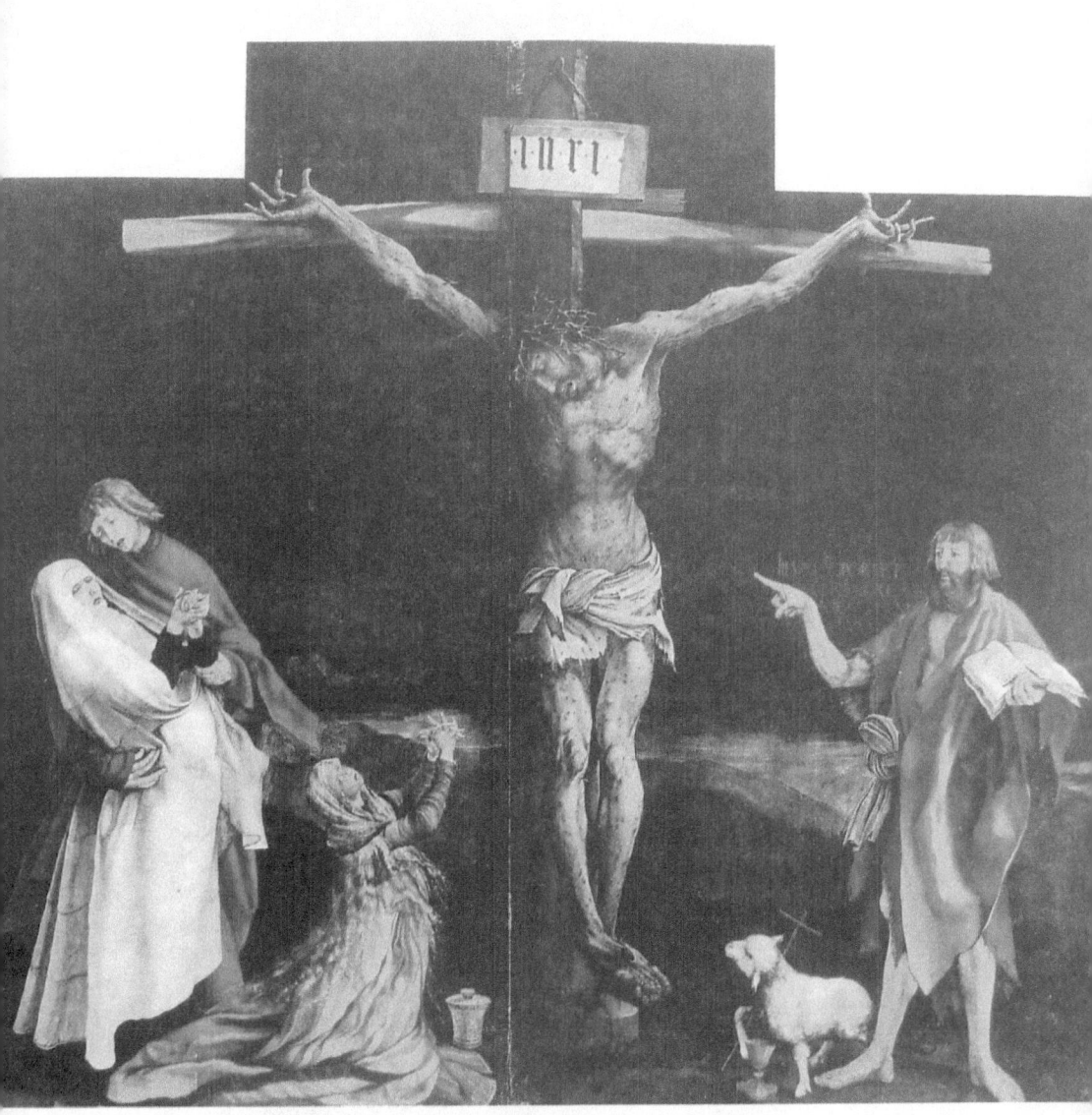
Matthias Grünewald, Crucifixion, Isenheim Altarpiece

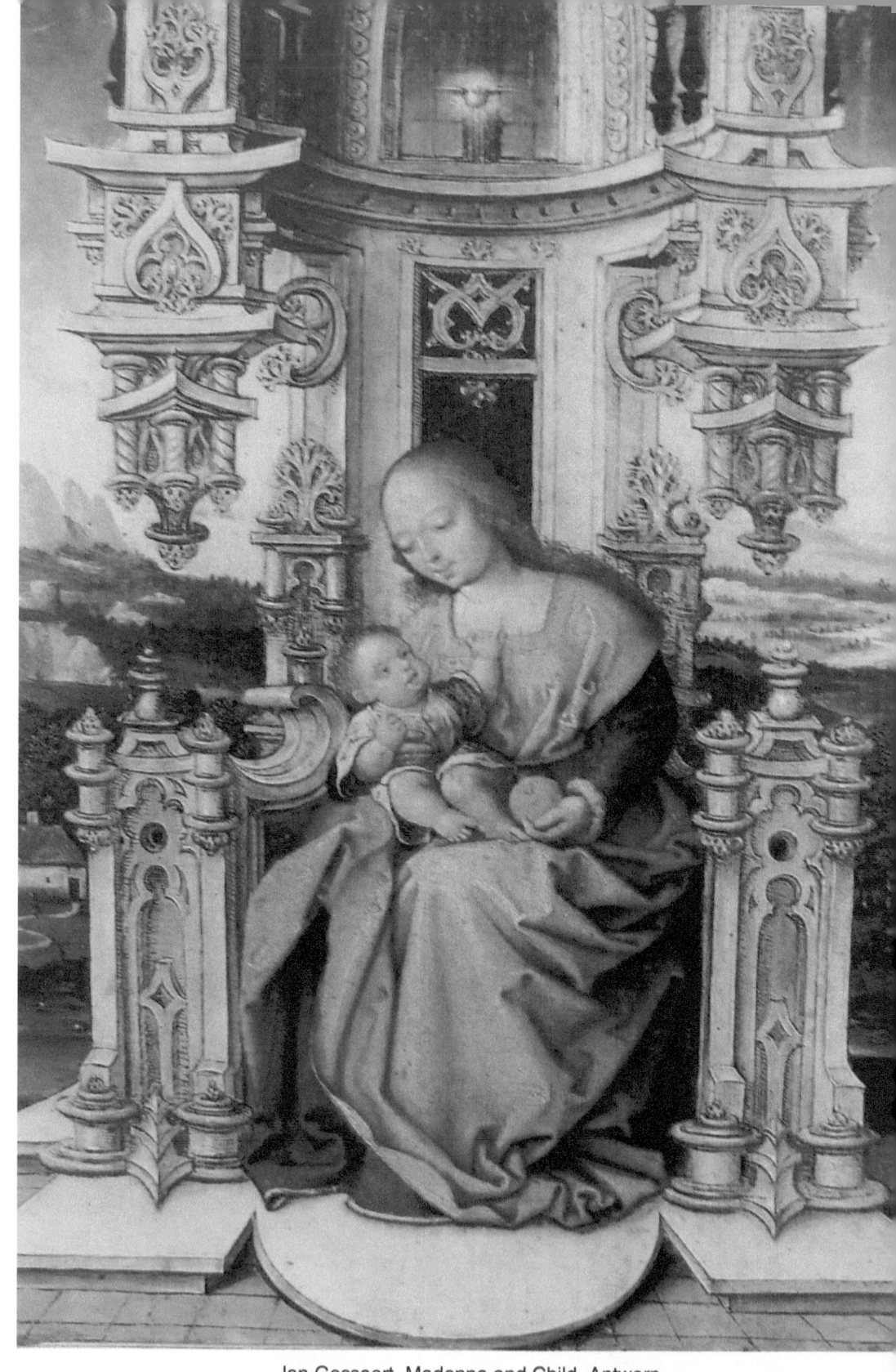

Jan Gossaert, Madonna and Child, Antwerp

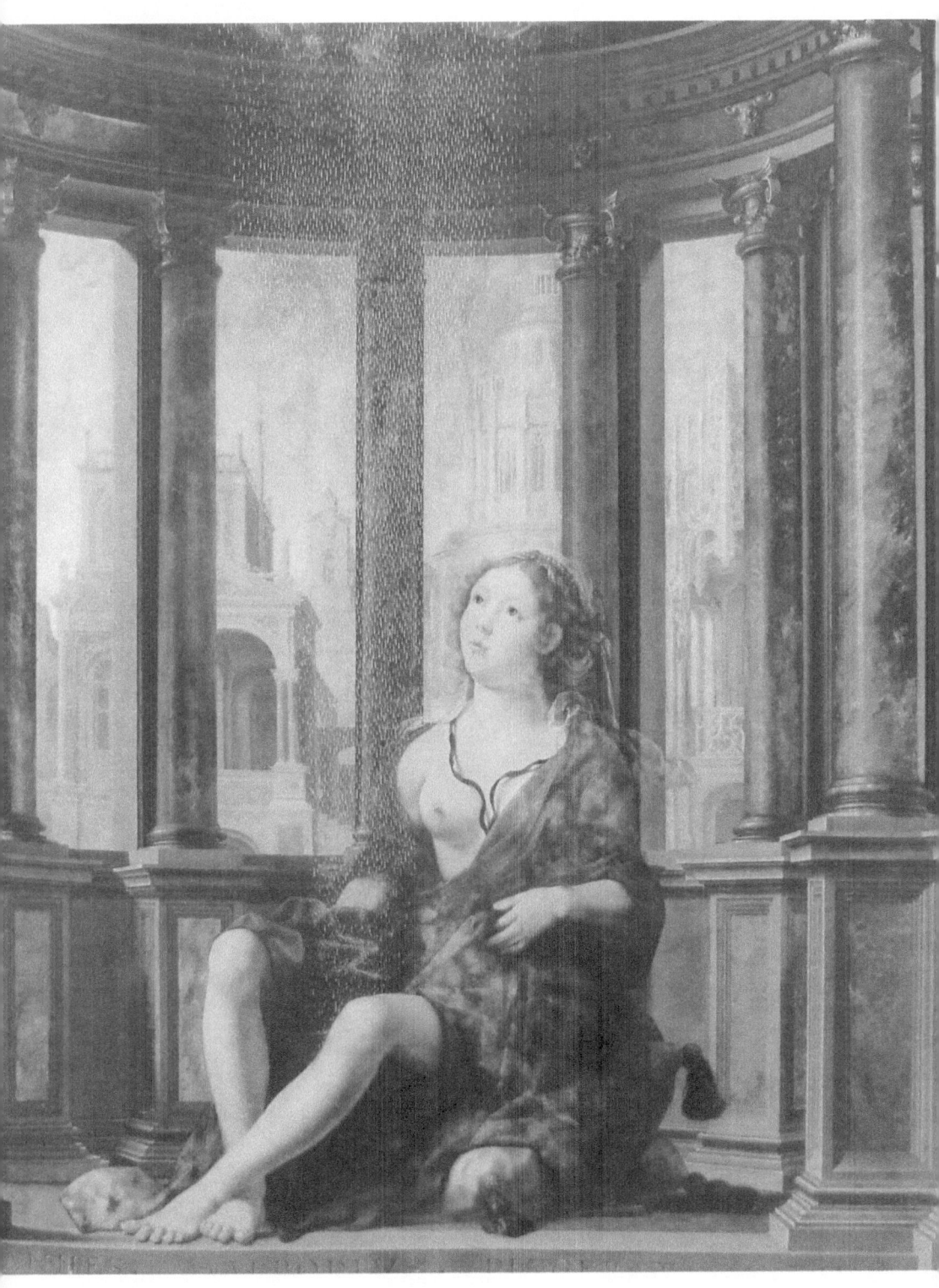

Jan Gossaert (Mabuse), Danae, Munich

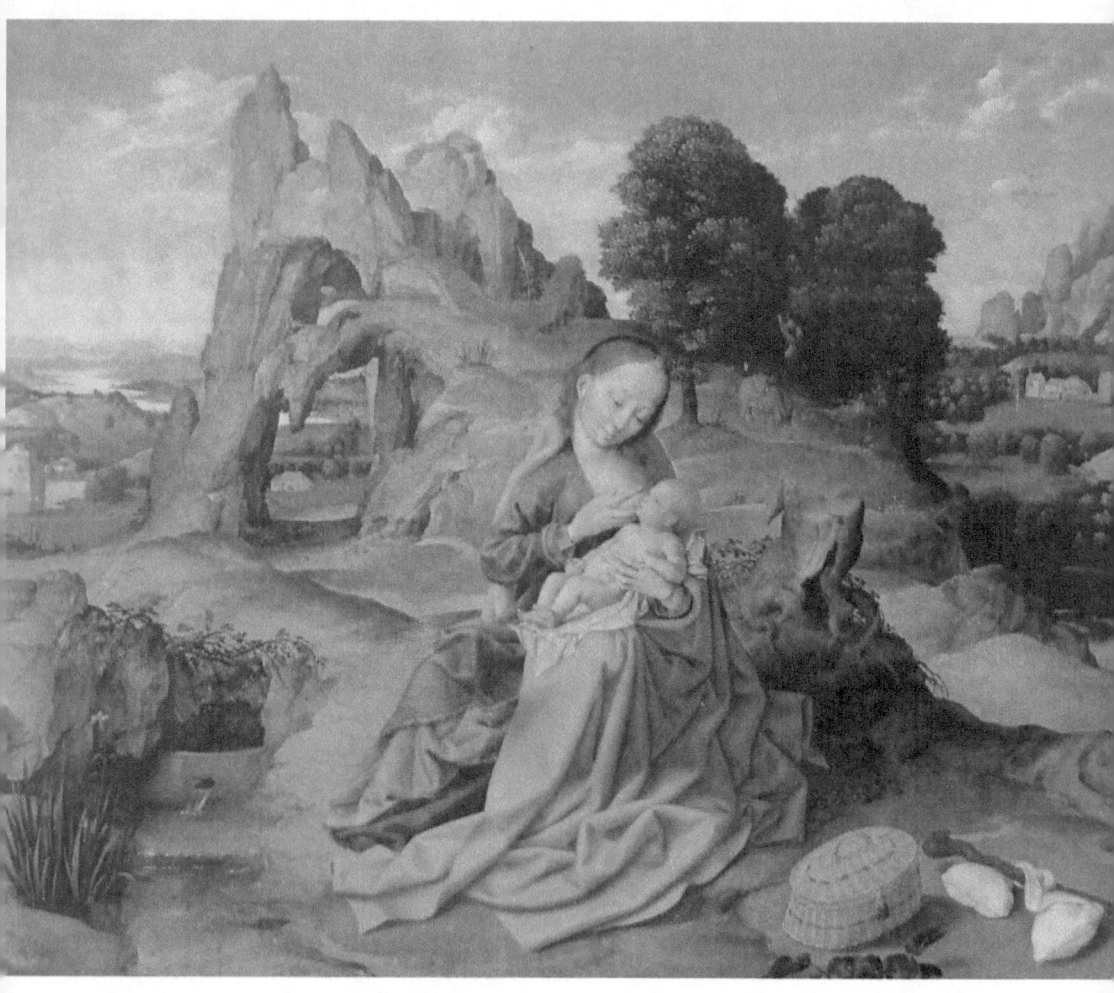
Joos van Cleve, The Rest on the Flight To Egypt, Brussels

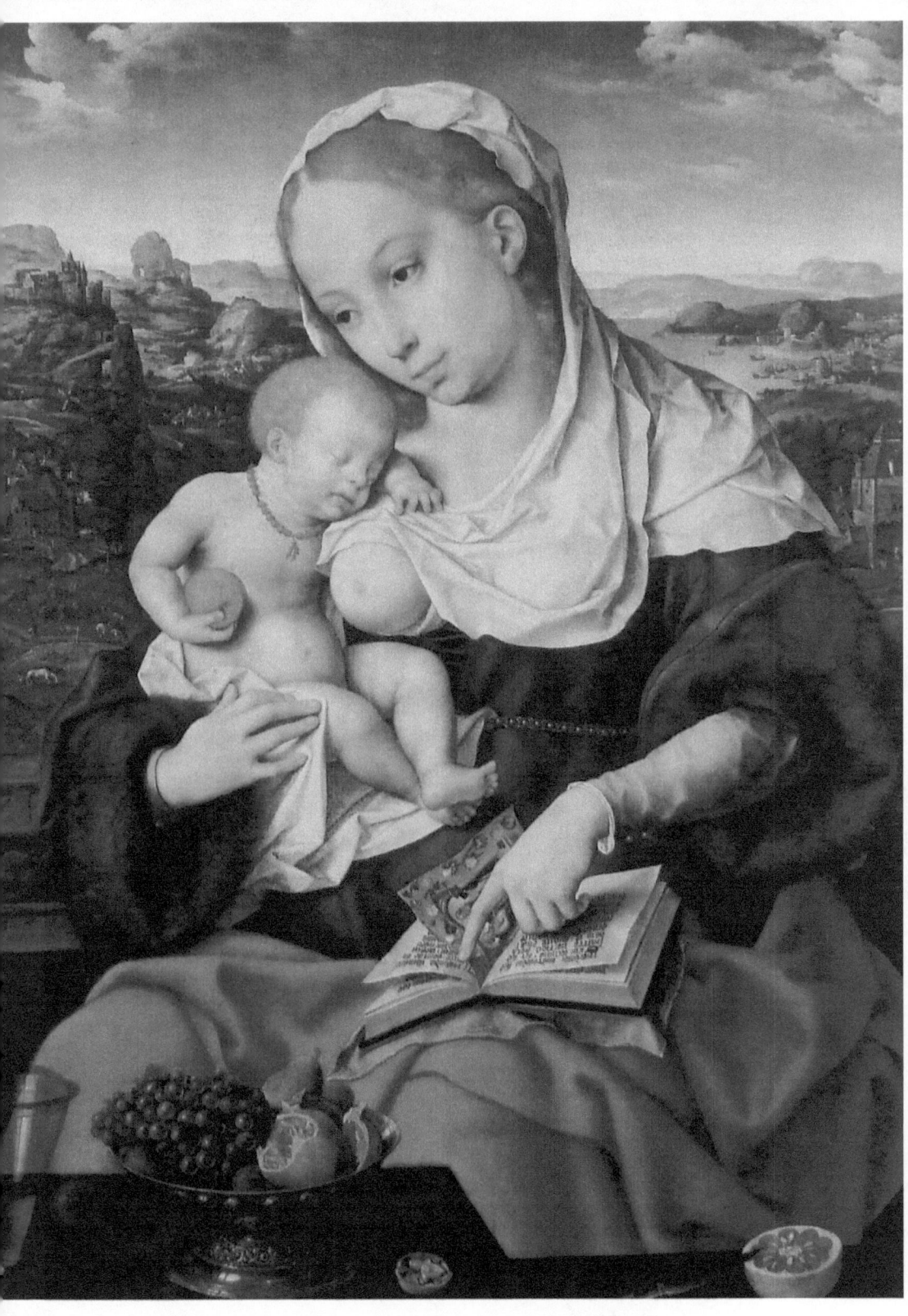

Joos van Cleve, Madonna and Child, Metropolitan Museum, New York City

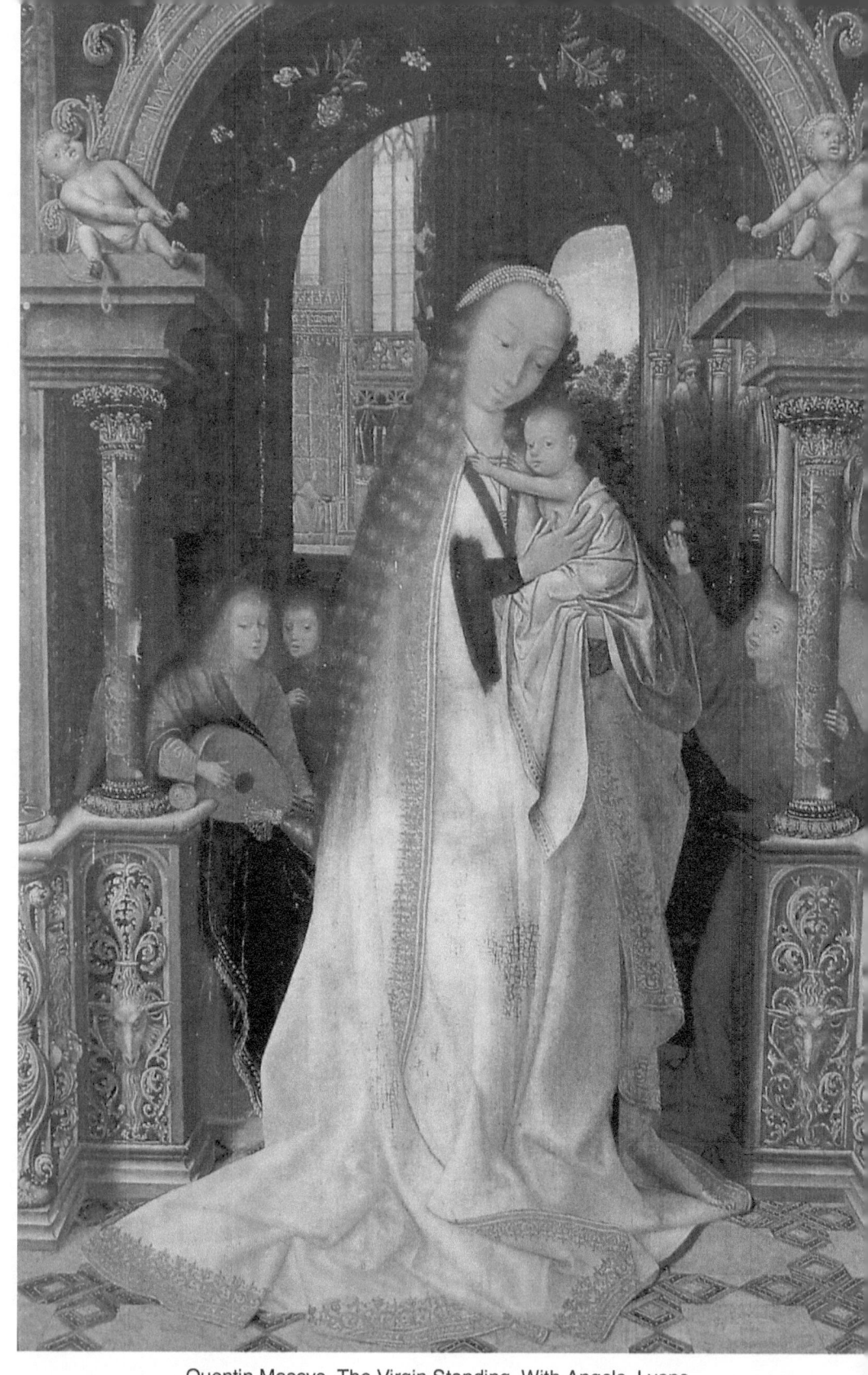
Quentin Massys, The Virgin Standing, With Angels, Lyons

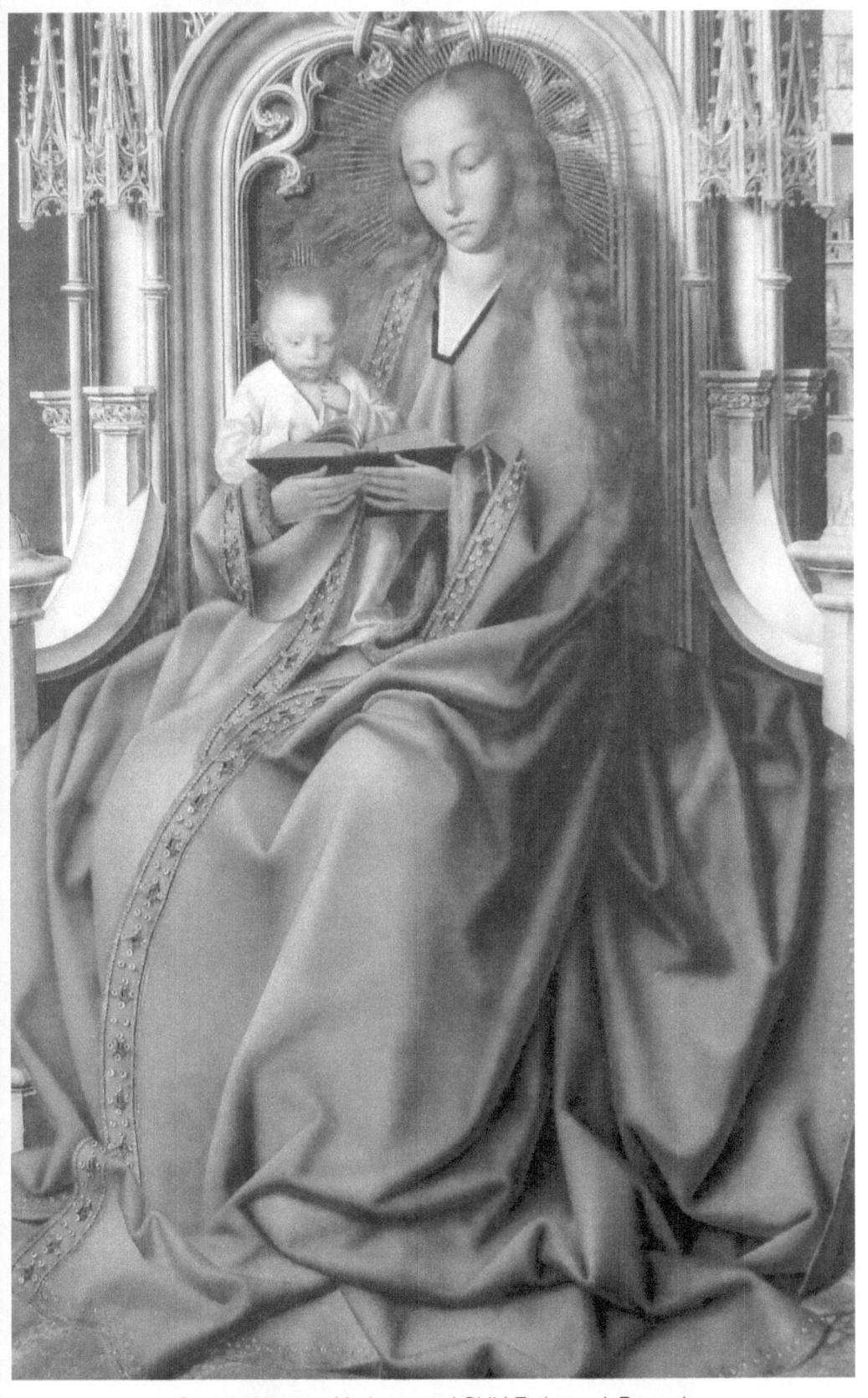
Quentin Massys, Madonna and Child Enthroned, Brussels

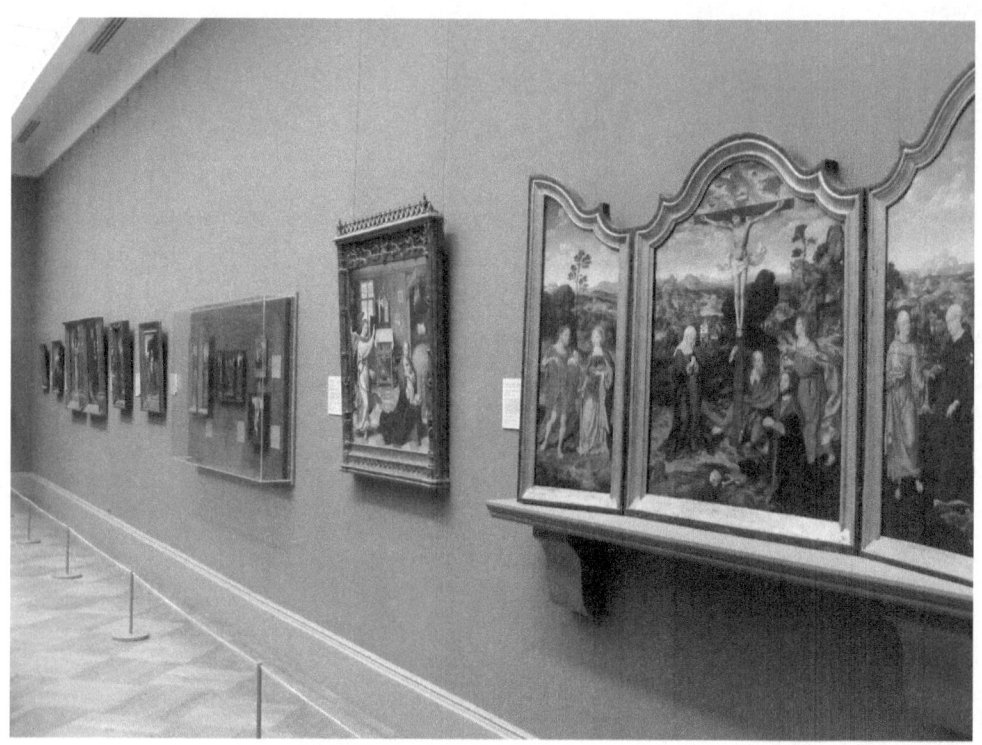

One of the Early Netherlandish galleries in the
Metropolitan Museum of Art, Gotham

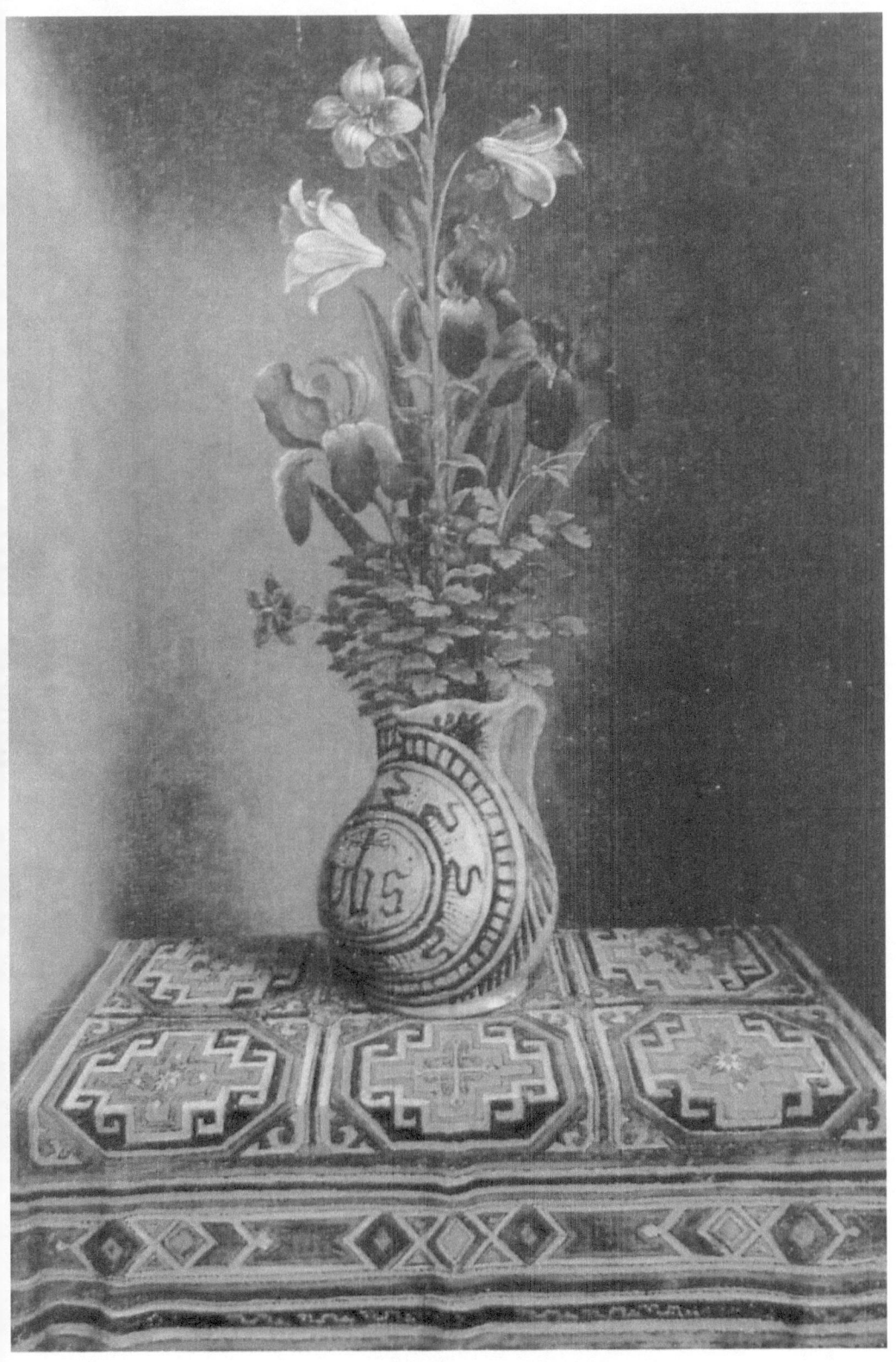

Hans Memling, Marian Flowerpiece, 1485,
Thyssen-Bornemisza Collection

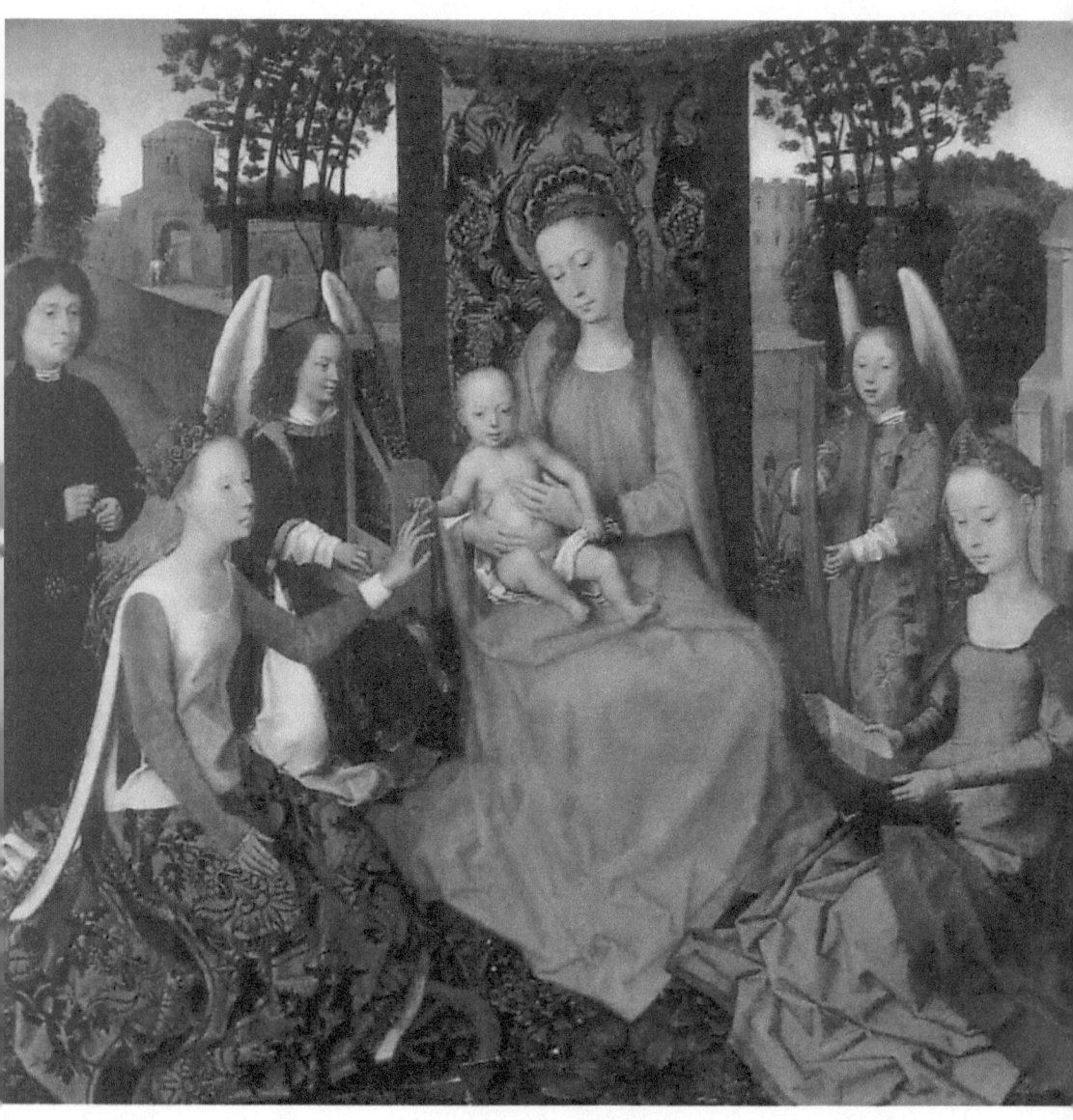

Hans Memling, The Mystic Marriage of St Catherine, Metropolitan Museum, New York City

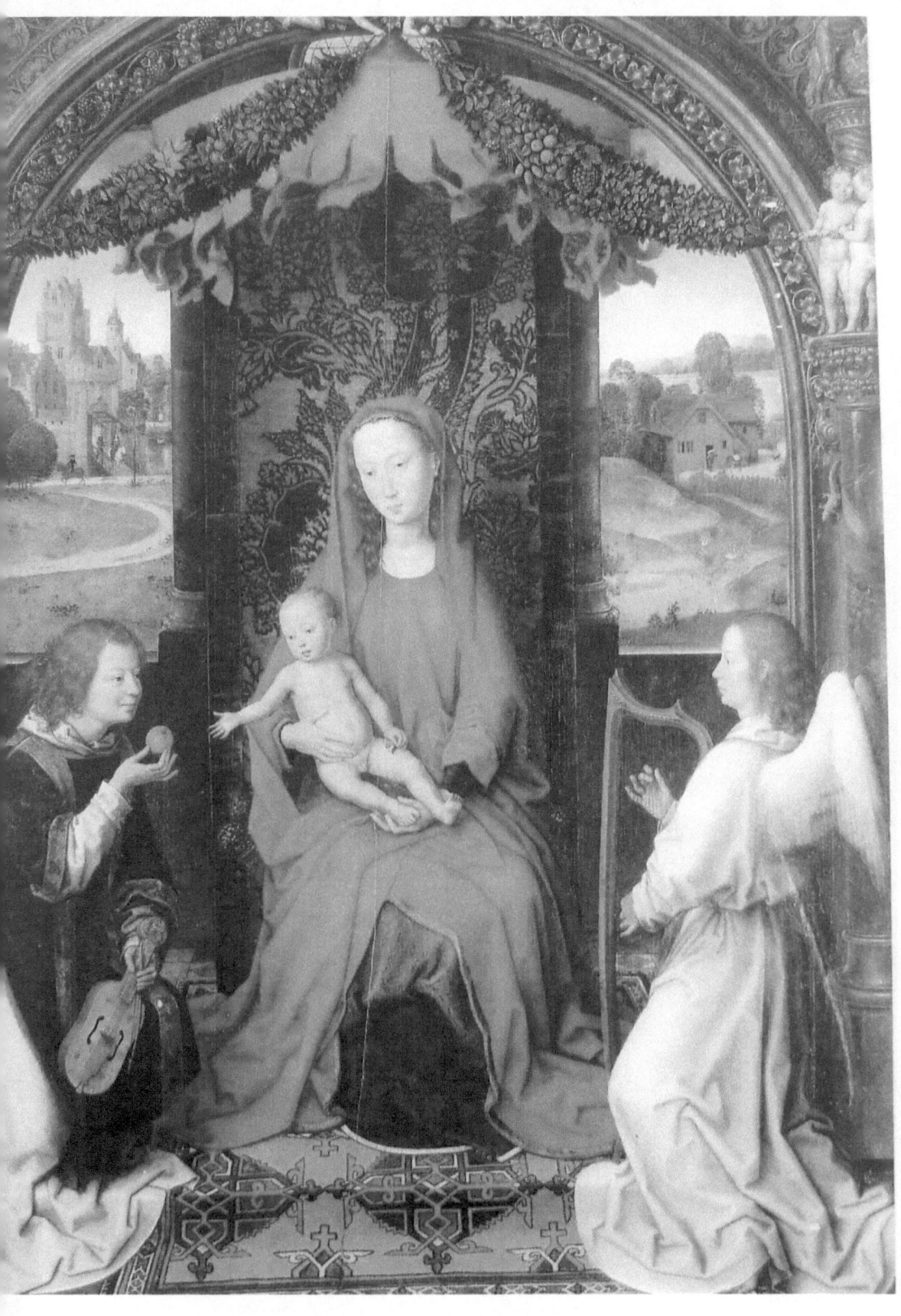
Hans Memling, Virgin and Child Enthroned, Vienna

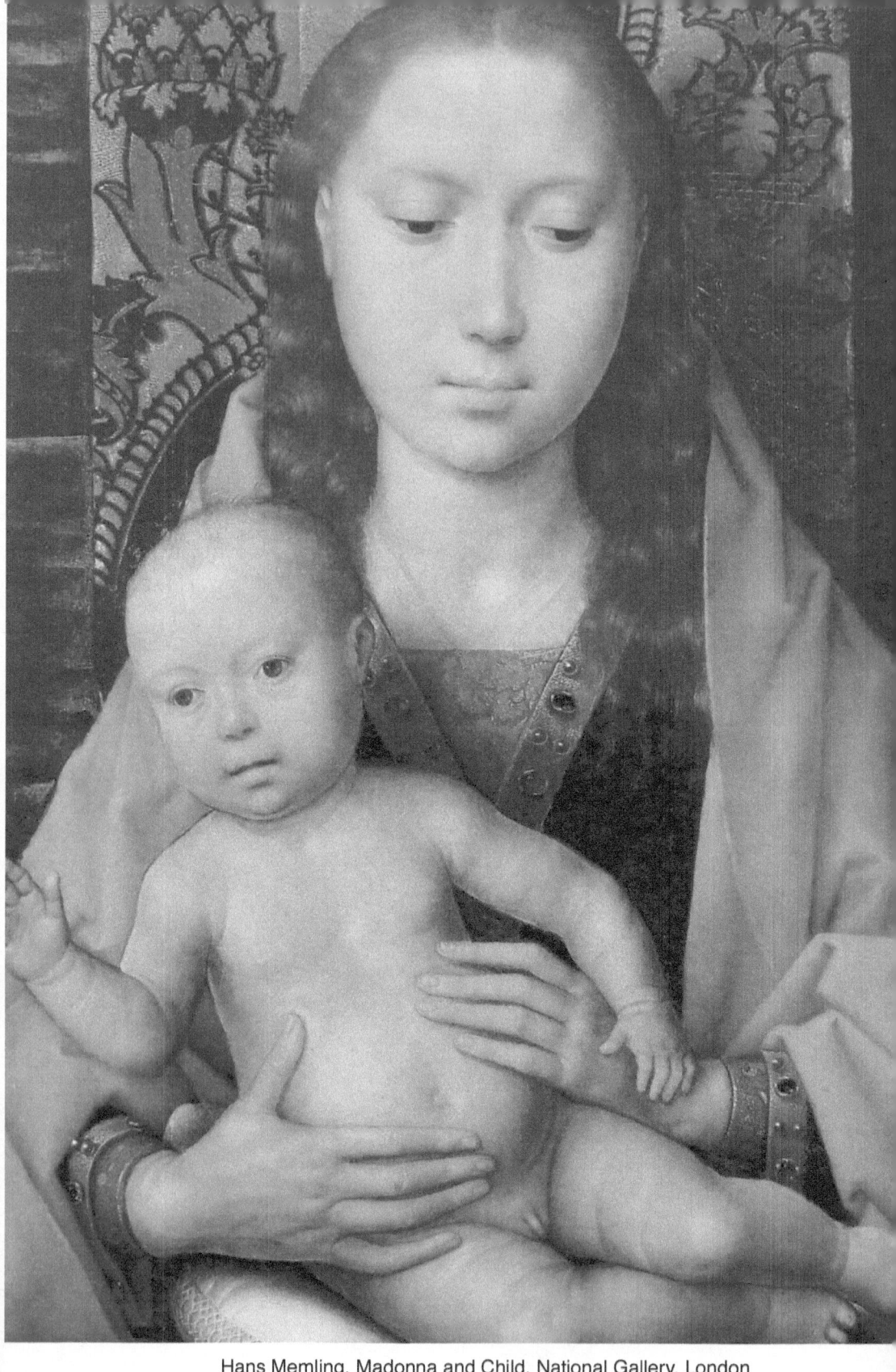

Hans Memling, Madonna and Child, National Gallery, London

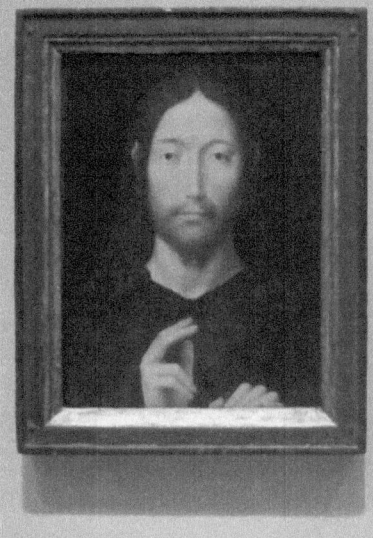

Hans Memling, Christ Blessing, Metropolitan Museum of Art

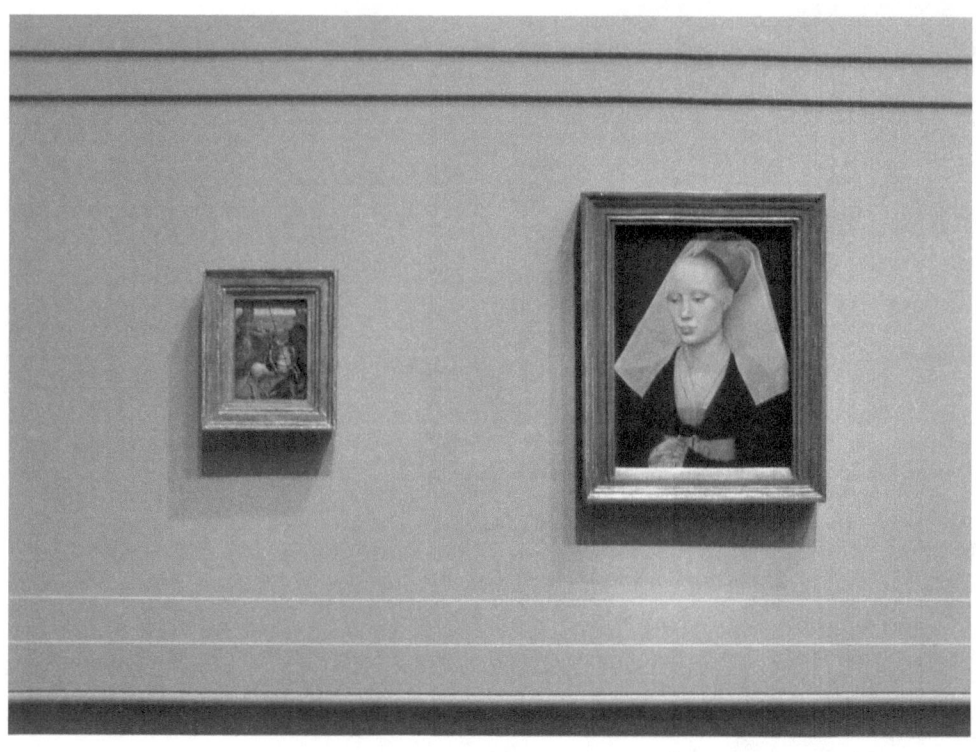

Rogier van der Weyden, National Gallery of Art, Washington, DC

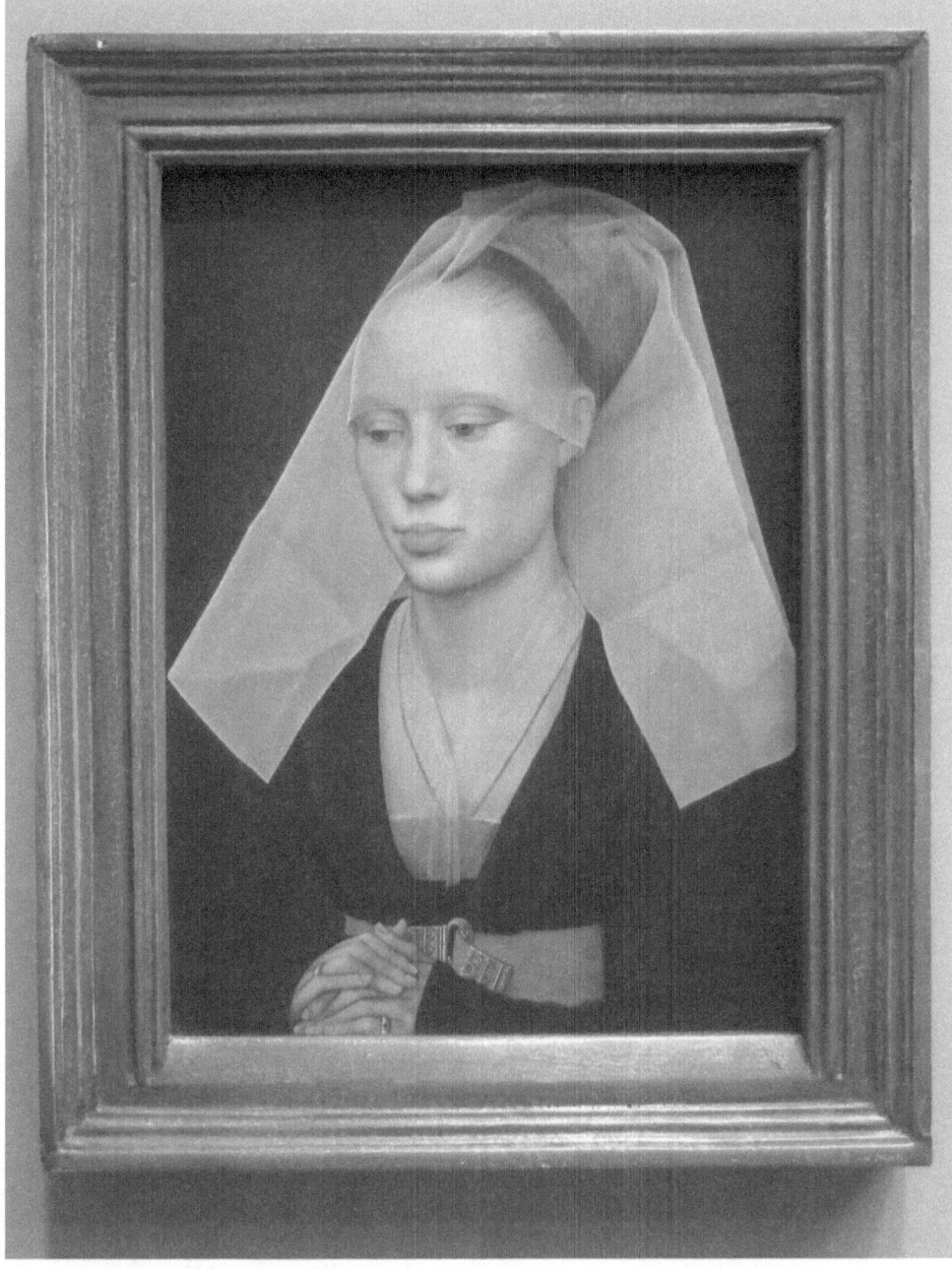

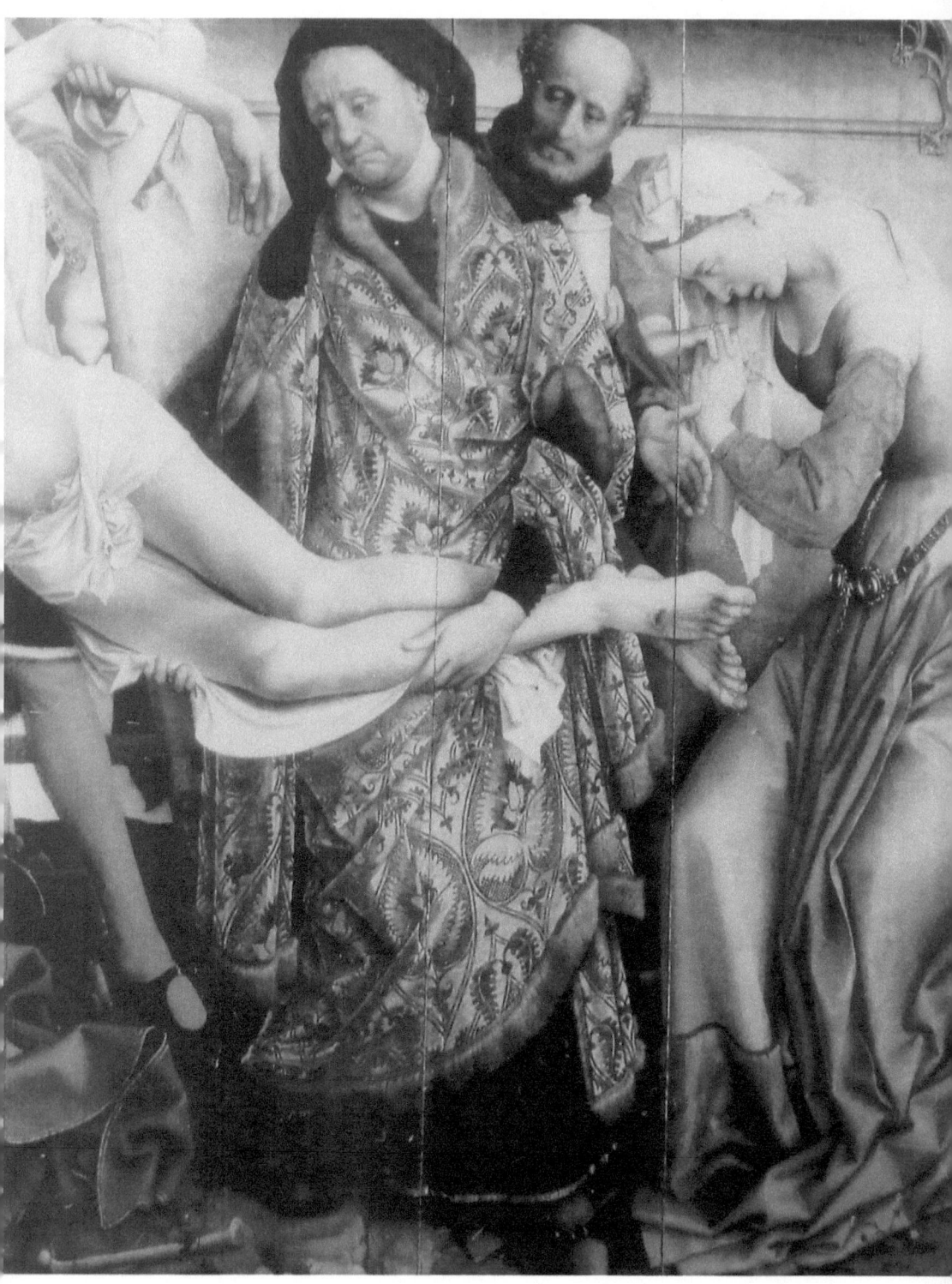

Rogier van der Weyden, Descent From the Cross, detail, Madrid

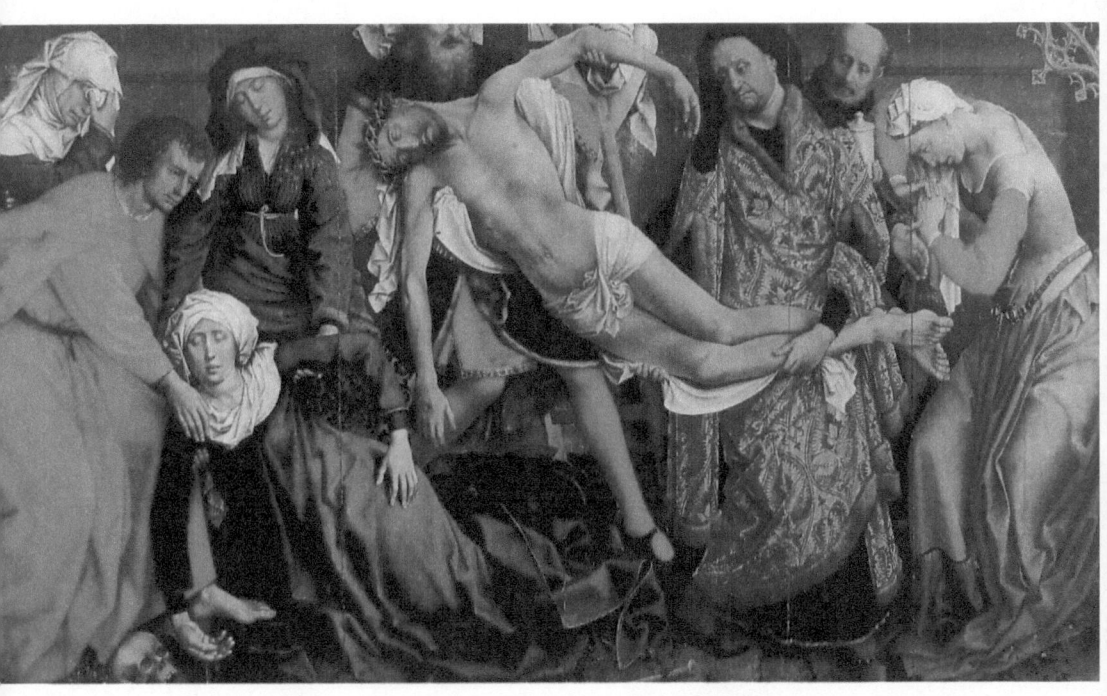

Rogier van der Weyden, Descent From the Cross, detail, Madrid

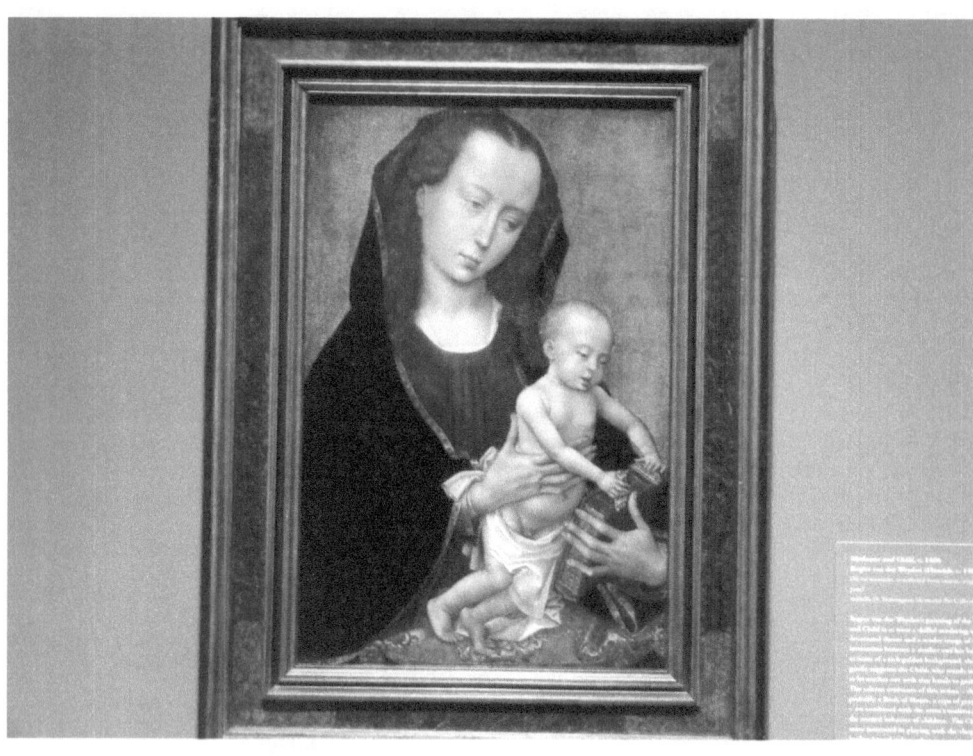

Rogier van der Weyden, Madonna and Child,
Metropolitan Museum of Art, New York

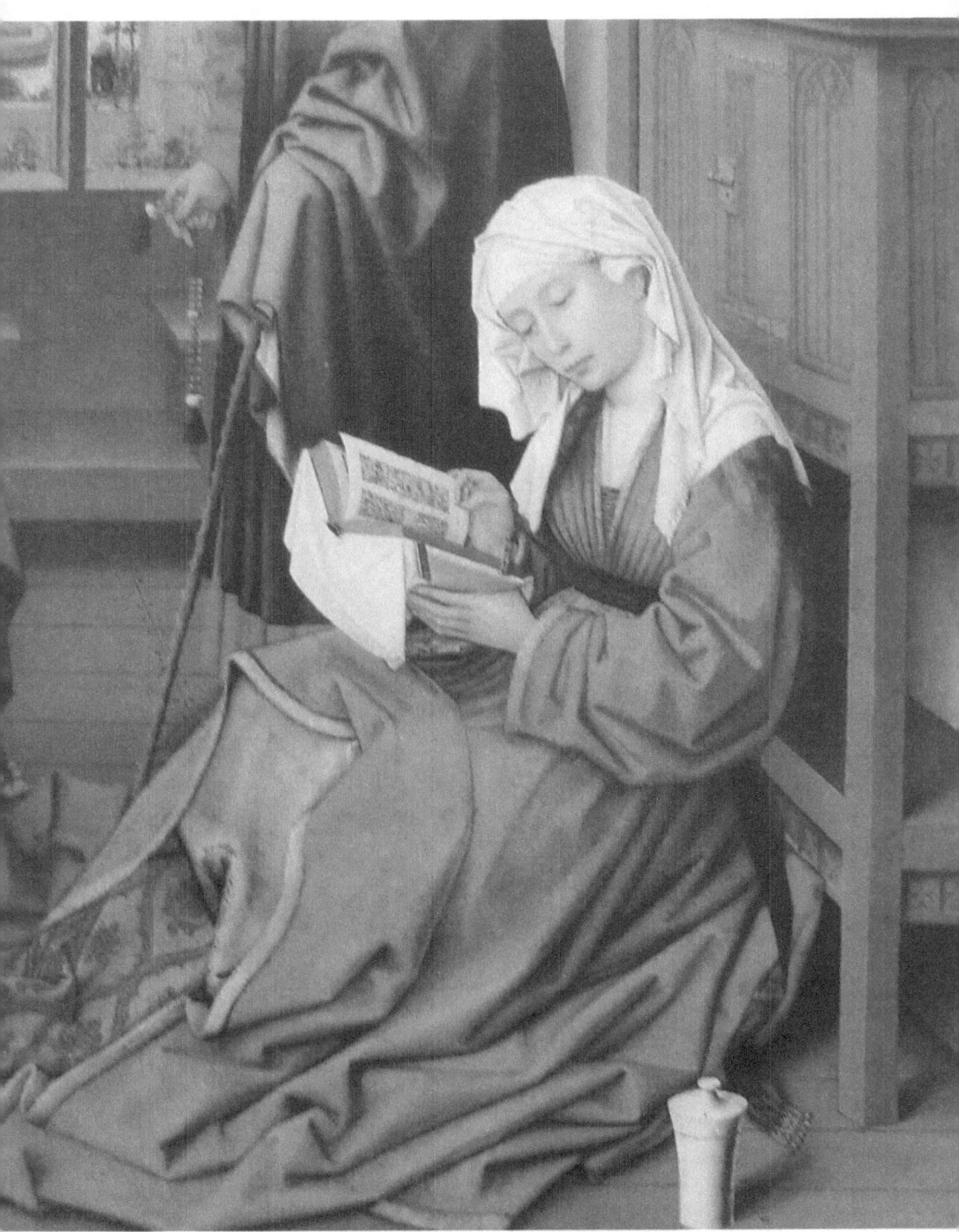

Rogier van der Weyden, Mary Magdalene Reading, detail, National Gallery, London

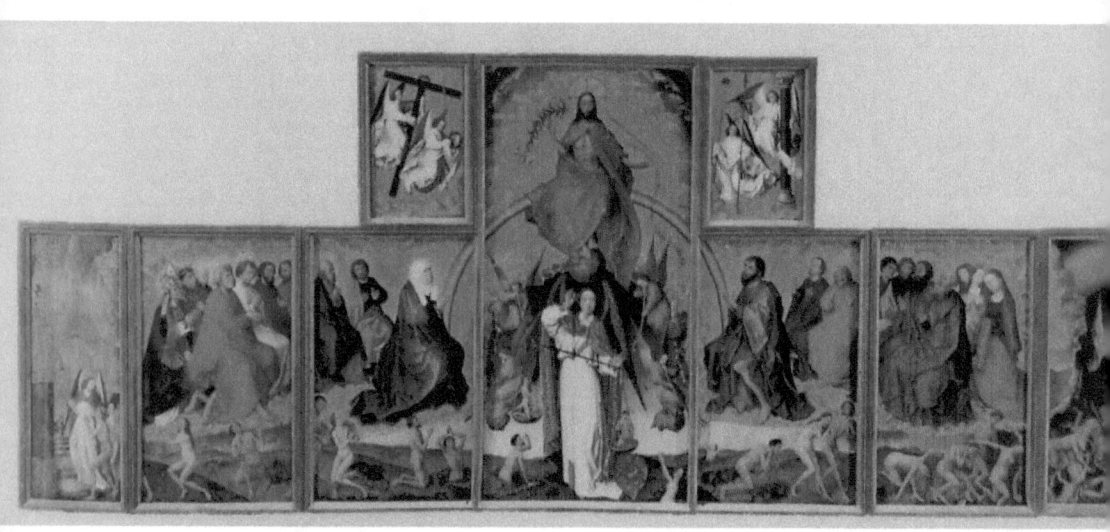

Rogier van der Weyden, The Last Judgement, 1445-49, Beaune

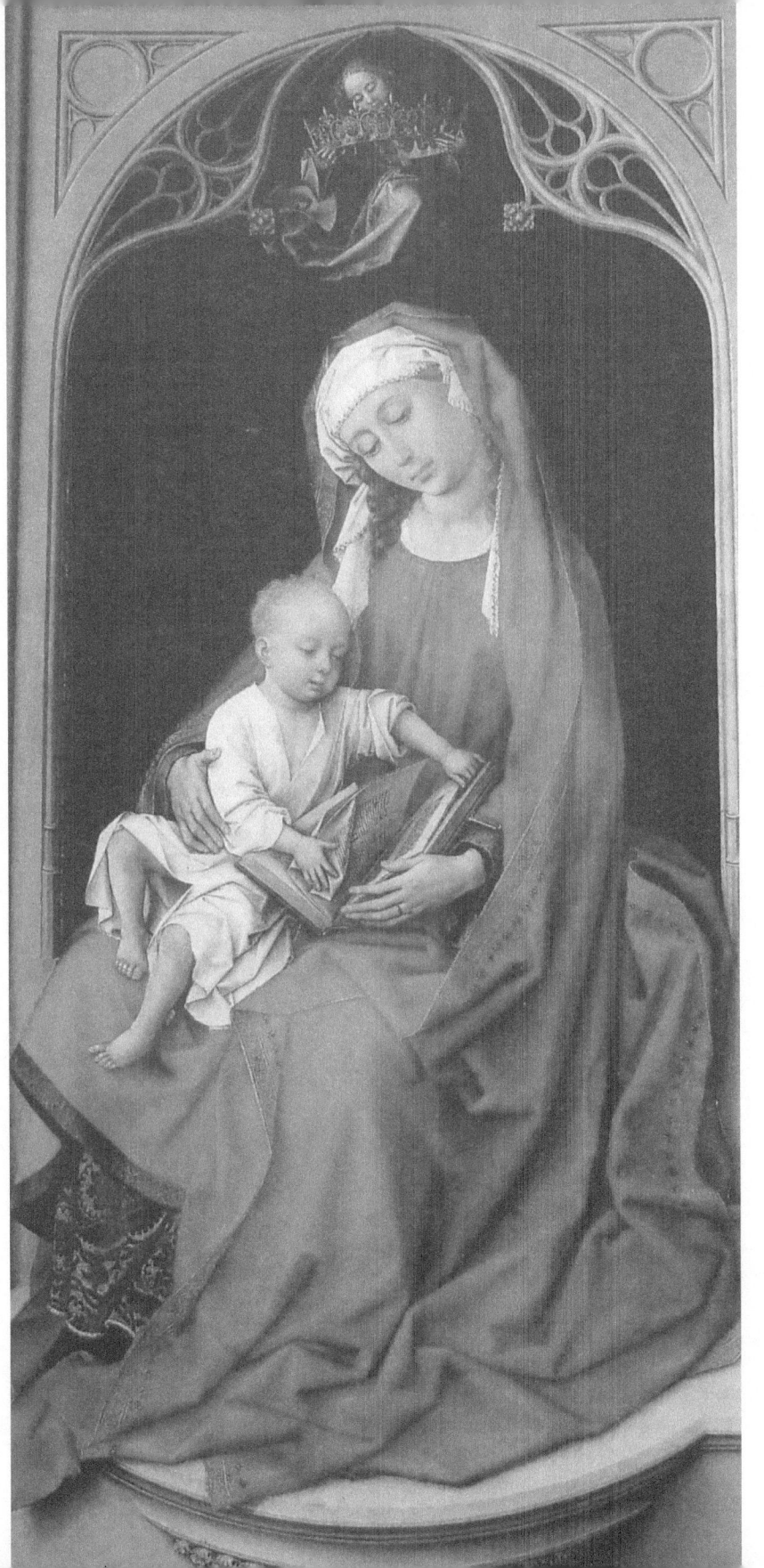

Rogier van der Weyden, Madonna and Child, Prado, Madrid

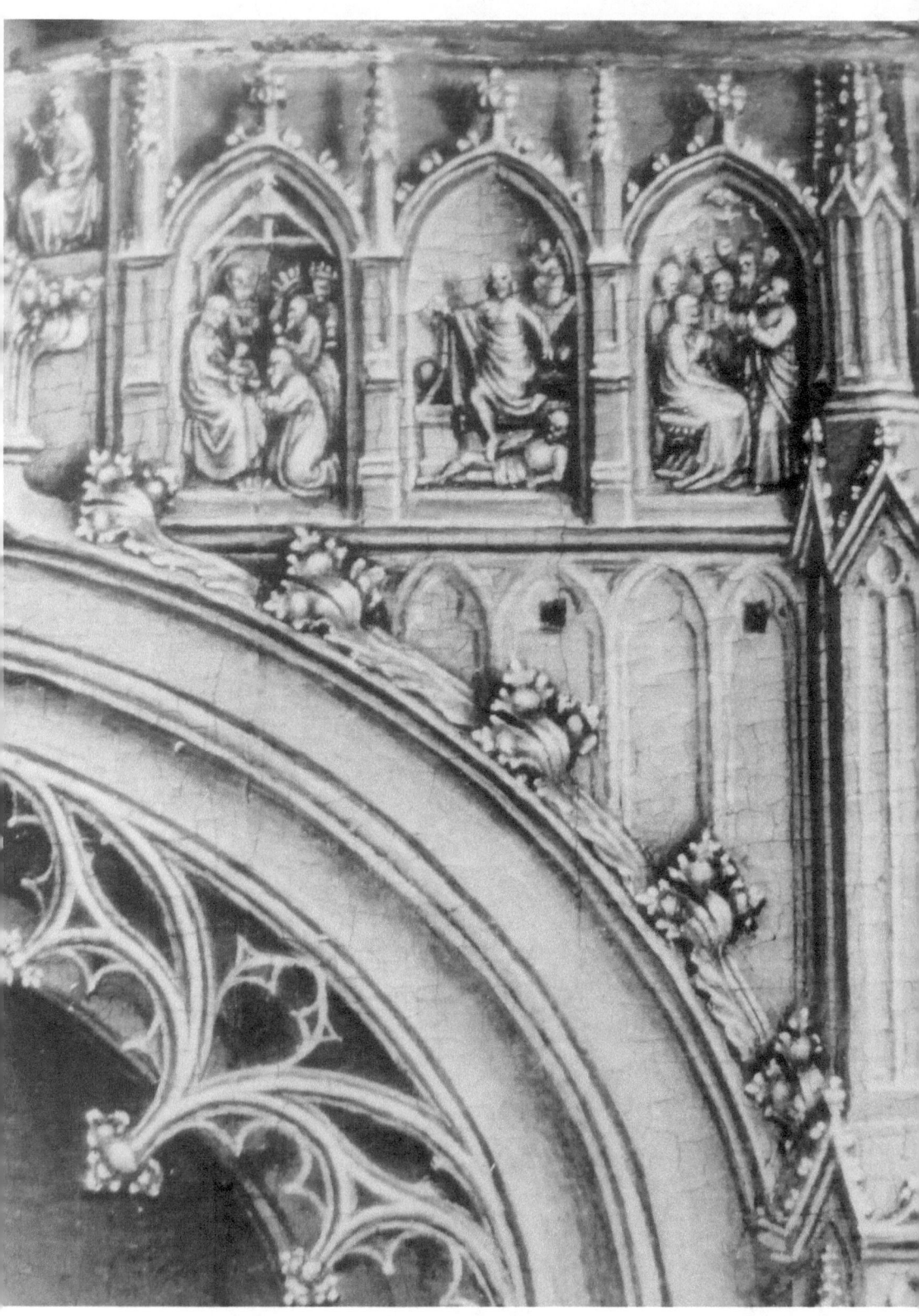

Rogier van der Weyden, 1433, detail, Thyssen-Bornemisza Collection, Madrid

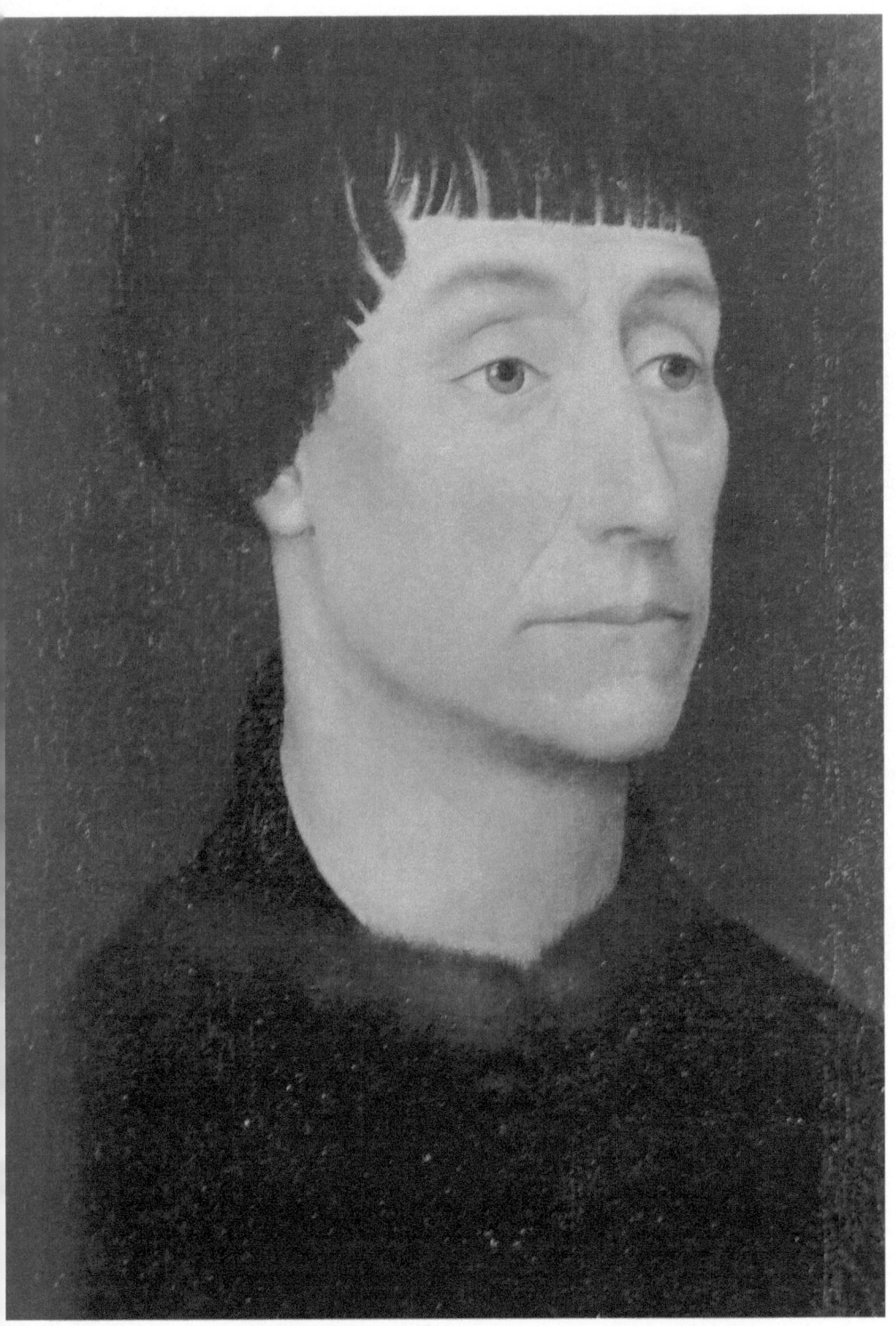

Rogier van der Weyden, Potrait of a Man, Thyssen-Bornemizsa

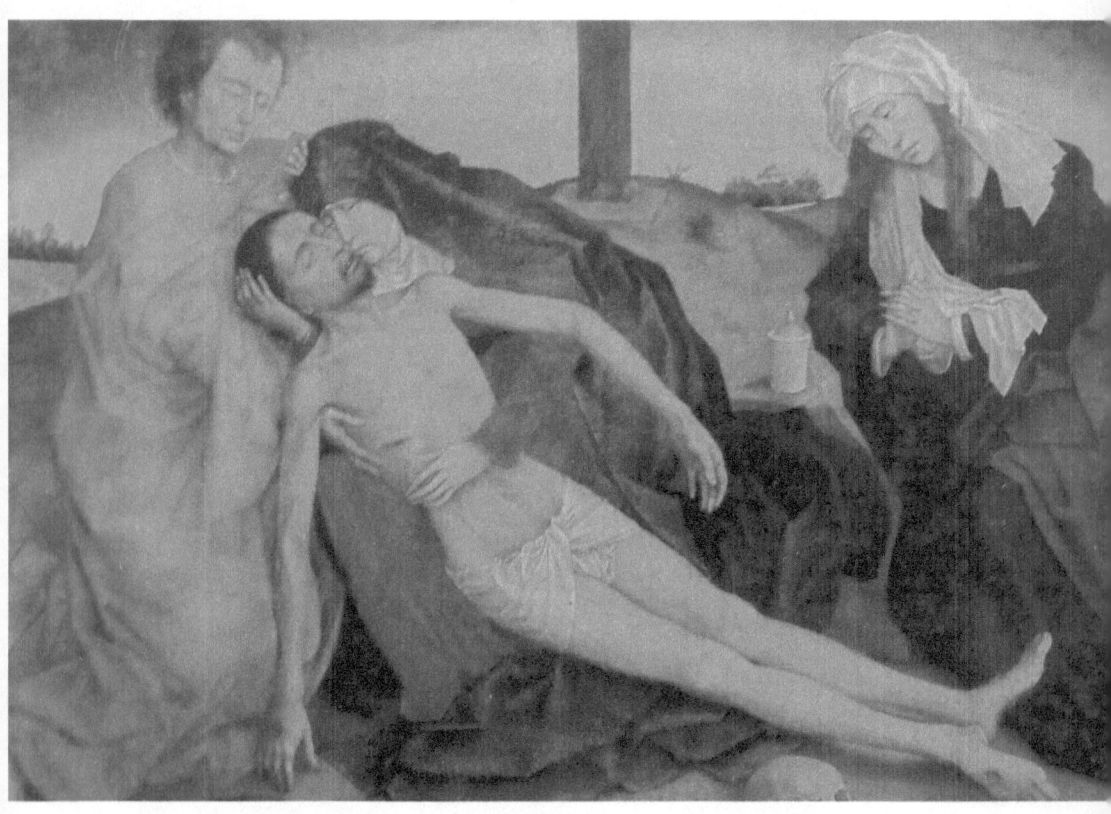

Rogier van der Weyden, Pietà, Brussels

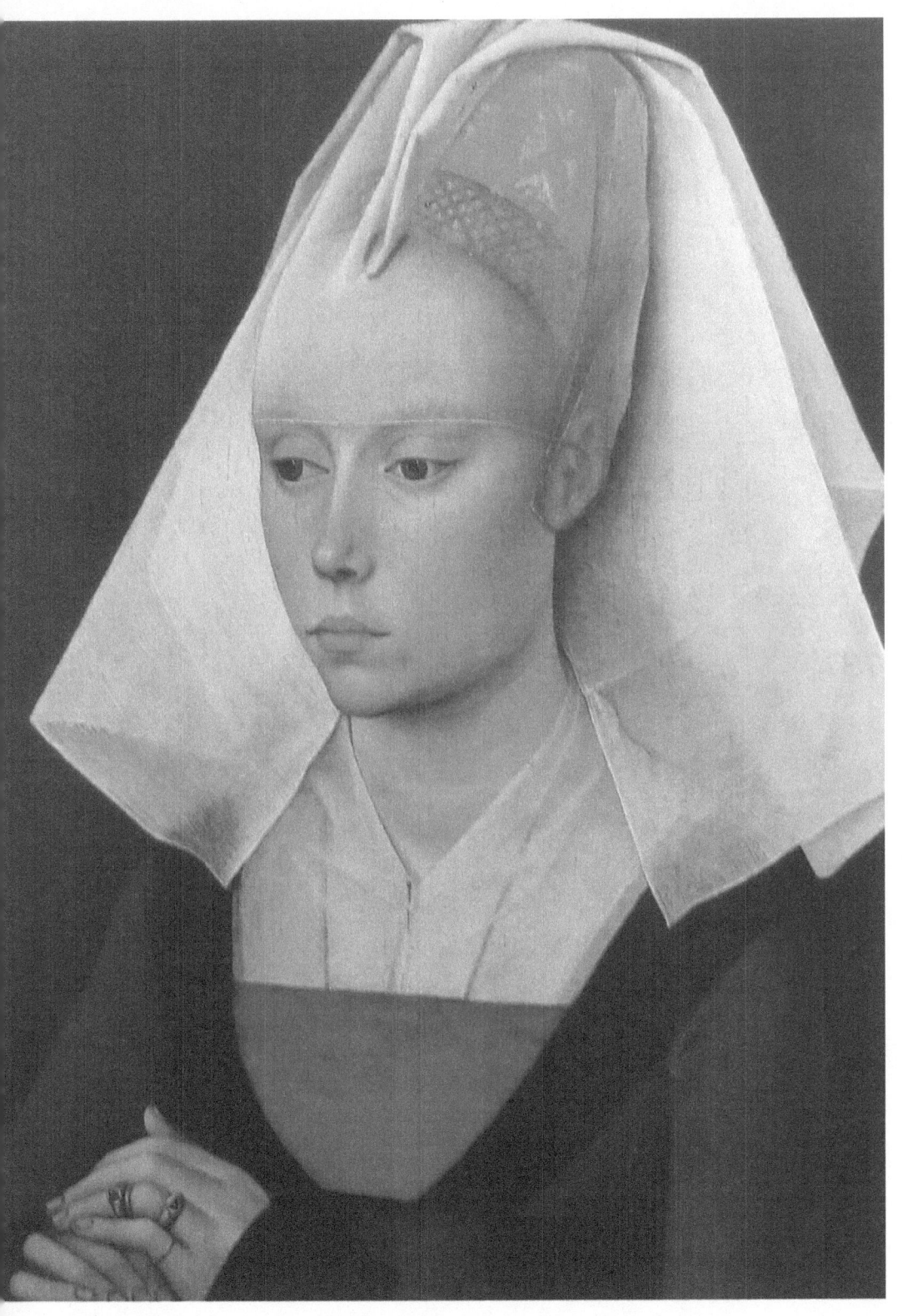
Rogier van der Weyden, Woman Praying, detail, National Gallery, London

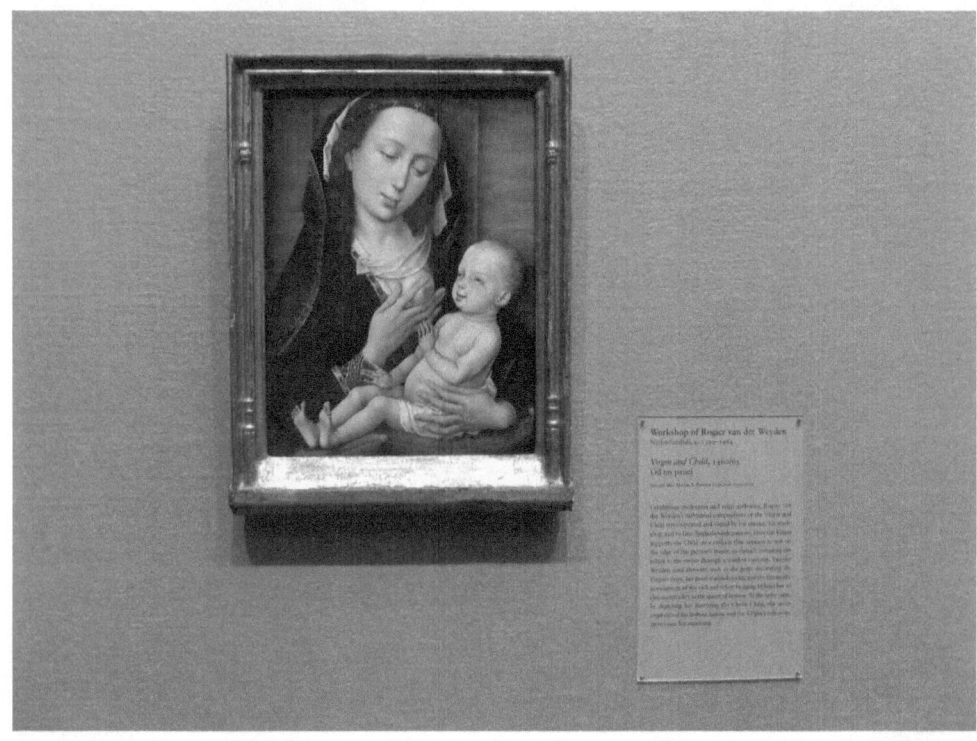

Rogier van der Weyden, workshop, Madonna and Child, Metropolitan Museum of Art, Gotham

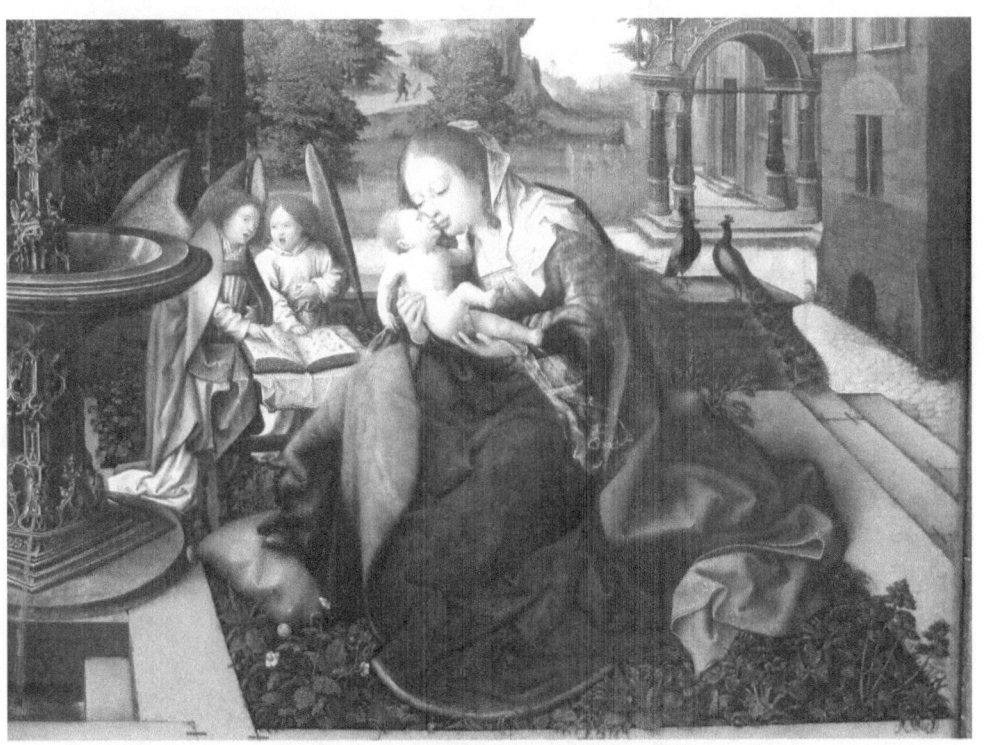

Bernard Van Orley. Madonna and Child,
Metropolitan Museum of Art, New York

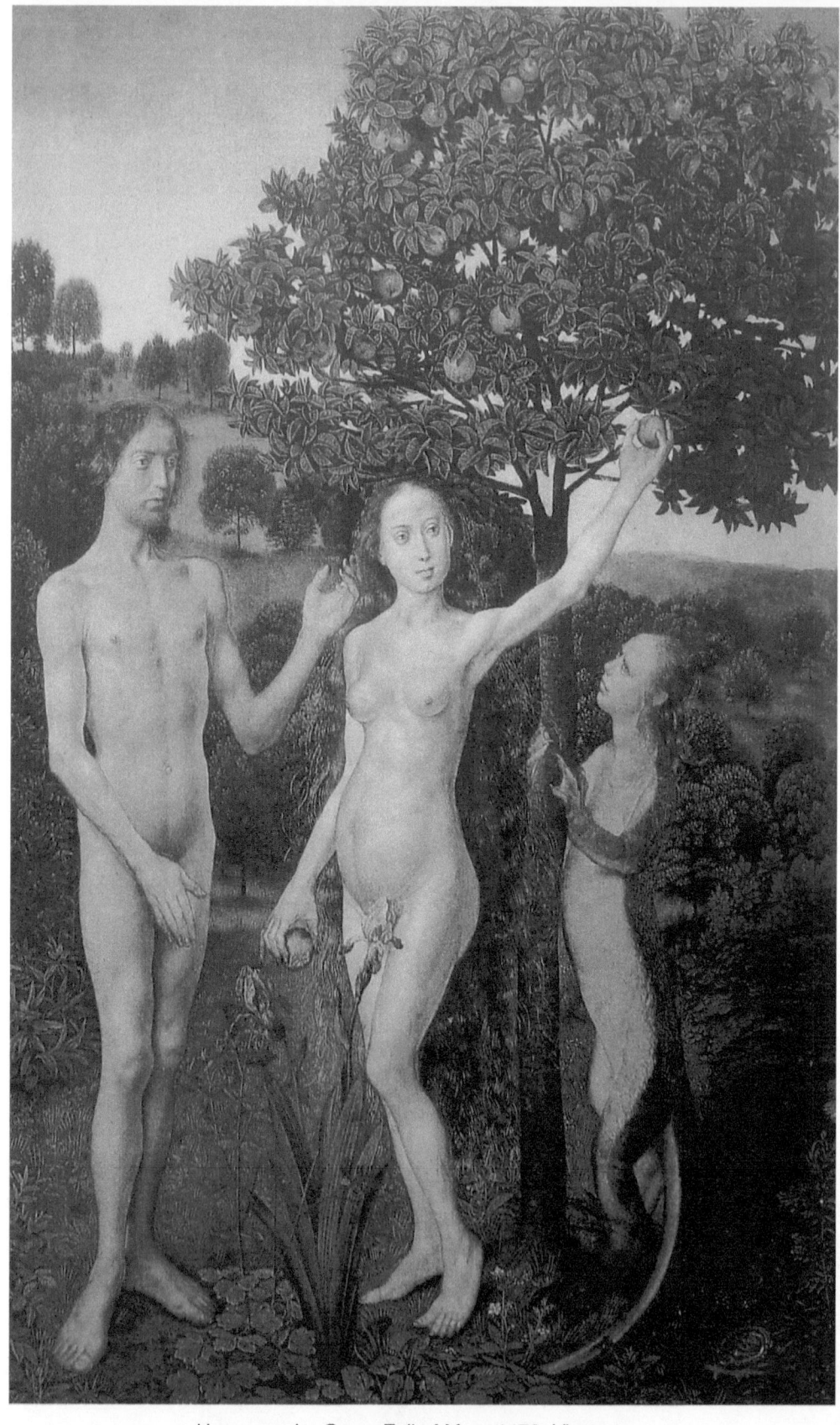
Hugo van der Goes, Fall of Man, 1470, Vienna

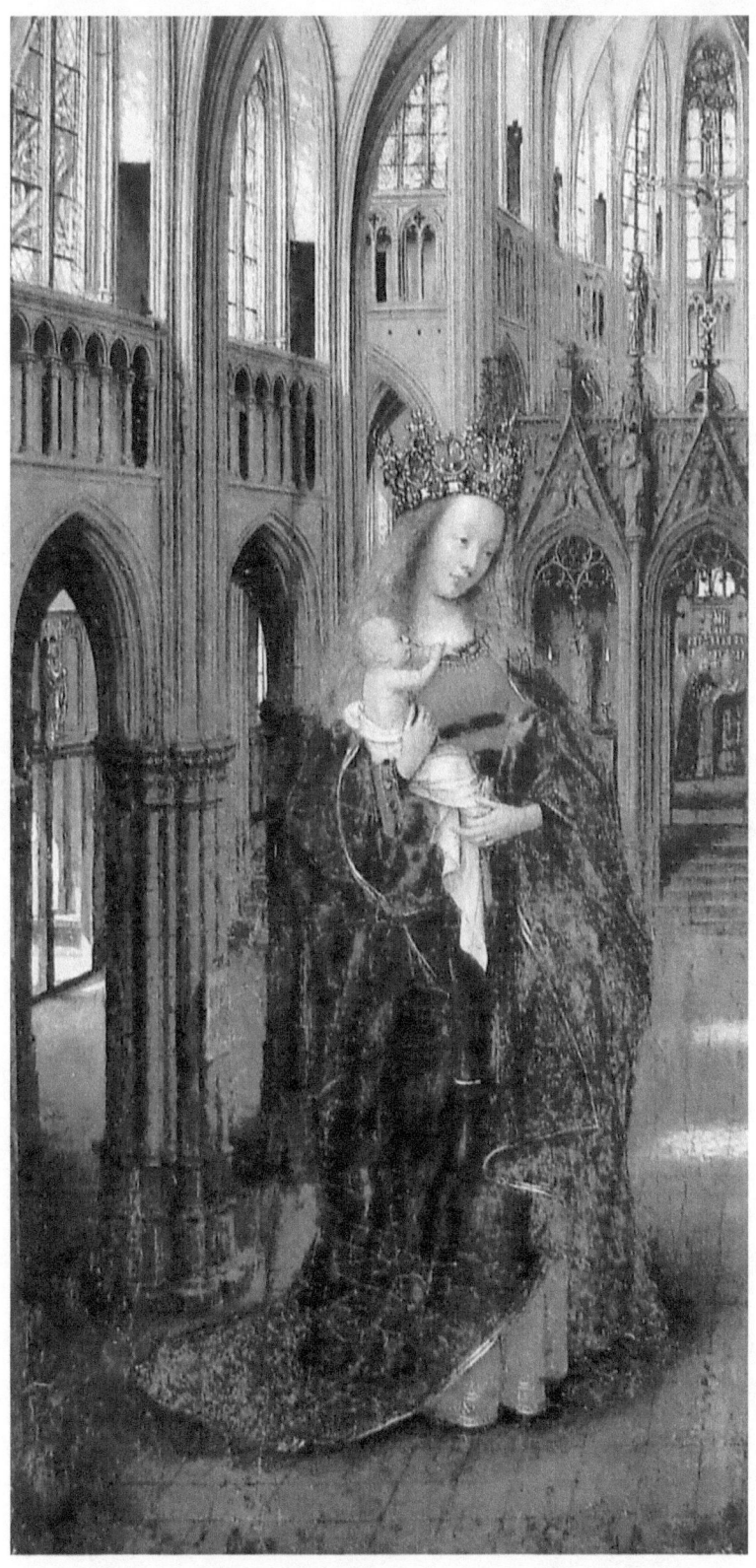
Jan van Eyck, Madonna In a Church, Berlin

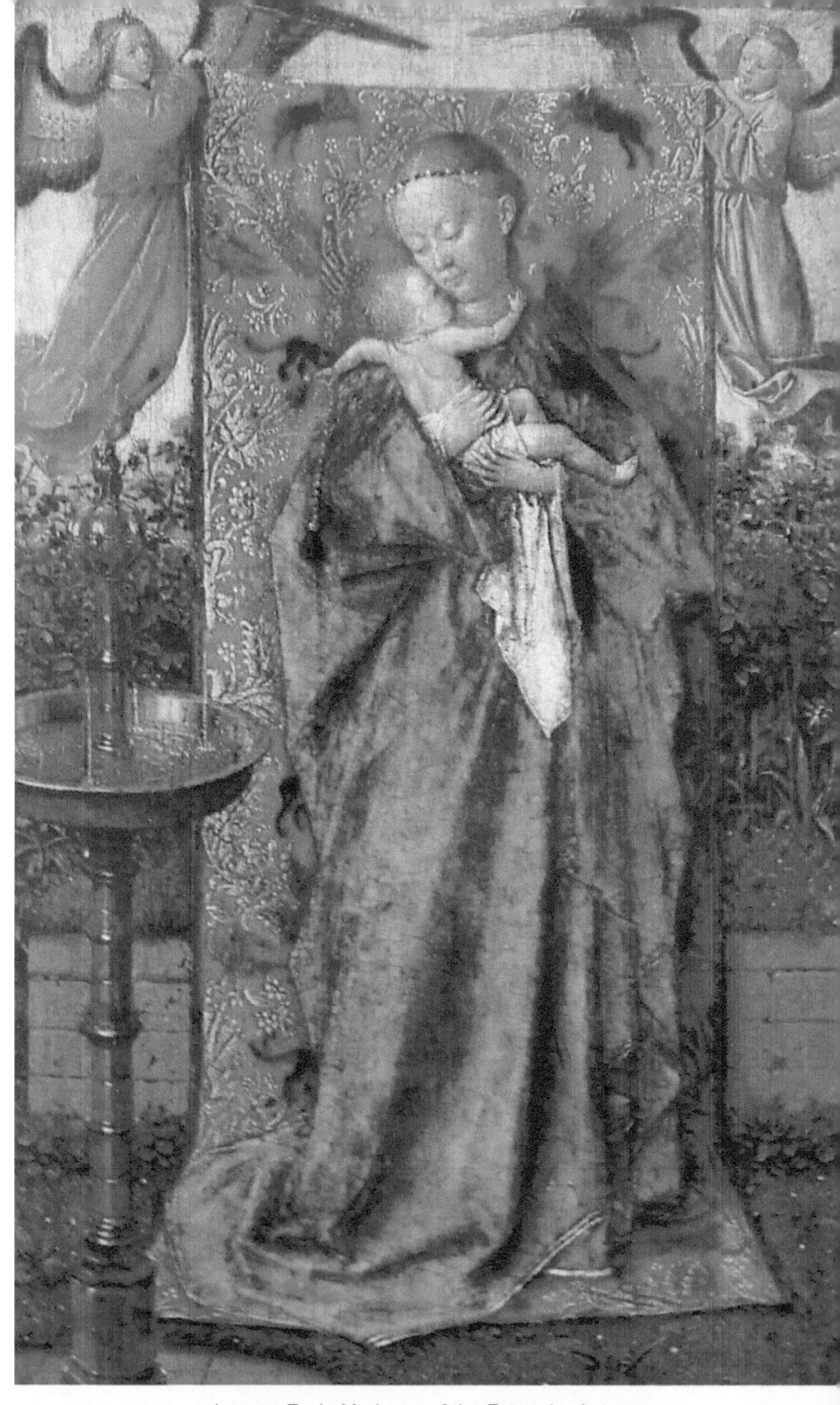
Jan van Eyck, Madonna of the Fountain, Antwerp

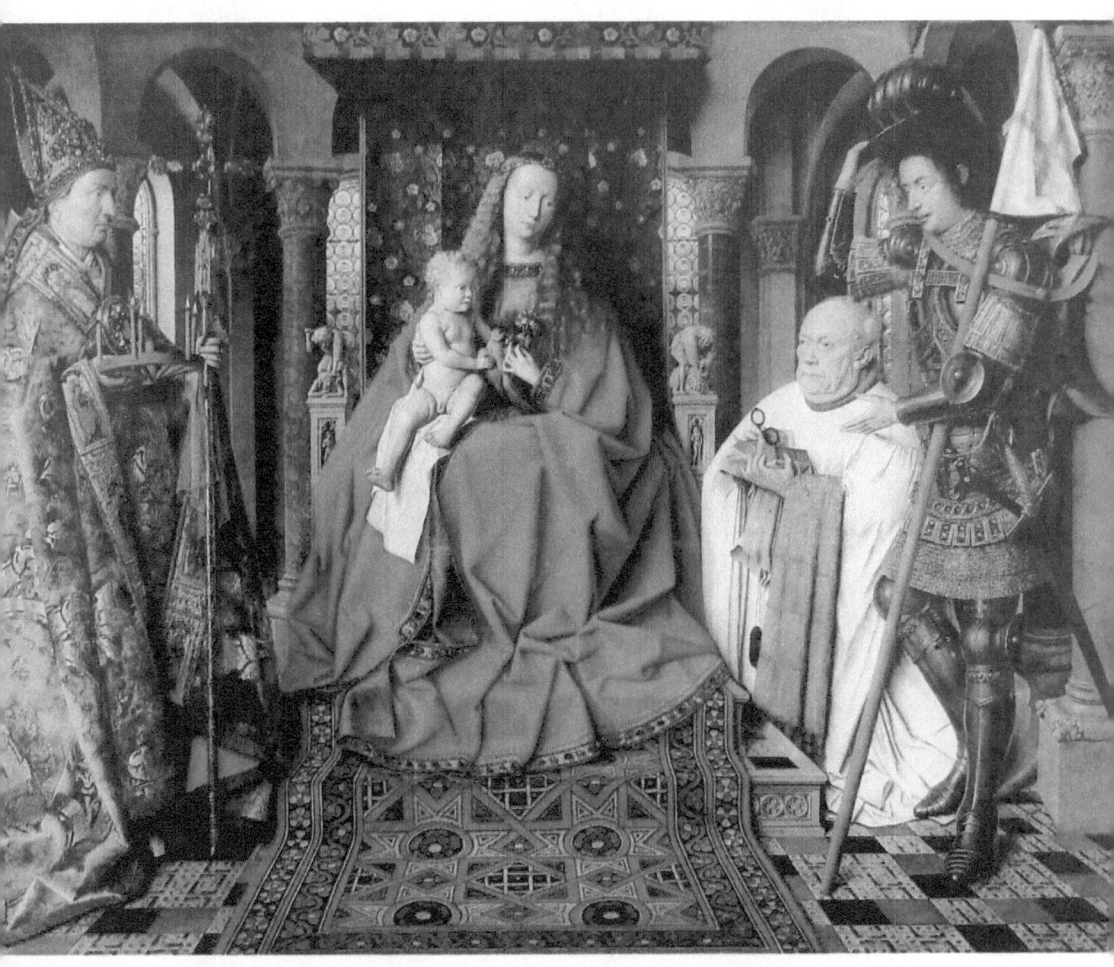

Jan van Eyck, The Paele Madonna, 1436, Bruges

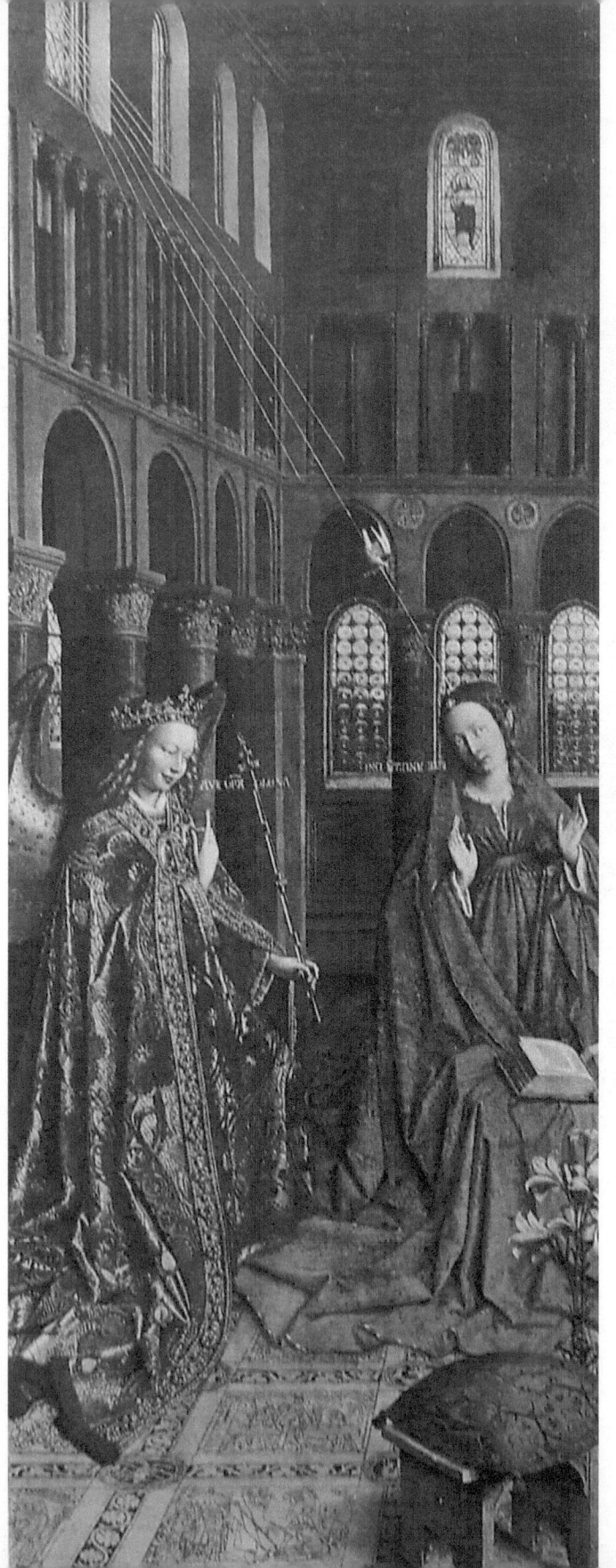

Jan van Eyck
The Annuncia-
tion, National
Gallery of Art
Washington, D

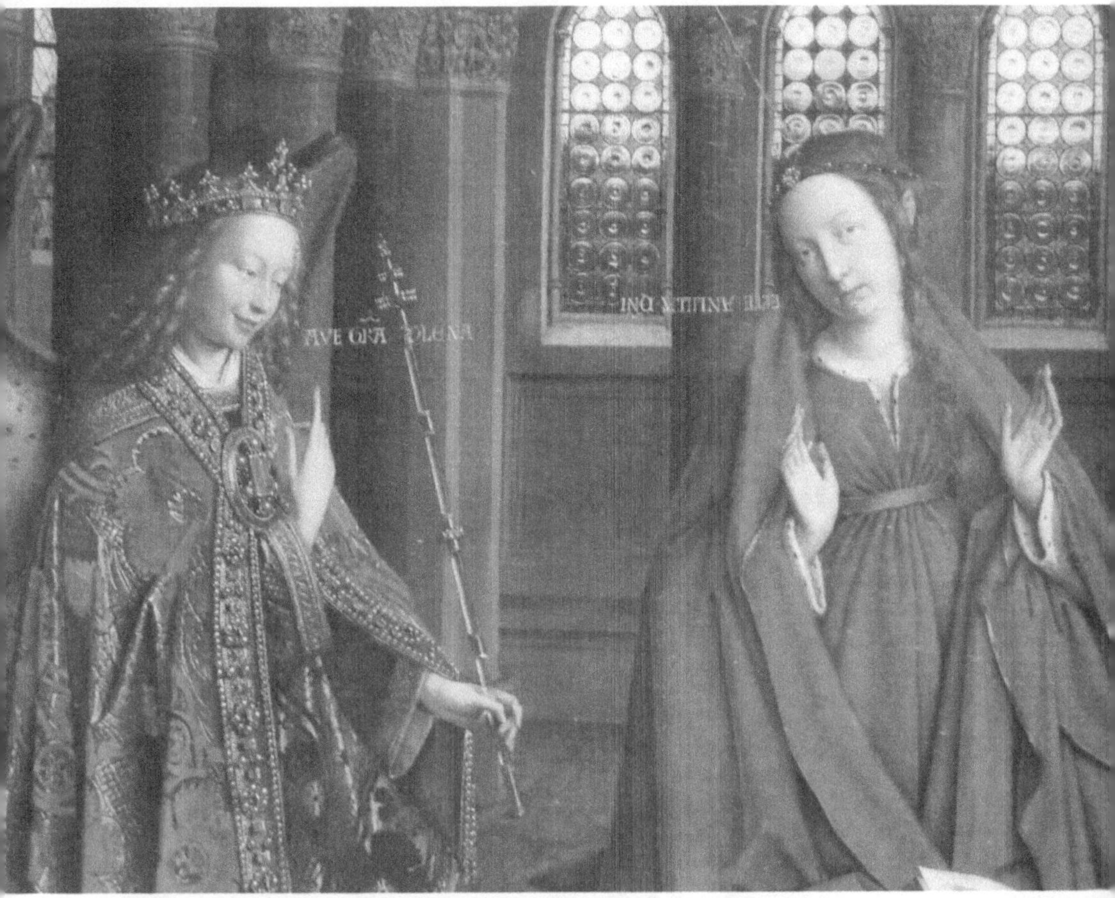

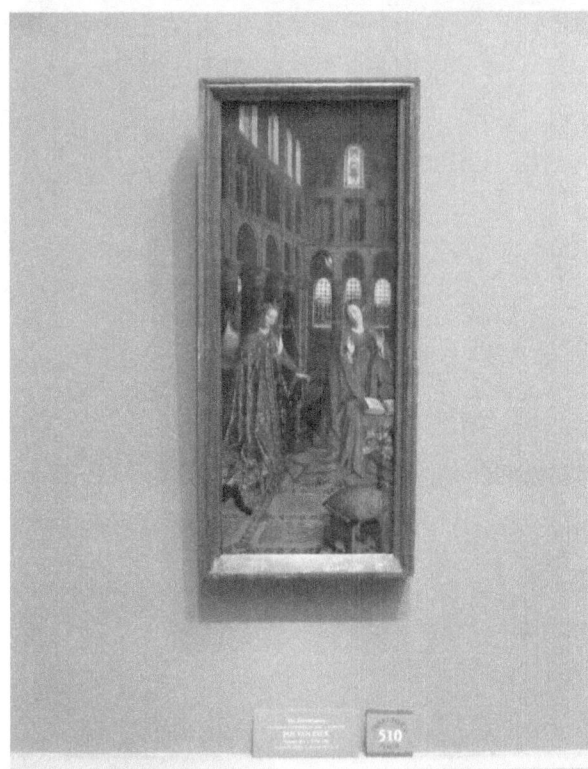

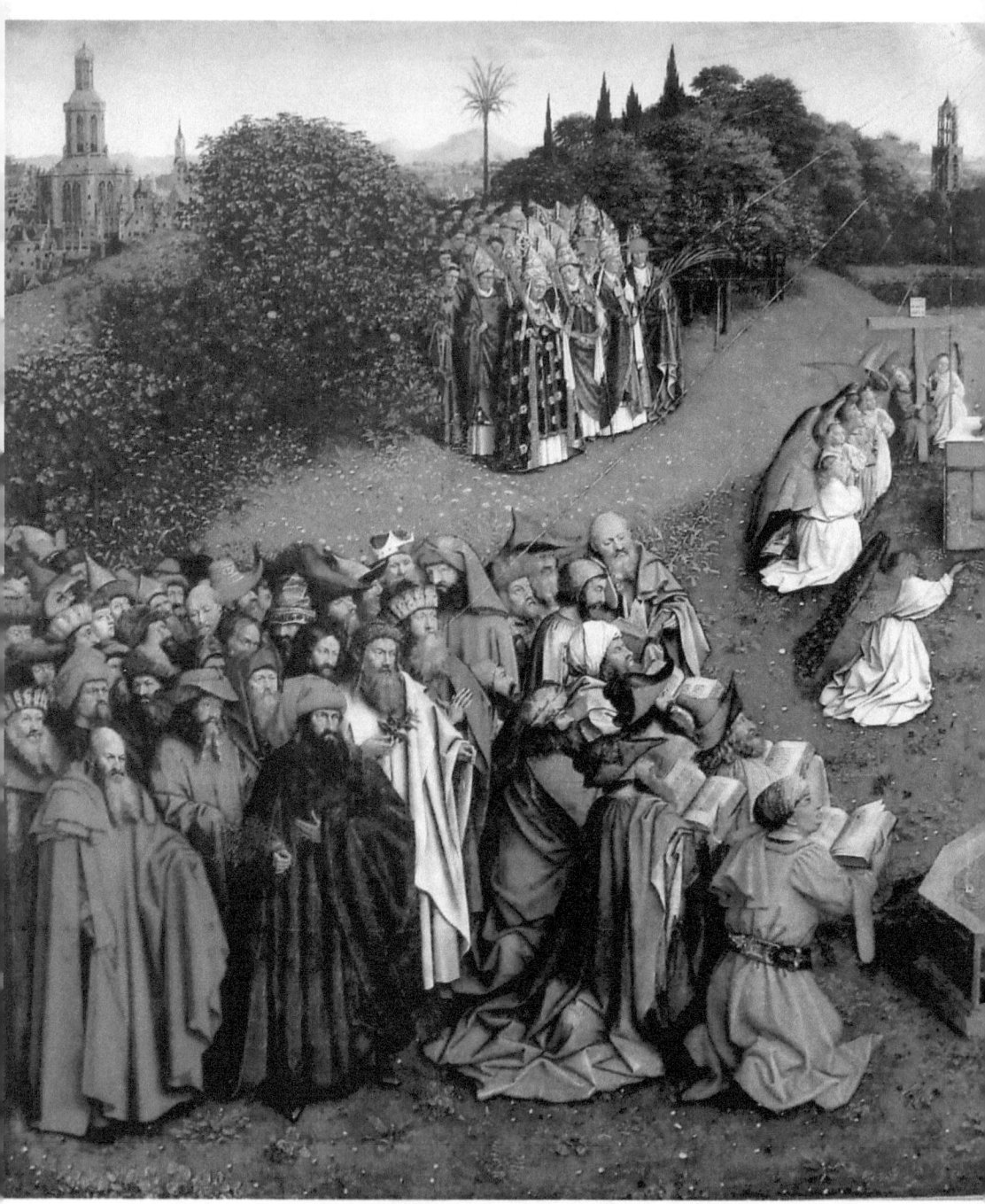

Jan van Eyck, The Ghent Altarpiece, detail

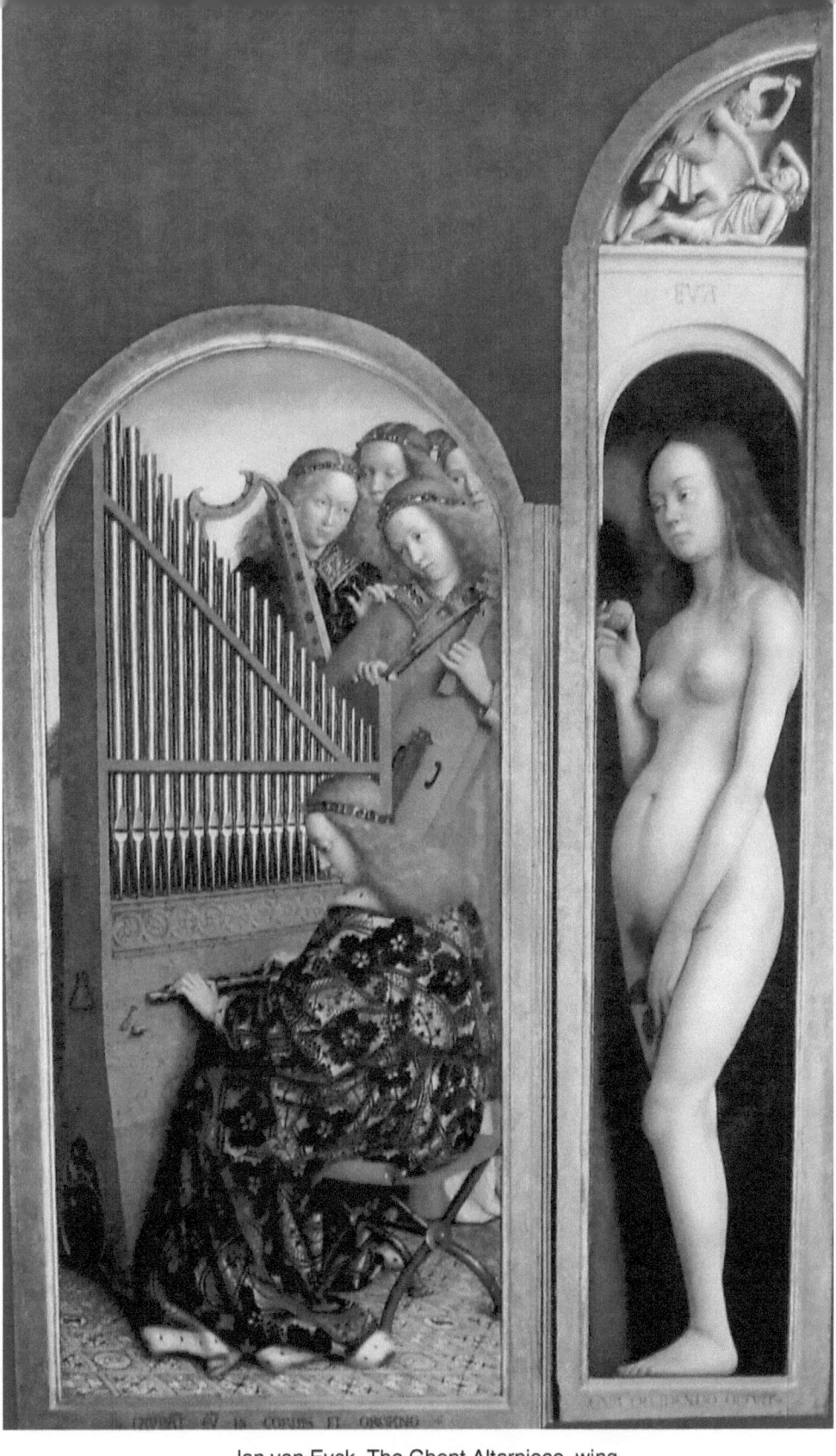

Jan van Eyck, The Ghent Altarpiece, wing

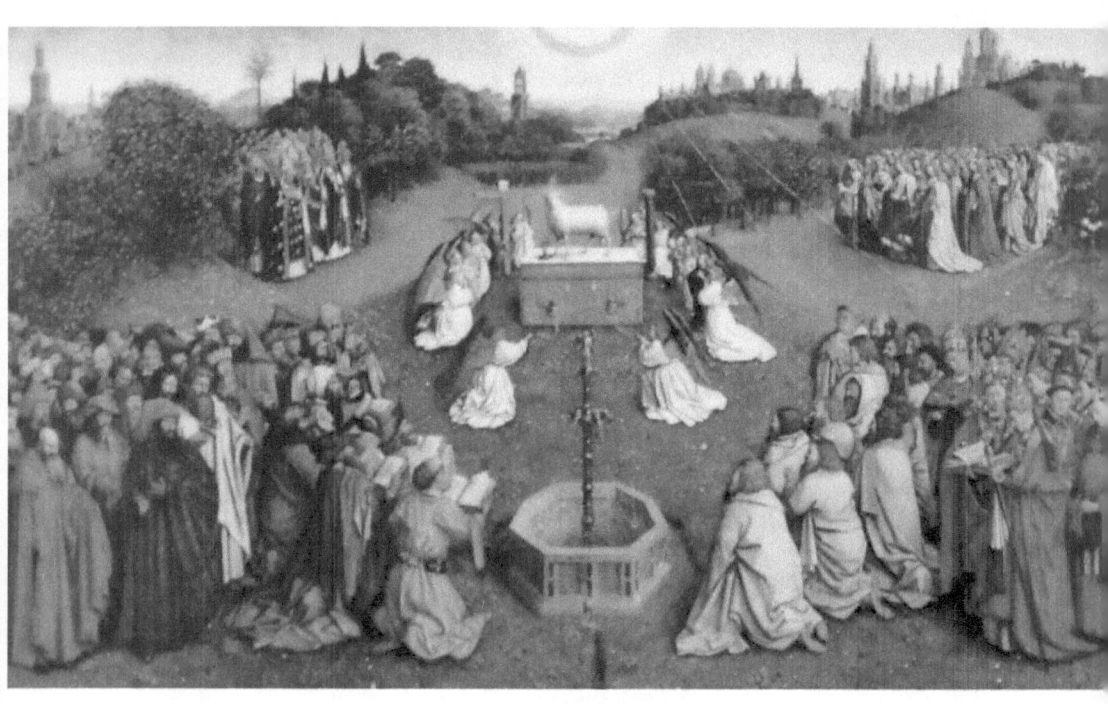

Jan van Eyck, The Ghent Altarpiece, detail

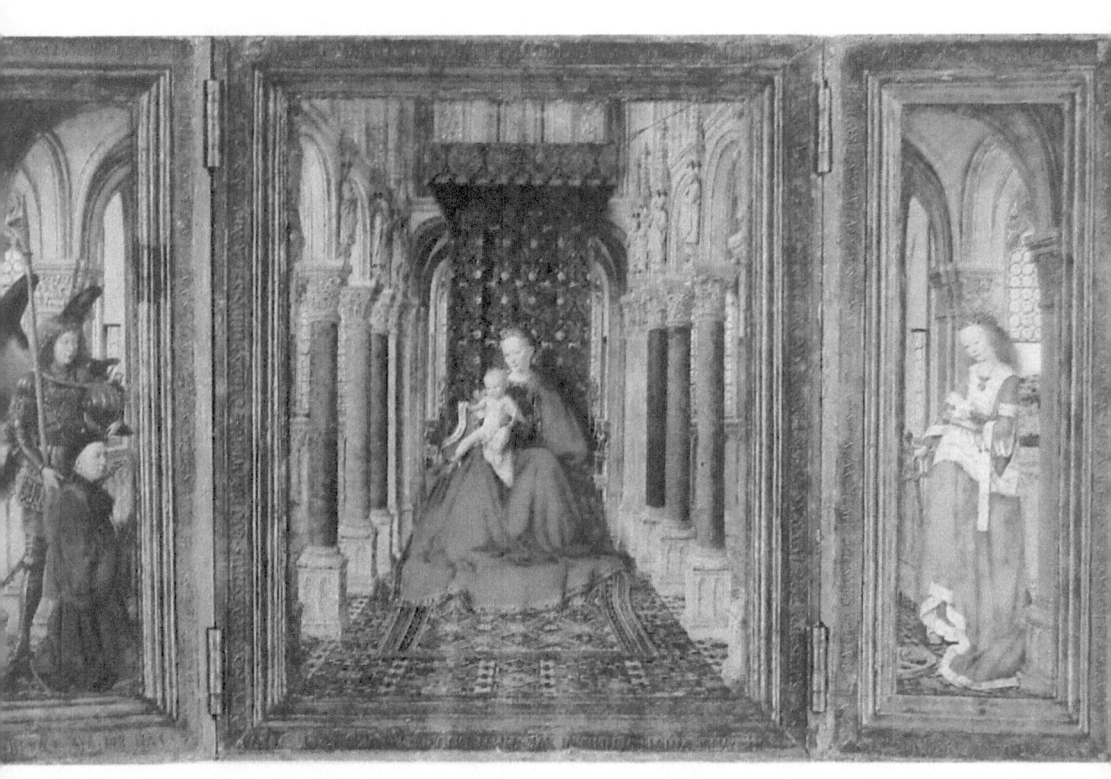

Jan van Eyck, The Dresden Triptych, 1437, Dresden

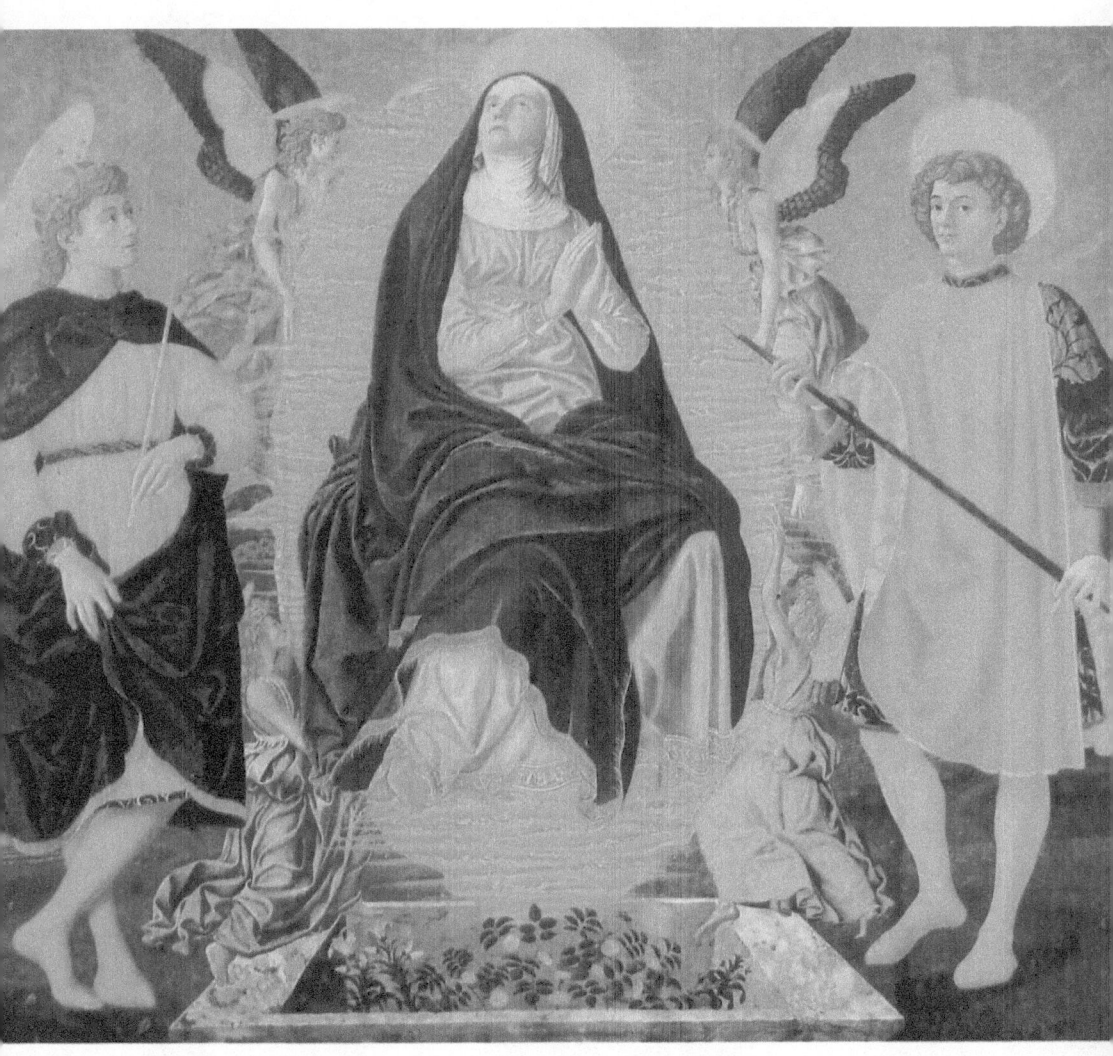

Andrea del Castagno, Assumption, Berlin

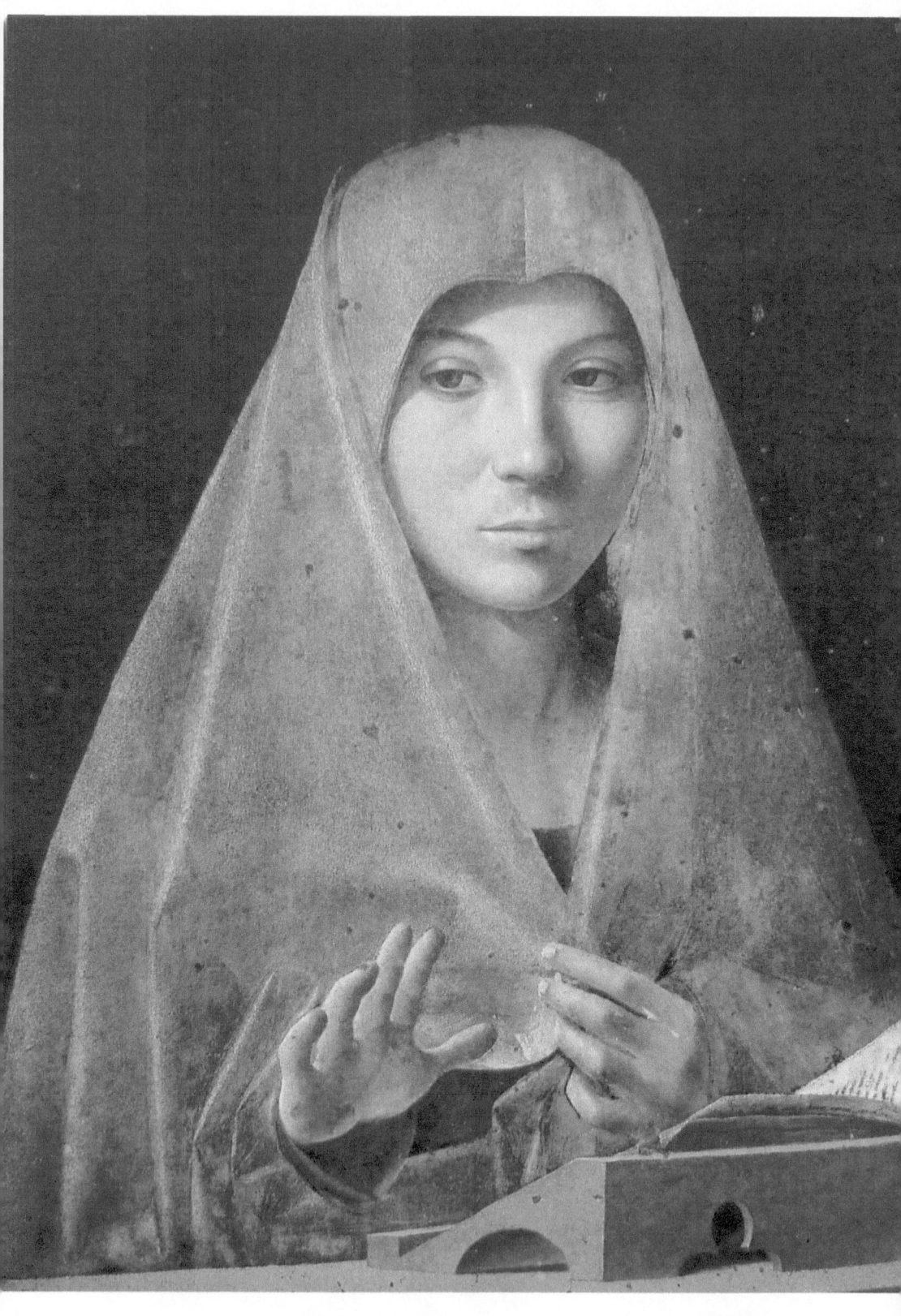
Antonello da Messina, The Virgin of the Annunciation, 1475, Palermo

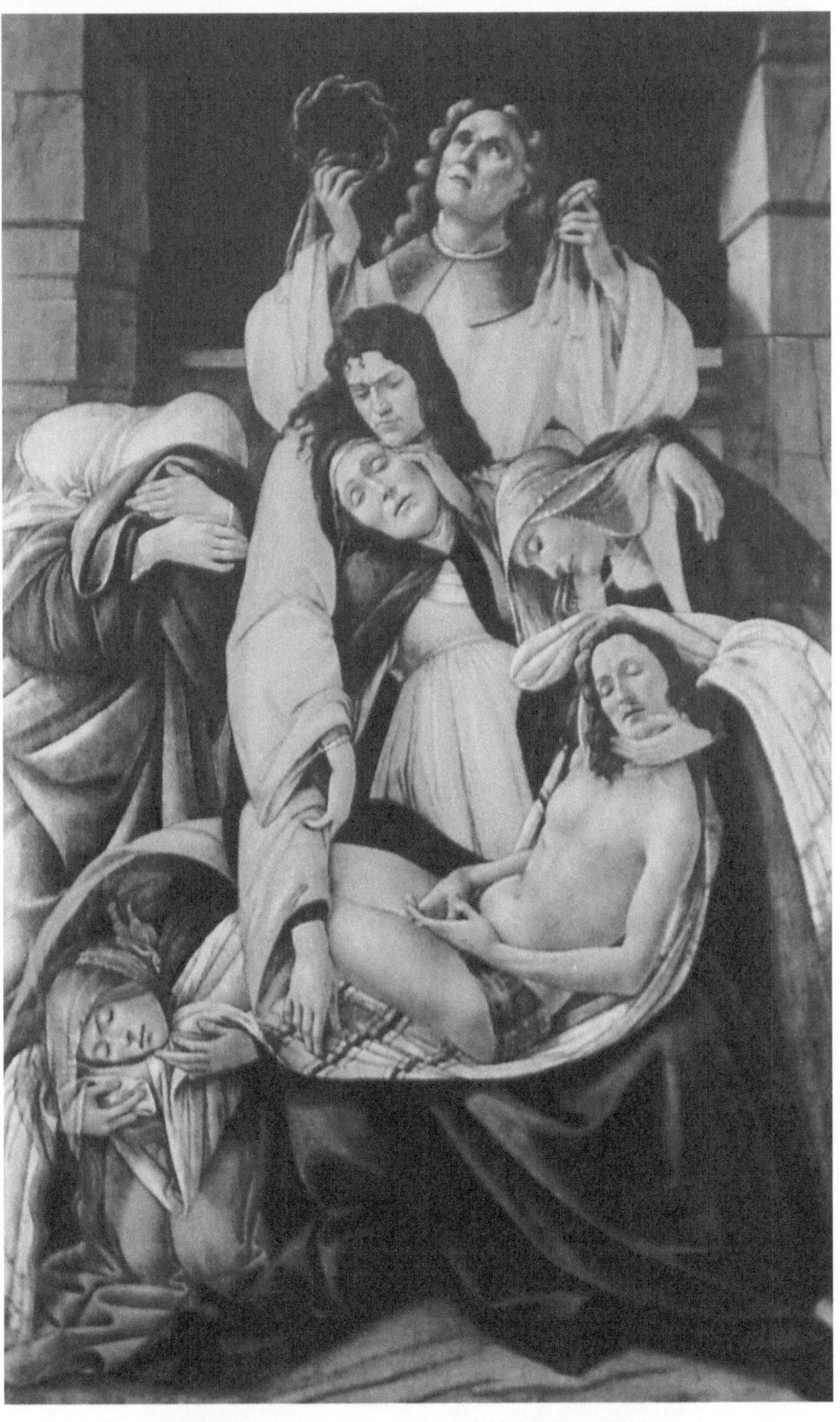

Sandro Botticelli, *Pietà*, Museo Poldi Pezzoli, Milan

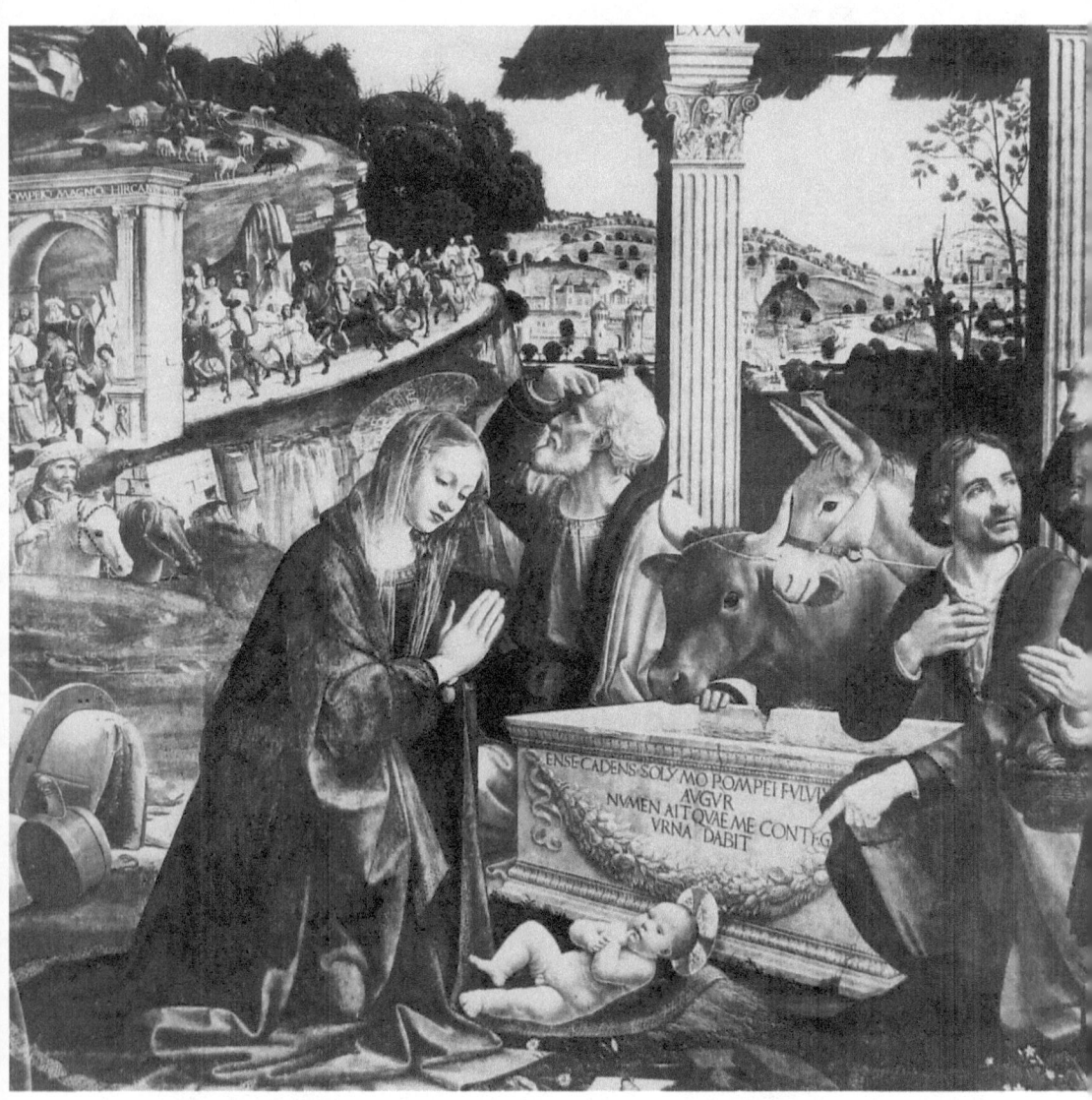

Domenico Ghirlandaio, Adoration of the Shepherds, 1485

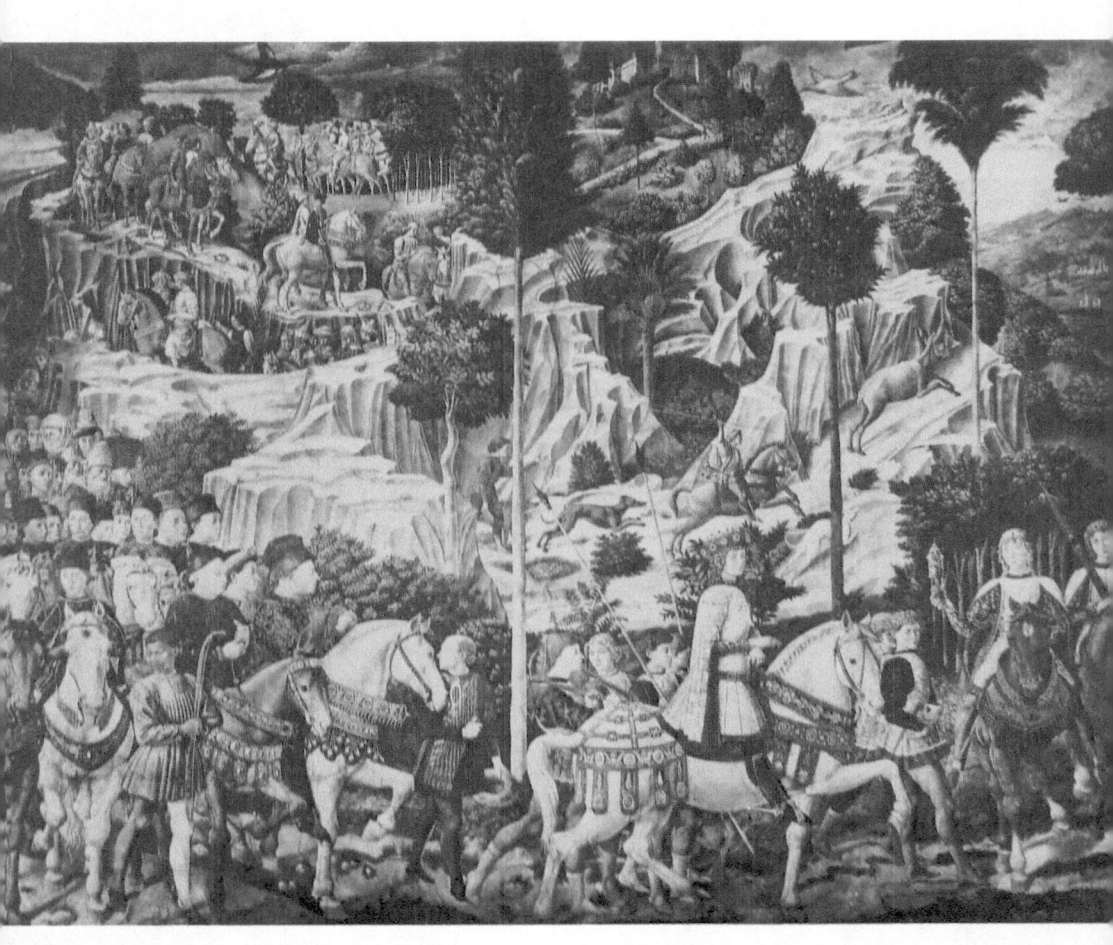

Benozzo Gozzoli, Journey of the Magi

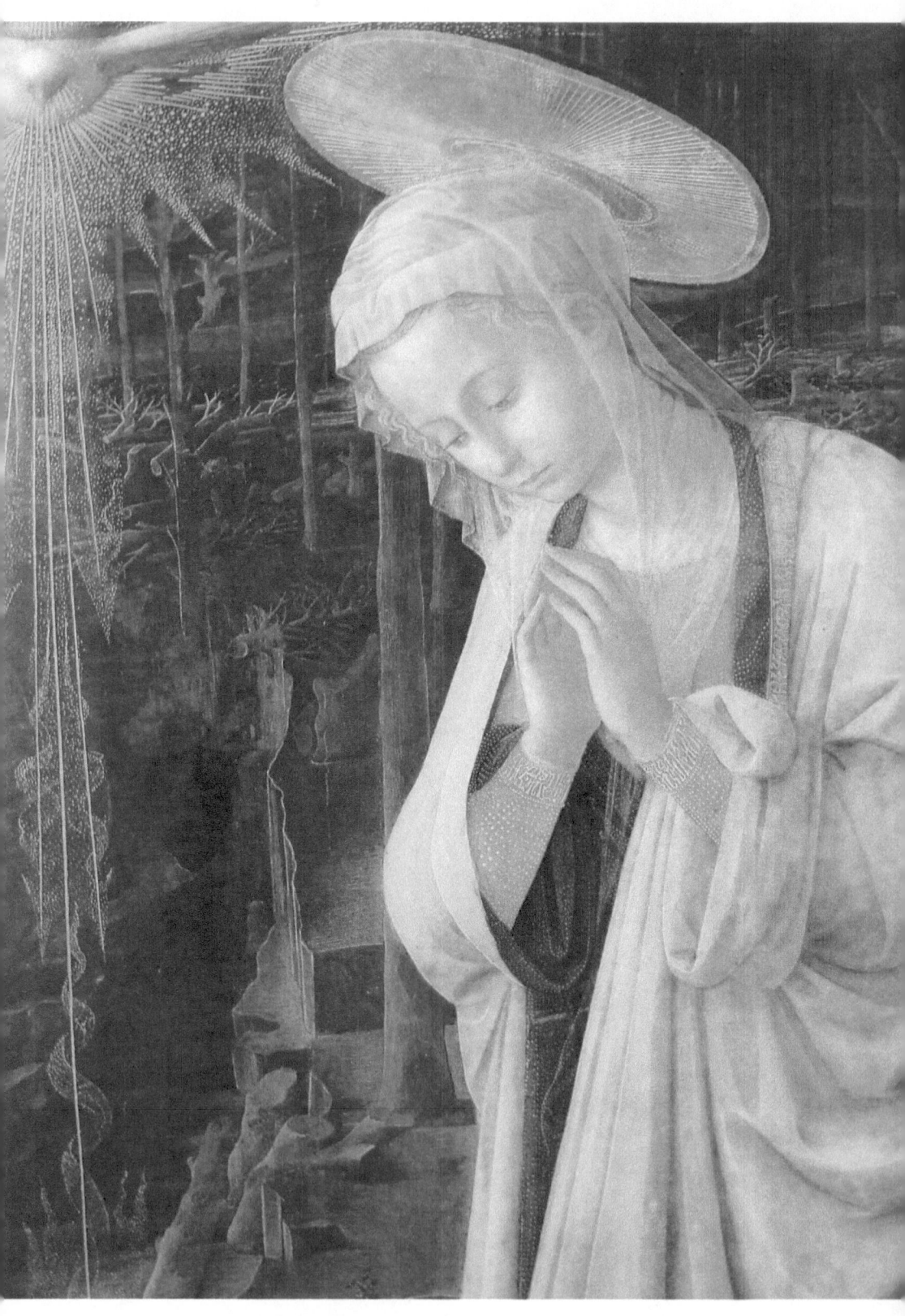

Fra Filippo Lippi, The Adoration of the Virgin, Berlin, detail

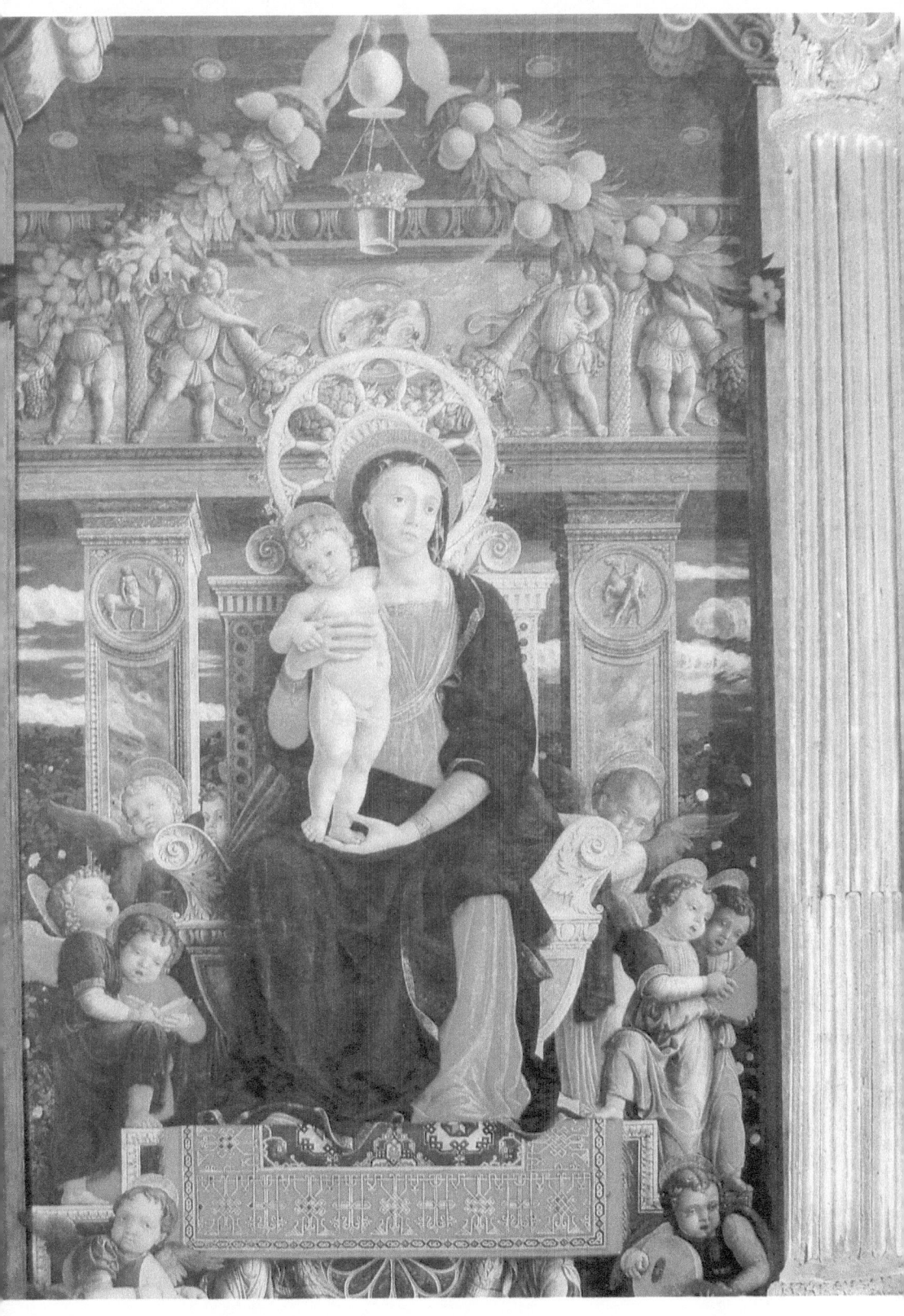

Andreas Mantegna, Madonna and Child Enthroned, 1457-60, Verona

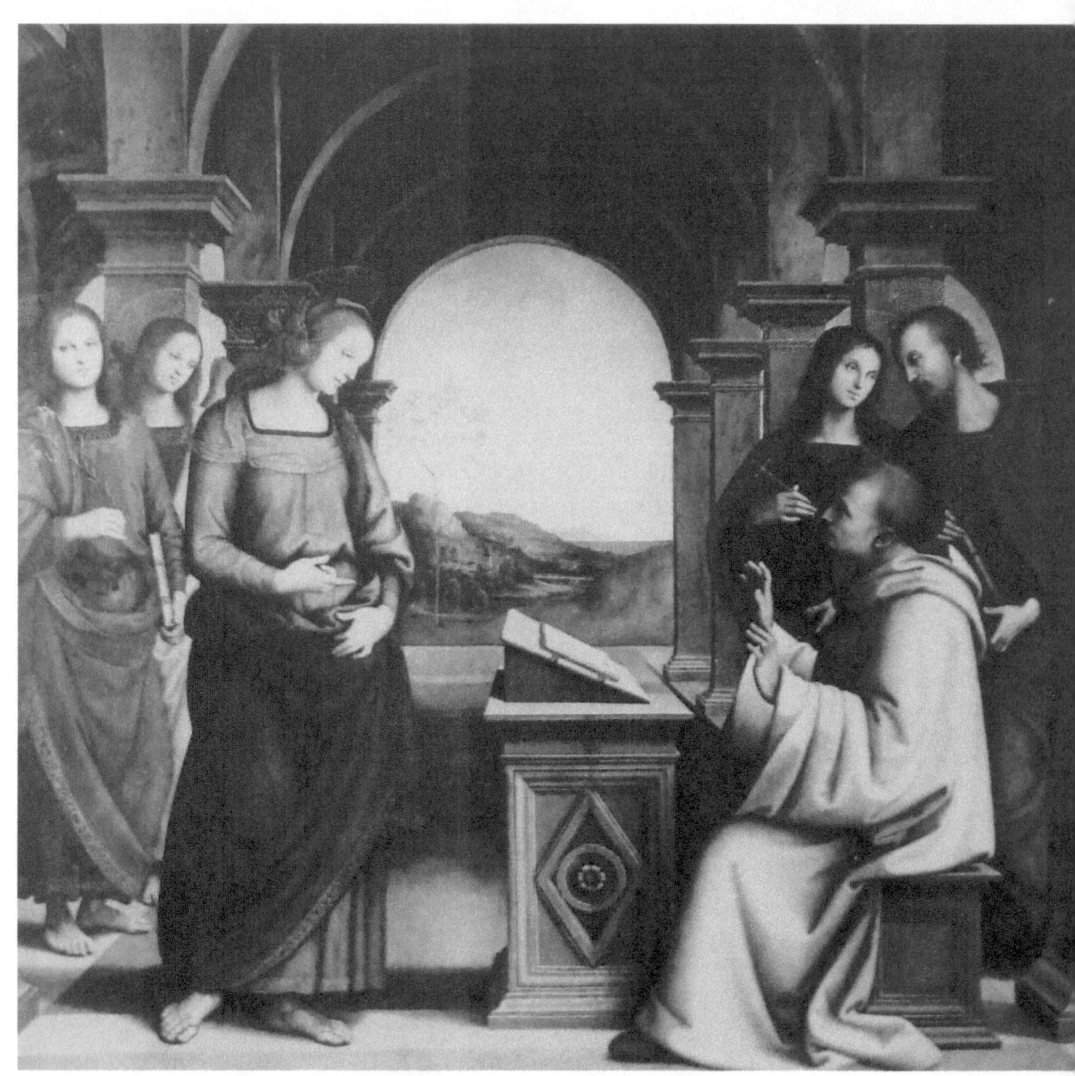

Perugino, Vision of St Bernard, 1488

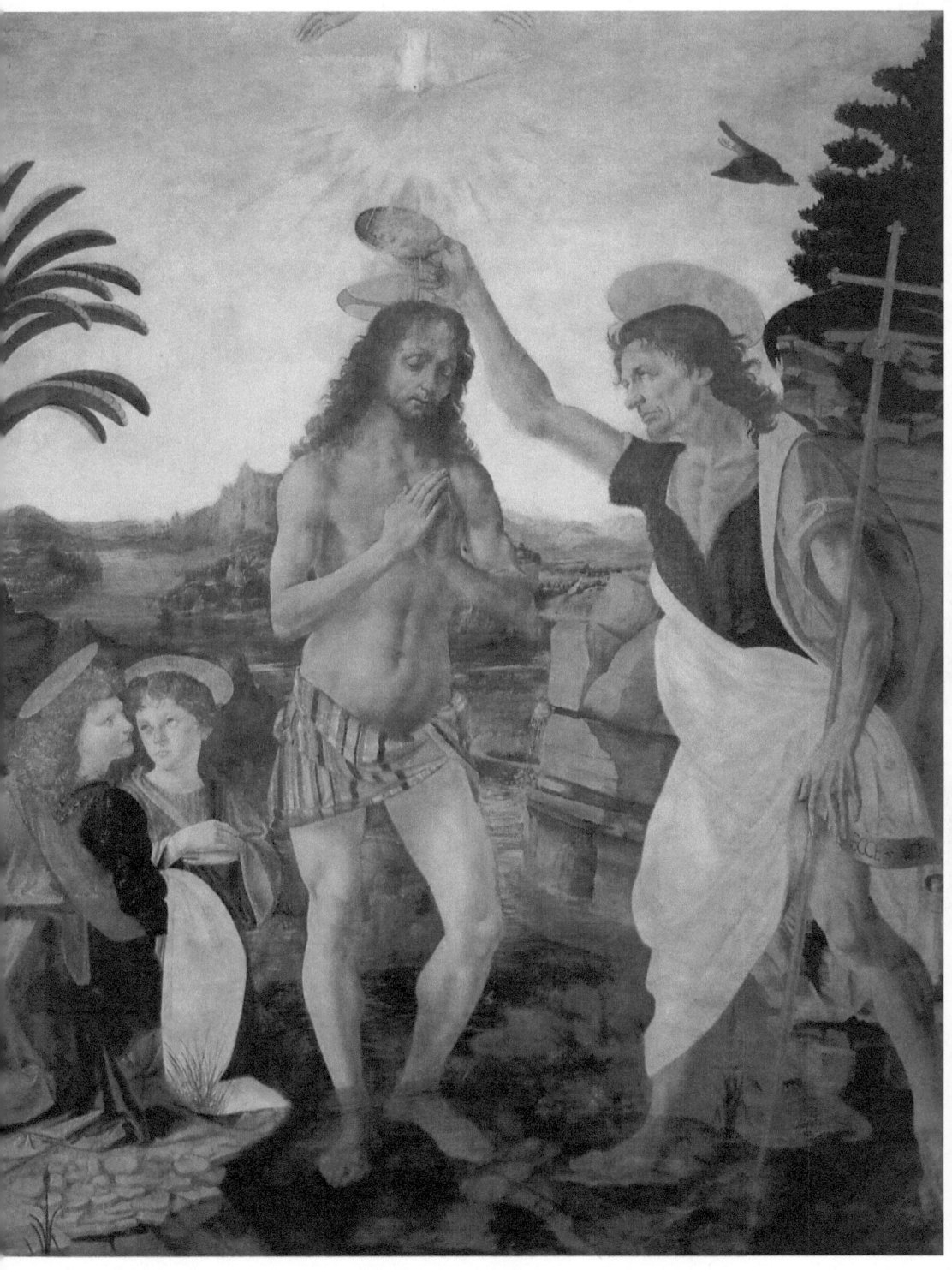

Andrea del Verrocchio, The Baptism of Christ

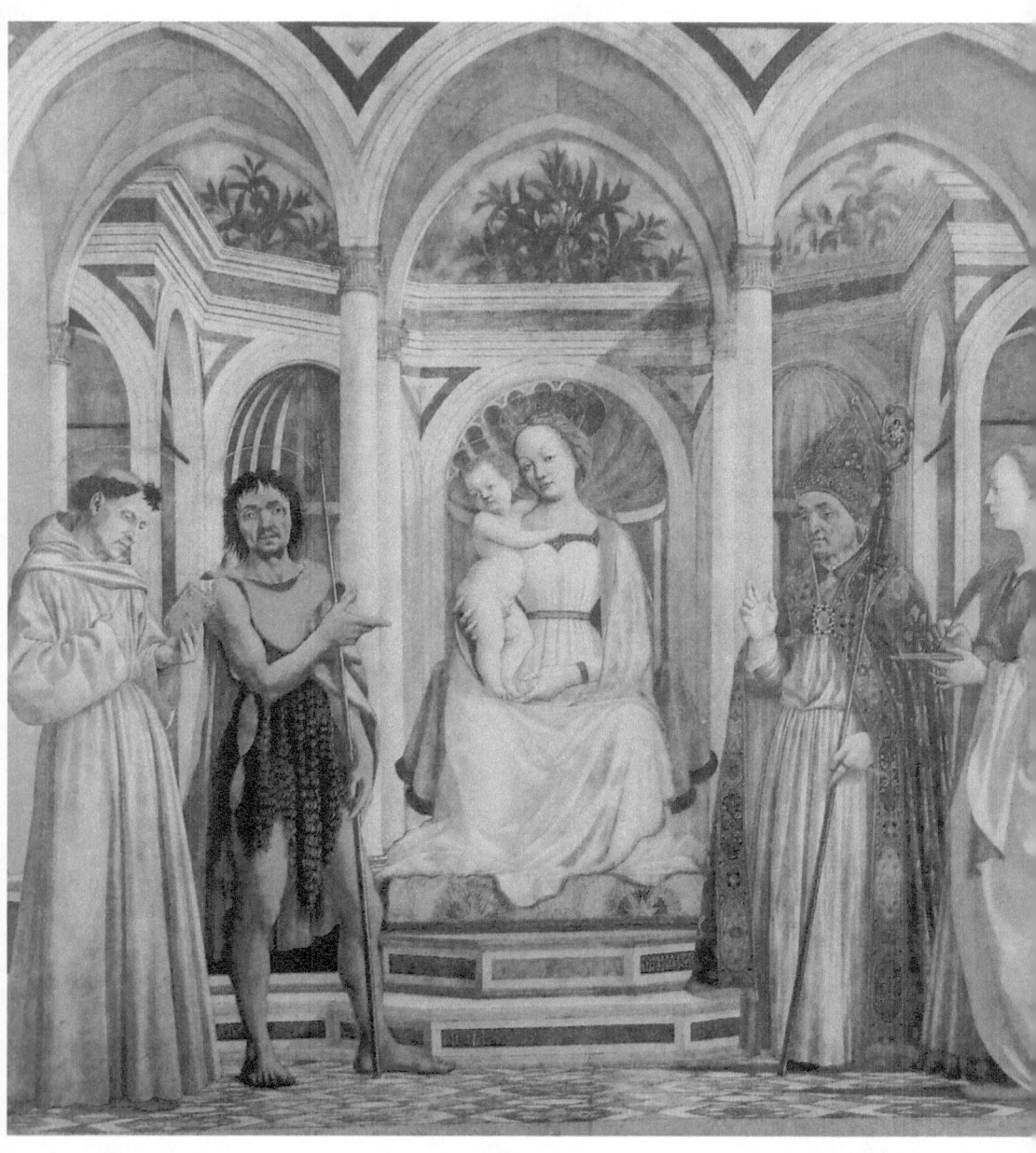
Domenico Veneziano, Madonna and Child With Saints, 1445, Uffizi Gallery

X
Jan Gossaert

THE INFLUENCE OF Italy is apparent in almost everything that Jan Gossaert, also known as Mabuse, painted. The Italian influence makes Gossaert's a quite different vision from the Early Netherlandish art of, say, the van Eycks or Rogier van der Weyden. The architecture, costumes, *mise-en-scène*, light, composition, tone, and other formal factors of Gossaert's art are quite different from Rogier or Jan van Eyck. Not so different as to be unrelated – there are many points of contact – but if one did not know Jan Gossaert was a Flemish painter, one might be forgiven for seeing him as Italian. The airy, spacious, relaxed, self-confident and open sense of space of the Italian Renaissance is very much apparent in Gossaert's *Venus and Cupid* (Brussels), *Neptune and Amphitrite* (1516, Berlin), and his erotic *Danaë* (Munich). In these works, the emphasis on the creation of a complex and Classical architecture is apparent. What strikes one about these paintings is the confidence of the architectural design: Gossaert clearly learnt much from the Italian masters about perspective, geometry and space.

Early Netherlandish Painting

ST LUKE PAINTING THE VIRGIN

Jan Gossaert's *St Luke Painting the Virgin* (National Gallery, Prague) is a bombastic rendering of a luxuriously ornate Italian Classical interior. It has that weight of wealth and state power of the Medici villas or Michelangelo's Laurentian Library in Florence. The difference between Gossaert's *St Luke Painting the Virgin* and Rogier van der Weyden's painting of the same subject is marked: where both depict a clever receding sense of perspective, Gossaert goes overboard with his architectural forms, which move back in ever-receding planes of shadow and light. The ostentatious architectural forms overwhelm the subject of the painting and the two people in the foreground. The Virgin Mary, despite having an enormous cloak that spreads outwards over the tiles, is subordinated by Gossaert's Italianate edifices. A later painting of the same subject, in Vienna (*St Luke Painting the Virgin*, c. 1525) has the Madonna appearing to the kneeling saint in a voluminous, billowing cloud, one of the most distinctive motifs of the idealizing, soaring Baroque era.

THE MALVAGNA TRIPTYCH

In *The Malvagna Triptych* (Palermo) we find the same subordination of human figures to architectural form. Here the late Gothic baroque dominates over half of the central panel, and seems as impossibly ornate as some of Gustave Moreau's visions. Few, if any, other Early Netherlandish paintings attain the same kind of over-the-top vision of architecture. *The Malvagna Triptych* is as extravagant in its architectonics as Hieronymous Bosch was in his apocalyptic imaginings. *The Madonna and Child* (Antwerp) boasts a similarly lavish setting for the Mother and

Child. In many paintings (the London *Adoration*, *The Malvagna Triptych*, *St Luke Painting the Virgin*, *The Virgin and Child* in Antwerp), we see Jan Gossaert moving towards a wholly Italian Baroque conception of space and form. This treatment applies also to his figures: – Venus, Neptune, Amphitrite, Adam and Eve are the monumental, idealized, heavy and sensuous figures of the Italian High Renaissance and Baroque period.

MADONNA AND CHILD WITH THE DONOR ANTONIO SICILIANO

Jan Gossaert produced a Virgin inside a church in the manner of Jan van Eyck, as part of the van Eyckian revival (*The Diptych of the Virgin and Child with Antonio Siciliano and St Anthony*, Rome), but Gossaert comes nowhere near achieving the same grandeur and sense of space and light that van Eyck's small, late panel seems to attain so effortlessly.

XI

Hans Memling

HANS MEMLING IS one of the great Early Netherlandish painters, but is generally felt by critics to have lacked an intensity of spiritual passion, which might have elevated him up to the stature of Jan van Eyck or Rogier van der Weyden. In contrast to painters such as Hugo van der Goes or Dieric Bouts, Hans Memling's art is quiet and contemplative. Memling (sometimes spelt Memlinc) worked best within narrow parameters and a humble vision – as in his many devotional panels of the Virgin Mary. Critics call his art 'harmonious, candid and serene' (K. McFarlane, 39), 'quiet and idyllic' (M. Whinney, 90), while Max J. Friedländer writes that

> Memlinc's faith is completely trusting, serenely confident, with no trace of fanaticism, melancholy or sentimentality, no feelings of guilt, no doubts, yearnings or driving ambitions. (1969, 46-47)

Hans Memling is deeply associated with Bruges, and with Rogier van der Weyden and Dieric Bouts, stylistically. It is true that Memling does suffer when compared to the intensity of earlier painters such as Jan van Eyck or Rogier van der Weyden. Yet he was a popular painter, and a rich one too. He owned four houses in Bruges, and was one of its wealthiest citizens. There were many painters who were influenced by him, which further attest to his significance. Friedländer is right to point out that 'over and above all change of taste his lovable and harmonious nature will ever continue to gain him friends' (ib, 47). This is true: Memling's style is reassuringly unthreatening. His style flattered the tastes of his patrons and admirers: there was little, it seemed, that was deeply disturbing in his paintings (unlike, say, Dieric Bouts, whose scenes of torture were unsettling). Yet this view of Memling's as the soft, serene artist of Early Flemish art is not entirely the case. The soft and serene description certainly applies to Memling's Madonnas, but then, most Early Netherlandish Madonna paintings are serenely unthreatening. That, indeed, is the point of them; to invoke a Paradisal early childhood when the mother's milk flowed freely, couching the babe in nourishing tenderness.

THE LAST JUDGEMENT

Hans Memling's *Last Judgement* (in Gdansk) derives from Rogier van der Weyden's masterpiece, but lacks the passion and visionary brilliance of the latter. But then, most *Last Judgments* would suffer in comparison with Rogier's painting. Seen in isolation (however culturally impossible), Memling's paintings do reveal a visionary strain as impressive as that in the art of Jaochim Patinir or Hugo van der Goes.

The Last Judgement, for example, increases the number of protagonists in Rogier's painting, and places them in a unified space, which was often Memling's preference. The increase in sheer numbers does not necessarily mean an increase in symbolic depth or sense of the epic. Yet the sight of so many souls being tortured by their own sins is compelling. Memling's introduction of devils beating and pulling at the sinners is a touch grotesque and macabre. The image of one of the Devil's minions with his club raised to smash the skull of a naked sinner is more than enough proof that Hans Memling was not always the quiet painter of soft and tranquil Madonnas.

ST JOHN ON PATMOS

Hans Memling's *St John on Patmos Contemplating the Apocalyptic Vision* (Bruges) presents in a high horizon vertical format a welter of fantastical images, worthy of Hieronymous Bosch. Great as Rogier van der Weyden's *Last Judgement* is, Memling's apocalyptic Bruges painting contains some innovations of Memling's own, which rival those of the older artist. For example, Christ and his vast retinue of angels, apostles and other honourable types appear in an enormous circular rainbow. Behind His throne are further circular rainbows, receding to the source of all light, which is God. The moons, flying Madonnas, seven-headed dragons, conflagrations, sea monsters, battles and giants show that Memling was not simply a painter of demure Madonnas.

St John on Patmos vividly manifests the relation between art and life, between imagination and reality. Hans Memling's painting depicts the power of the imagination. St John has a book on his knees: his head is raised: it is as if he has just been reading of the Apocalypse, lifts his head, and sees it all. *St John of Patmos* is structured around the visionary powers of people, the ability to conjure visions out of the air. Rarely has this link between imagination and reality been so dexterously handled, in this lifted head of the saint and the visions beyond.

Early Netherlandish Painting

THE MARTYRDOM OF ST URSULA

Further extraordinary scenes in Hans Memling's œuvre include his series of works on St Ursula (the famous 1489 reliquary casket in Bruges). These are not, as Max Friedländer maintains, images in which the pain of martyrdom is superseded by beatitude: rather, the lightness and lyricism of the *Martyrdom of St Ursula* paintings adds to their impact as images of horror. The vision of the group of soldiers surrounding the boats and firing arrows at St Ursula's companions is particularly effective and moving. It is the way the soldiers in their armour stand so nonchalantly on the quayside and fire their crossbows into the flesh of the praying virgins that is arresting. The tragic passivity of the oppressed, already seeing themselves as 'victims', is contrasted with the mechanical detachment of the militia.

SCENE FROM THE PASSION AND THE VIRGIN

One of Hans Memling's specialities as an innovator in painting were his large scale visions of a vast panoply of figures and architectural elements, such as in the *Passion* panel in Turin, and the superb *Scenes From the Life of the Virgin and of Christ* (in Munich). Memling's *Scenes From the Passion* is a view of the world as a whole, ranging from a host of figures in the middle ground, to distant vistas which include a tiny but detailed Crucifixion group. The physical size of the *Passion* panel (21.5 × 35.5 inches) does not hint at the vast scale of the world depicted in it. Memling's stroke of genius was to place all the scenes of Christ's Passion into a unified space. Few painters of the same era could equal this 'epic' sweep of narrative and symbolic discourse. It is a marvel, this painting, and its companion panel in Munich: the eye happily ranges over an

Early Netherlandish Painting

amazing number of integrated scenes. One has to keep wandering over the painting, to pick up new details, from the large peacock on top of the wall in the front of the town, to scenes at the edges, such as Christ praying in Gethsemane, on the extreme left, to Christ appearing to the Magdalene, on a hill, in the top right section. Then there are the scenes in the windows and doors of the architecturally complex town, which require further slow exploration.

In the panel of scenes from the life of the Virgin Mary and Jesus, the unified space is more harmonious, and even richer in detail. The painting is larger (31.8 x 74.4 inches) and needs to be seen in the flesh to be able to appreciate the many scenes depicted, and the way they interrelate spatially and symbolically. *Scenes from Life of the Virgin Mary and of Christ* is one of the most engaging of Renaissance paintings, one in which the viewer can lose themselves for long stretches of time. Here art is a vision all things under Heaven: it is very much a vision of life on Earth: Heaven itself is only suggested, not depicted (although various ascending deities are shown). The sky in fact is a narrow strip across the top of this wide, horizontal format painting. A series of crucial life-experiences are shown, including birth, death, preaching, betrayal, torture, motherhood, confession, prayer, joy, mourning and voyaging. Memling's *Scenes From the Life of the Virgin and of Christ* is one of those all-inclusive paintings that one could package up and send out into space as a portrayal to aliens of life on Earth. Memling's image would not be any less informative than other images that have been launched by rockets into the cosmos.

Early Netherlandish Painting

THE DONNE TRIPTYCH

Hans Memling is famous for his Madonna paintings, and rightly so. A typical rendering of the Virgin Mary occurs in his *Donne Triptych* (London). The Mother of God holds the Child on Her lap, and is flanked by angels and saints, with the donor and his wife. The symmetry and perspective of the painting is relatively simple; the light is limpid; the colours are heraldic (azure and crimson for the costumes). It is a tranquil, sombre scene, played in utter silence. The only sounds would drift into the semi-open interior from the landscape beyond, which's kept at a respectful distance. The female saints, as so often in Memling's art, recall the Flemish *virgo inter virgines* type. In the wings the barefoot Baptist and the Evangelist look forlorn. The painting is all balance and harmony – perhaps it is too harmonious: nothing is introduced to upset the visual symmetry and the symbolic tranquillity of the scene. Negative images are included only on a minor level (Christ reaching for the fruit the angel offers, for example).

THE FLOREINS ALTARPIECE

The face of the Madonna in *The Donne Triptych* – gently oval, flat, with a small, shy mouth and a narrow nose, the eyes turned downwards – is found in most of Hans Memling's paintings. Sitting at the centre of the centre panel of *The Floreins Altarpiece* (*The Virgin and Child with Jan Floreins, his Family and Saints James and Dominic*, painted for Brother Jan Floreins, master of the Hospital of St John in Bruges), the Virgin Mary's face is exactly the same as in *The Donne Triptych*. Her downcast eyes make her look oblivious of the attention Her son is attracting. As in *The Donne Diptych*, the baby seems wondrously happy. Memling's altarpiece depicts a gathering of people around the Madonna and Child in a partially open ecclesiastical interior, an image that recalls Jan van Eyck's Virgins in church interiors (though Jan van Eyck's interiors were never as densely populated as this). Again, the glances of every participant in this silent rite are at anything but their neighbours. *The Adoration of the Magi* presents humanity caught up in the solemnity of worship. No one looks at any one else, just as one is not supposed to stare at people praying next to oneself in a church. It is improper to stare at a praying person. Hence, in Memling's altarpieces, as in most Early Netherlandish altarpieces, the participants look down, across, sideways (never up – looking up is not sombre enough), anywhere, in fact, but at another person.

THE MYSTIC MARRIAGE OF ST CATHERINE TRIPTYCH

Painted for the high altar of the Hospital of St John in Bruges, Hans Memling's *Triptych of the Mystic Marriage of St Catherine* (1479) is a more ornate and bold composition than the earlier *Donne Triptych*. The central panel depicts the familiar placid hierophany of the Madonna and Child surrounded by various saints and virgins and angels. St Catherine, one of the symbolic brides of Christ (like the Magdalene, and the Virgin Mary in Her coronation mode), is seen on the left embroiled in the ring-giving ceremony with the baby Jesus.

The seated virgin saints again echo *virgo inter virgines* paintings, with the interior again half open to reveal a background landscape in which a town is prominent. The dainty central scene, though, is radically modulated by the wings of *The St Catherine Triptych*: on the left is the beheading of the Baptist (recalling Rogier van der Weyden's *St John Altarpiece*), while on the right is the vision of St John the Evangelist (described above). The niceties of the spiritual marriage between a virginal martyr and a baby God in the central panel are overwhelmed by the violence of the imagery in the outer wings.

THE MADONNA AND CHILD ENTHRONED

There are a number of paintings of the Madonna and Child Enthroned (not all of them autograph works by Hans Memling). The many works from Memling's studio inevitably include many Madonna paintings, such as *St Anne, the Virgin and Child* in Munich. *The Madonna and Child Enthroned* (Vienna) a triptych, has much the same structure as *The Donne Triptych*. Again, an angel offers the god-child an orange (a bridal symbol of purity and fruitfulness, but also, as ever, symbolic of the Fall). Two depictions of the Madonna and Child Enthroned (both entitled *The Madonna and Child with Angels*, both of them *circa* 1485, one in Washington, the other in Vienna) feature again the symbolic act of the angel offering the baby the fatal fruit. This act featured in a late work, *The Diptych of Martin von Nieuwenhove*, although it is the Virgin Herself who offers the fruit. It is a tribute to Hans Memling's greatness that he can make this act both simple and symbolic, both natural and of religious import. In his paintings, the child reaches for the fruit in a natural way, as babies are attracted to bright objects, especially ones in their immediate vicinity. Memling shows how these seemingly simple acts – of reaching for an apple – also have an immense religious weight attached to them. For the Fall is *the* primal myth not only of Christianity, but of Western religion. It lies at the heart of the Judæo-Christian tradition. Memling's angels do not seem to be aware of the tragic symbolism of offering the fruit; neither does the baby, who smiles as a baby would; only the Virgin Mary seems fully aware of what is going on. Her expression shows it: She looks down, off and away to a point in the distance, behind the viewer.

Early Netherlandish Painting

In speaking of Hans Memling's symbolism and compositions, we have neglected to mention his colour, which is especially fine. His landscapes, for example, are as wistfully blued-over as Joachim Patinir's or Gerard David's: in Memling's Vienna *Madonna and Child Enthroned*, for instance, there is a very pleasasant green land, with a river and swans, a horseman, a distant town, a parkland and trees. It is pure pastoral sublime, three hundred years before the Romantics turned it into the departure for their voyages into the unknown.

THE DIPTYCH OF MARTIN VAN NIEUWENHOVE

A late Madonna, in *The Diptych of Martin van Nieuwenhove* is one of Hans Memling's most successful paintings (paintings associated with it include the Berlin triptych of Benedetto Portinari). The format is a standard one in Renaissance art, putting together the donor and the Mother of God and Her son into the same place. The donor's worship of the Virgin and Child (his hands clasped together, his face sombre but rapturous) by extension helps his own veneration. The *mana* of the deities depicted on one wing in diptychs rubs off on the human donor. The half-length Madonna in *The Diptych of Martin van Nieuwenhove* is one of Memling's best: he displays how much he has learnt from van Eyck. The stained glass and the reflections in the mirror behind the Virgin show how carefully Memling has absorbed van Eyck's motifs. The painting is full of Eyckian richness, apparent in the costumes, the brocade, the stained glass and the jewels. The Virgin Mary's form is pyramidal and huge: She reaches up to the top of the painting. In Her face, in the long, narrow nose, the little bud of a mouth, and Rogieresque eyelids, Memling goes beyond van Eyck and creates his own form of painterly mariolatry. *The Diptych of Martin van Nieuwenhove* recalls another Memling *Madonna* (in London), where the

Virgin and Child are shown in close-up, in half-length, the Child resting on a cushion, hand raised to bless the spectator. This half-length Madonna seen against a cloth of honour recalls Giovanni Bellini's paintings, where the Child is presented on a marble ledge right at the base of the picture area.

THE MARIAN FLOWERPIECE

A painting related to *The Diptych of Martin van Nieuwenhove* is in the Thyssen-Bornemisza Collection. This depicts a praying man, in the manner of the praying Benedetto Portinari (Uffizi) or Martin van Nieuwenhove. It is the *verso* of this painting, however, that is interesting. It is a flowerpiece, which at first does not seem that remarkable. However, this is the earliest extant still-life in Flemish painting.[1] It depicts some flowers in a jug, set in a shadowy recess on an Turkish rug. Again, there seems nothing to interest the casual viewer here – but then, painters such as Vincent van Gogh and Henri Matisse could make flowers radiant subjects for painting. As an example of painting, Memling's *Marian Flowerpiece* is among his finest work. The play of light and shadow in the little corner is exquisitely rendered. Memling proves himself to be a master of every nuance of light. The suppleness of his depiction is sumptuous. The flowers seem to be placed on the carpet in this niche for the purpose of quiet contemplation.

It is the symbolism of the flowers themselves, however, that does much of the expressive communication of *The Marian Flowerpiece*. For this is no ordinary still-life but, unusually, one with an explicit religious programme. The flowers are those related symbolically to the Virgin Mary. Most conspicuous is the white lily, which refers to the Virgin's purity, Her virginity, to the Annunciation and Immaculate Conception. There is a purple-blue iris here too, and a columbine. The shapes and textures of the petals lyrically connote the 'feminine'. There are three or four stages of symbolism and abstraction between the viewer and the final goal, which is the Virgin Mary. The mysticism of Memling's painting is founded on painterly abstraction: the viewer must look through the oil paint, through to the flowers, then to the symbolism of the lily, columbine and iris, making the cultural connections between these particular flowers and the Virgin Mary, then to the Madonna Herself, and beyond Her, to God. It is a journey of cultural abstraction, in which the mysticism of the painting is only meaningful if the viewer has the right cultural understanding to make the abstract connections. In this sense, Memling's *Marian Flowerpiece* is a vivid form of religious abstraction. Although representational, Memling's *Marian Flowerpiece* requires a sophisticated knowledge of symbolism and art to make sense of it.

XII

Gerard David

THE MYSTIC MARRIAGE OF St CATHERINE

GERARD DAVID IS not as hard-hitting or as visionary as Jan van Eyck, as plangent or tragic as Rogier van der Weyden, nor as showy and self-confident as Hugo van der Goes. Nevertheless, David is the author of some very fine works of art, and the overseer of an influential workshop.[1] One of his best is in London's National Gallery, *The Virgin and Child with Saints and Donor*, also called *The Mystic Marriage of St Catherine* (1505). The painting depicts a silent *sacra conversazione* lit by a soft iridescence which picks out the details in the opulent costumes and jewellry. The figures seem frozen in poses and gestures of timeless stillness. There is no breath of wind, not a thing moves, not the dog, nor the bushes and trees in the background. The figures have an uncanny, disturbing immobility which is enhanced by the dark, staring eyes. The two saints on the right, Barbara and the Magdalene, in particular have strange, blankly staring eyes. There is a series of interconnected hands and gestures. The donor prays, as donors tend to do; St Catherine gestures towards the donor with one hand, with the other she takes the ring from Christ. The infant offers the ring with one hand, the other rests on His lap. The Virgin Mary's fingers are interlinked as She clasps the child around the waist. St Barbara holds a book. Mary Magdalene reaches out to St Barbara, her other hand clutches her urn.

Everything in the painting seems lifelike yet emptied of emotional weight, rather like those paintings of deserted American streets in Superrealist paintings. The setting seems 'realistic' – the enclosed, walled garden looks real enough, and the city – Bruges – behind the garden is a faithful rendition. Yet the city is like a ghost town, showing blank windows like those in a Magritte painting, or perhaps like the one-sided buildings on a movie set. There is a disconnectedness to the painting. There is a plastic sheen to objects. Significantly, none of the figures is looking at anyone else. They each look in a different direction (generally, they look down). They each seem to be lost in their own thoughts and worries. No one smiles. No one speaks. No one moves.

As with Rogier van der Weyden's paintings, Gerard David's *Virgin and Child with Saints and Donor* has a beautiful sense of surface. Not a millimetre of the surface is left unfinished. The painting is polished, with a high degree of finish to it. No part of it is skimped, every section is worked up to the same level of finesse. Not all of Gerard David's paintings display the same high degree of accomplishment. His Winterhur *Pietà*, for instance, is marred by the stiffness of the figures, in particular Mary and Christ. Often we see the Early Netherlandish painters striving to achieve a poignant realism as well as idealism in the portrayal of suffering in the *Pietà* scene. It is a challenge to draw Christ dead, slumped, His body showing much pain, perhaps going stiff after death, and the Virgin encircling Him, Her arms around Him, His body half over Hers. It's a scene that causes painters many problems of line, space, form and light, as well as achieving the required sense of tragedy and sublime, noble suffering. David does have problems with scale, as in his *The Virgin and Child with Angels* (New York).

Early Netherlandish Painting

THE VIRGIN AND CHILD WITH SAINTS

The Rouen *The Virgin and Child with Saints* (1509) is another one of those *sacra conversazione* in Gerard David's sculptural style. The weight of seriousness is the painting is palpable, as in the London *Virgin and Child with Saints and a Donor*. The Rouen painting displays no inappropriate behaviour, nothing is out of place in the formal *sacra conversazione* setting. The painting is constructed with a rigid formality, a sense of decorum and *gravitas*. As with David's other paintings of groups of people, everyone looks in a different direction, remaining aloof of the others, yet aware of their presence. The modelling and colouring is as precise as ever, and the interweaving of a largish number of figures is accomplished. Like the London picture and *The Marriage at Cana*, the Rouen *Virgin and Child with Saints* depicts people as statues, flesh and blood beings reduced to finely sculpted forms in a hieratic, ritualized scene.

It is the same in Gerard David's *The Marriage at Cana* (1503, Louvre), which is not, as one might expect, a joyous celebration, but more of the same preoccupied introspection and solemnity. Most of David's major paintings have a dominant central vertical line (*The Virgin and Child with Saints*, London, *The Baptism, The Rest on the Flight to Egypt*), but *The Marriage at Cana* breaks with this Davidan tradition, and places the composition off-centre. The challenge of depicting a group of people sitting at a table, where the sheer mundaneity of the subject can produce wooden renditions, is surmounted by David employing a calculated choice of viewpoint and perspective.

Early Netherlandish Painting

THE JUDGEMENT OF CAMYSES

Another crowded painting, the earlier *Judgement of Camyses*, made for the town hall of Bruges, also uses an off-centre composition. The scene in the second panel, where Cambyses is flayed alive, is one of those particularly horrible Renaissance images. It's all the more gruesome for its rich setting, the way the tortured near-naked man is surrounded by the wealthy and noble, who soberly look on while Camyses's flesh is peeled off his leg. Violence is undertaken with the authority of God in David's Eyckian *St Michael* (Vienna), where the archangel, clad in a gigantic robe, destroys the fiends of Hell.

THE CRUCIFIXION

Gerard David's Genoa *Crucifixion* is a powerful painting, small-scale in conception, but with its own sense of sorrow and poignancy. One little gesture of Christ's is unusual: He is seen blessing with His right hand. The lighting is unnatural: the sky darkens behind the Cross, as in so many *Crucifixions*, but the three figures are lit frontally. David rationalizes the landscape, creating a small mound on which the Cross and figures stand. The simplicity of the design and the symmetry focusses the viewer's attention on the subject matter, which is Christ's Passion. Nothing is allowed to distract attention away from the central mystery of Christianity.

Early Netherlandish Painting

THE BAPTISM OF CHRIST

Gerard David's *Altarpiece of the Baptism of Christ* (in Bruges) made for Jan de Trompes of Ostende, fuses the secular and sacred, the personal and the public. De Trompe's first wife, Elizabeth van der Meersch, appears on the right wing, while his second wife, Madeleine Cordier, is on the reverse of the right wing. The details of the plants in the foreground, which take up a sizeable portion of the composition, are painted with a van Eyckian precision.[2] The colours in *The Baptism of Christ* are particularly beautiful: the deep scarlet of the Baptist's robe, the brocade of the angel's costume. The poverty of Christ's attire (the simple loincloth) contrasts markedly with St John the Baptist's opulence, though the Baptist is often portrayed as a wild, ragged figure. The space of *The Baptism* is intriguing: a large foreground and middle ground, which is populated by the donor and family, and figures under the trees. The abundance of trees, rocks, flowers, plants and flowing water make this *Baptism* especially languidly pastoral. The presence of Nature is very great here, though the would-be celebratory tone of the painting is punctured by the very direct and sombre look of Jesus, which stares directly at the viewer out of the exact visual centre of the triptych. His look is unsettling. At each point in the Christian story, Gerard David, Rogier van der Weyden, Jan van Eyck and the other Early Netherlandish painters portray the events as sombre. So Christ's blank, serious stare is interpreted as an essential element in the Christian pageant. For Christ's baptism is the point in which His holiness is made publicly clear. It is the point in which He is pointed out to all and sundry as the messiah. It is the seriousness of the baptismal act, and Christ's recognition of it, that makes this painting so solemn.

Early Netherlandish Painting

THE REST ON THE FLIGHT TO EGYPT

One of Gerard David's masterpieces is *The Rest on the Flight into Egypt* (1510, Washington DC), There's so much blue in fact the painting moves into abstraction. The colour blue pervades the shadows on the grey rocks, the grey soil in front of the Virgin, the hazy landscape beyond, the sky and of course the Virgin Mary's cloak and dress. Instead of contrasting the Madonna's blue outer robe with a red inner dress, as in so many Renaissance paintings, David has a blue robe and a blue cloak. Red is apparent in a section of the Virgin Mary's undergarments.

Gerard David's *The Rest on the Flight into Egypt* is an exercise in landscape painting, but the Madonna is very large in the frame, so that the painting is more of a *Madonna and Child* than the usual *Flight into Egypt*. Joseph, as so often, is a slight presence in the background, flicking a tree with a stick. The focus of the painting is the two faces of the Madonna and the baby Jesus. They both look down at the grapes (alluding to the Passion), tilting their heads in the same pose. It is an image of emotional and spiritual harmony. The grapes look forward to Christ's suffering, but the significance of the grapes is secondary to the image of the fruit as connoting abundance. Here, motherhood, as so often in Renaissance painting, is portrayed as a loving, bountiful experience for both child and mother.

Early Netherlandish Painting

ANNUNCIATION AND MADONNAS

Gerard David's *Annunciation* in (Frankfurt) is a work that circumscribes melancholy and spiritual feeling. David's Brussels *Madonna and Child* shows the *jouissance* of the maternal world in full swing, though depicted with David's usual restraint. The young mother is shown feeding the Child milk, while the baby plays with a small spoon. It is an image of domestic union: there are seemingly 'mundane' details in the foreground: a bread roll, an apple, a knife and a wooden cutting board. Here it seems as if a diligent mother is giving a child breakfast: both seem caught up in the warmth and beauty of their emotional symbiosis. Only when one considers the Christian context of this mother and child image do the symbolic meanings of the knife, the apple and the bread become apparent. The painting is dark, and very soft – one of David's softest, most deliquescent images.

Gerard David's *Virgin and Child with Angels* (Metropolitan Museum, New York) depicts the Madonna holding the baby extremely closely, so Her face is touching His. He, meanwhile, is more intent on turning round to look at the viewer, than cuddling His earthly mother. She stands in an ecclesiastical doorway which opens out onto an enclosed garden with the ubiquitous Early Netherlandish town seen beyond the walls. In the Louvre *Virgin and Child with Angels Playing Musical Instruments*, the centre panel shows again the self-conscious humility of David's participants, as each one pointedly (and humbly) looks away from the others. Despite the presence of the musical angels, this is one of the quietest of Northern Renaissance paintings. Gerard David was certainly no ordinary painter of domestic scenes: the detail and control of large scenes in his Brussels *Adoration of the Magi*, for example, is superb. He knows how to portray large crowds, as deftly as any other Renaissance painter.

XIII

Joachim Patinir

JOACHIM PATINIR'S SPECIALITY was to set figures in a landscape, but it was a landscape which he made all his own. Patinir's worldview is dominated by landscape, so that the figures diminish in size until they are seen in long shot. He is regarded as the first Western landscape painter – Albrecht Dürer described Patinir as a 'good landscape painter.'[1] Patinir's colouration is instantly distinctive. He uses large doses of pale cerulean and ultramarine. His rivers and seas, which he loves, are pale turquoise and azure. His skies are equally saturated with blue, but not the clear blue skies of Tuscany which we associate with the Italian Renaissance painters. Patinir's skies are overcast and stormy. Banks of black and grey clouds loom on the horizon. Under them, a liquid luminescence, of light blue and white. It is a watery light, as after rain. There are usually rocks in the Patinir landscape, as with Leonardo da Vinci, piles of battleship grey rocks. And dark trees, underneath which are deep shadows.

Joachim Patinir's landscapes are wonderfully, magically realized worlds, clearly deriving, as with Claude Lorrain or Thomas Girtin, from a lengthy and careful observation of the natural world. True, Patinir does idealize the landscape, as Claude or Nicolas Poussin did, but with Patinir's art there is always that sense of reality, whether it comes from the luminous backlighting, the stormy clouds, or the little rivers and streams that snake though the scenes.

THE REST ON THE FLIGHT INTO EGYPT

The subject of the flight to Egypt was an excuse for a landscape study, but Joachim Patinir went much further, and many of his paintings looked like versions of *The Rest on the Flight to Egypt*. Patinir's *The Rest on the Flight into Egypt* in Antwerp (Musée Royal des Beaux-Arts, c. 1515-20) is all landscape and hardly anything of the Madonna, Joseph and Child. The grandeur of the natural realm becomes the true subject of the painting. In Patinir's Prado *Rest on the Flight into Egypt*, the Madonna sits breast feeding Christ in a large, rocky landscape. There is a welter of incidental detail: huge cumulus billow in the sky; there's a farm where workers are harvesting the crops and ploughing the fields; the trees are intricately portrayed; – they are not stereotypical trees – Patinir has studied Nature as carefully as later painters such as Jean Baptiste Camille Corot, William Turner and Claude Monet, painters who also made painting trees one of their specialities.

Joachim Patinir's forms are taken from nature, and his motifs – rocks, trees, rivers – appear differently in each painting. His landscapes are generalized, though they might be slightly idealized. The lighting of the Madrid *Rest on the Flight into Egypt* is cloudlight, the sort of light that comes from a brisk wind and sunlight, the clouds moving across the sun rapidly. Thus, the farm and its golden corn glows yellow in the sun to the left, but in front of the field is a rocky outcrop, which is in shadow. In the far distance there are sunlit hills. The Virgin Mary and Jesus, however, are of course brightly illuminated in the foreground. A heavily shadowed Virgin and Child is unthinkable in Renaissance art. The Virgin wears predominantly white, which luminously reflects the patch of sunlight in which She sits. In the background, walking through the rocky landscape is Joseph. He is relegated to the position of a subordinate, someone who waits on the Virgin and Jesus. He is indistinguishable from the farm workers.

CHARON CROSSING THE STYX

Joachim Patinir's *Charon Crossing the Styx* (also known as *The Passage of the Infernal Regions* and also in the Prado, Madrid), features that beloved Patinir motif, the large river estuary opening out onto the sea (also found in Patinir's *St Christopher, The Baptism of Christ*). Charon ferries a soul across the mythical river. On the left, a riverbank and world of angels; on the right, a Boschian world of monsters and destructive fire. The landscape in *Charon Crossing the Styx* is as visionary and splendorous as anything in J.M.W. Turner or Rembrandt van Rijn. Patinir's landscapes, the more one looks at them, are impressive expressions of a visionary imagination. What is striking about *Charon Crossing the Styx* is that it is a Last Judgement picture, a picture of Heaven and Hell. Yet the vision of a landscape predominates. It is not a thoroughly 'pastoral' landscape, in the manner of ancient Arcadia and the Old Testament Paradise. Always there is a transplendent light in the painting, in most of Patinir's landscape paintings, so that, no matter how hideous Hell is, it is always transcended by the warmth and hope of the light.

Early Netherlandish Painting

ST JEROME AND ST CHRISTOPHER

Joachim Patinir's *St Jerome* portrays the saint in the usual manner, in a lean-to shack next to a cave. But the landscape dominates the painting: St Jerome and his dwelling takes up only one quarter of the composition. The rest of the painting is a loving exploration of the Low Countries landscape: always the sea, always rivers and lakes, always little towns with their churches, always trees and fields, always rocky outcrops. Patinir's colouration is masterly. Not for him one or two colours, but a host of hues between each of his major groups of colours (brown, blue and green). In Patinir's *St Christopher*, as in Quentin Massys' *St Christopher*, the saint is seen wading across a river holding a staff. The painting is one of Patinir's busiest, with a scale, from foreground to background, as vast as the history paintings of John Martin.

THE BAPTISM OF CHRIST

Joachim Patinir's *The Baptism of Christ* places the messiah in the centre of the composition, as in most *Baptisms*, staring at the viewer. Knee deep in cool blue water, he is baptized by a Baptist looking much poorer than the red-robed saint in Gerard David's *Baptism of Christ*. As in other *Baptisms*, part of heaven opens up to let God through, Who casts down the dove. But behind Jesus is the vast world, the calm waters and the reflections of hills and trees, and distant vistas of mountains and valleys. Patinir's is a view of the world as infinitely rich and varied, where the chief wonders are not always the traditional ones of God and Christianity. Just as wondrous in Patinir's views are the hills and rivers. However beautiful and important the Madonna, Jesus and God are in the scheme of things, the natural world is just as crucial, if not more so, in Patinir's nature mystical worldview.

Early Netherlandish Painting

THE TEMPTATION OF ST ANTHONY

Perhaps the largest and the most far-reaching of Jaochim Patinir's landscapes occurs in the painting he worked on with Quentin Massys, *The Temptation of St Anthony* (c. 1520-24, in the Prado). The painting is another of Patinir's strange blends of Christian and Classical elements. Dark pockets of shadows drift about the painting, while the sky just above the horizon is, as so often in Patinir, incandescent. There are plenty of middle ground details to satisfy the viewer, and the distant views of the river are as pleasing as any in Patinir's landscapes. St Anthony is not having a particularly horrible time. A monkey pulls his coat, a hag bares her breasts and grimaces at him, and a woman offers him an apple (as in the Judgement of Paris). St Anthony turns his head and looks imploringly at the spectator. Patinir's image is not the most severe of depictions of the theme of St Anthony's torments – such as Matthias Grünewald's painting, and the most horrific, which is of course Hieronymous Bosch's *The Temptation of St Anthony*.

XIV

Bernard van Orley

THE JOB ALTARPIECE

BERNARD VAN ORLEY is one of the most baroque of Early Netherlandish painters ('baroque' is probably the incorrect art historical term here, just as calling Van Orley 'Early Netherlandish' may also be incorrect). Van Orley was thoroughly an Italianized Northern painter, sometimes he is called a 'Romanist'. His *The Trials of Job* (Brussels) is a very busy picture; there is really too much going on, too much vyng for attention, to make the painting successful. It is an overload of imagery and gesture, which actually suits the subject of the painting, which is violent disruption. The eye darts from one hand thrown up in horror to heads thrown back in grief, to running figures. The humans, however, are only part of the subject of the painting: much of Van Orley's concern is with elaborate architectural detail. The design of *The Trials of Job* is extremely bold: the composition of the painting can be seen as a piece of bombast which looks forward to the airy idealizations of the High Baroque era.

Early Netherlandish Painting

THE LAST JUDGMENT

Bernard van Orley's large (the central panel is 8.2 by 7.2 feet) triptych of the Last Judgement (Antwerp) employs the compositional stratagems of Joos van Cleve and Jan Provost, among others. That is, the central panel is a vision of a vast landscape, with Christ riding high above the assembled throng. At least in Van Orley's *Last Judgement* Christ looks as if He means business, whereas in Joos van Cleve's *Last Judgement* he looks more like Adam reclining on pillows of clouds in Michelangelo's Sistine Chapel ceiling. These Mannerist Flemish/ Dutch paintings of the Last Judgement (by Van Orley, Joos, Provost), however, have none of the terror and grandeur of the *Last Judgements* by Rogier van der Weyden or Hans Memling.

THE HANNETON TRIPTYCH

Bernard van Orley's *Pietà*, the centrepiece of *The Hanneton Triptych*, is a tight grouping of mourners about the diagonal, slumped body of the Saviour. Beyond the figures is a flat gold background which recalls Rogier van der Weyden's *Descent From the Cross*. As with Jan Mostaert's *Passion Triptych*, there is none of the intense tragedy of Rogier's Escorial painting in Van Orley's *Hanneton Triptych*. But then, very few paintings before or since have contained the kind of scorching emotion of Rogier van der Weyden's Escorial *Descent*.

Early Netherlandish Painting

THE VIRGIN AND CHILD

There are softer, less grandiose images in Bernard van Orley's art than *The Last Judgement* or *The Job Altarpiece*, of course. His Prado *Madonna and Child*, for example, finds the painter on familiar Renaissance ground. However, Van Orley still seems concerned with showing off his Italianate/ Raphaelesque flourishes: the angel who flies in crowning the seated Virgin is not the tiny fairy-like angel of Jan van Eyck or Petrus Christus but a full-size figure whose clothes billow Botticelli-like as he soars in through the open window. Such an extraordinary occurrence – this dynamic angel floating into the room horizontally – naturally arrests the Child's attention: instead of going to His mother's proffered breast, he gazes up at the airborne angel.

THE VIRGIN AND CHILD WITH ANGELS BY A FOUNTAIN

One of Bernard van Orley's most successful works is his *Virgin and Child with Angels By a Fountain* (New York). The painting depicts pure bliss, and every aspect of the painting is intended to evoke various aspects of bliss: the bliss of Paradise (the enclosed garden, the softly playing fountain, the sunny sky, the peacocks and flowers); the bliss of childhood (the baby cavorting with His mother, enshrined in Her body); the bliss of motherhood (the Virgin clasps the boy to Her bosom, Her face pressed up against his like lovers); the bliss of art (the angels singing from a songbook, the voluptuousness of the painting itself). Van Orley curbs his usual tendency to create bombastic, unbelievable architecture, and concentrates on the depiction of the enclosed garden and its top-ranking inhabitants. Having said that, the wall and doorway of the *hortus conclusus* is fiddly, as if the painter cannot help making elaborate any block of stone, and the palatial building on the right is also luxurious.

The overall atmosphere of Bernard van Orley's *The Madonna and Child By a Fountain*, however, is of maternal ecstasy: the colours are muted greens and blues, the whole painting is suffused with an underwater green light, distinctly recalling uterine, pre-natal and oceanic pleasure. The baby is scooped up in His mother's arms; but She too is enfolded by the plants which grow profusely around her body.

XV

Hugo van der Goes

THE ADORATION OF THE SHEPHERDS

ONE OF THE stranger altarpieces of the Early Netherlandish Renaissance is Hugo van der Goes' *Portinari Altarpiece (The Adoration of the Shepherds)*, painted before 1476. The central 'adoration' is not that of the shepherds, however, but of a mother for her son, in this instance the most special Mother and Son of the Western world. She kneels, hands gently touching, in front of a tiny child. As with Leonardo's *Adoration*, also in the Uffizi, the Virgin Mary and Her heavenly offspring are the tranquil centre of a busy, noisy composition. Unlike Leonardo's masterly portrayal, van der Goes does not keep to a precise, geometric sense of proportion and perspective. Instead, the scale is all over the place, creating some skew-whiff perspectives, from the high viewpoint of the floor of the stable, to the Flemish town house beyond. The angels in the foreground are conflicting sizes, while the flying angels in the sky are also out of proportion. The scale of Jesus is tiny compared to that of the towering Virgin Mary. But none of this matters one iota, because the tenderness and sweetness of the evocation of the Adoration transcends the demands of formalism. These notions of scale and proportion become niggling beside the intensity of the emotional scene portrayed.

Early Netherlandish Painting

THE MONFORTE ALTARPIECE

Another *Adoration* by Hugo van der Goes, this time of the Magi (*The Monforte Altarpiece*, Berlin) depicts a more unified and 'rational' space, with the dignitaries again approaching from the right. As with the *Portinari Altarpiece*, van der Goes fills his frame with many details and moving passages of paint, from the gifts set down by one of the kings who kneels before the Christ child, to the landscape in the background. The pale skin of van der Goes' figures was called 'chalky, silvery, bloodless, of aristocratic pallor' (by M. Friedländer, 4, 18).

Hugo van der Goes proved to be one of the most accomplished painters of landscapes behind the hieratic scenes occurring in the foregrounds of Renaissance art. The right wing of the *Portinari Altarpiece*, for example, has a highly populous landscape, with the Magi on horses, peasants, and townsfolk going about their business in a hilly landscape dotted with bare, wintry trees.

THE ADORATION OF THE SHEPHERDS

Something of the unreality and bedazzlement of Leonardo da Vinci's *Adoration of the Magi* appears in Hugo van der Goes' *Adoration of the Shepherds* (c. 1480, Berlin). The theatricality of the scene, with the prophets on each side drawing back a drape, is not the most remarkable aspect of the painting (though the use of curtain in this manner is unusual in Early Netherlandish painting). What is striking is not the wide horizontal format, though this too is unusual. It is shepherds themselves, two of them in particular, who are stumbling into the holy scene from the left. The cluster of figures around the crib is the traditional grouping, but these two shepherds, their kinetic energy and poses, set the painting quite apart from other *Adorations of the Shepherds*. In contrast to the solemn, static Magi in so many other *Adorations*, including Hugo van der Goes' other versions, the two shepherds in the Berlin *Adoration* bring with them a sense of vitality and transience into what is usually an eternally motionless scene.

THE DEATH OF THE VIRGIN

In Hugo van der Goes' *Death of the Virgin* (Musée Communale des Beaux-Arts, Bruges), the space of the painting is much tighter than the *Portinari Altarpiece* or the *Monforte Altarpiece*. It is compressed space, a little awkward, cramped, perhaps disturbing.1· In these religious paintings, van der Goes combined his 'visionary ecstasy' with 'naive and artless demeanour' (M. Friedländer, 51). I do not regard van der Goes as 'artless', however: like the other Early Netherlandish painters, he was full to the brim with art. As with others depictions of the end of the Virgin's earthly life, a cluster of figures gather around the bed, shown in various states of mourning. Many of them grasp the bedclothes, or hold up their hands in grief, or pray. Here the power of the Mother is demonstrated, as these grown and noble men kneel and crouch, bow their heads and subjugate themselves before the Virgin. Van der Goes depicts mature men acting in that strange, obsequious, fawning fashion that occurred in the courtiers surrounding female monarchs such as Elizabeth I or Cleopatra, Queen of Egypt. But if the awkward foreshortening of *The Death of the Virgin* is not enough, with the abasement of the mourners, to make this an idiosyncratic rendering of the theme, the arrival of Christ in a huge bubble of heavenly light is. With angels gathering up his massive robe like a wedding gown, Jesus in glory flies above the Virgin's head, ready to accept not only Her soul, but also Her actual body into Heaven. The inrushing of such an abundance of divine power into a sombre domestic interior is indeed an unreal event, and van der Goes manages to convey the miraculous nature of the deity's approach.

THE FALL OF MAN

In earlier works, such as the diptych of *The Fall of Man* and *Lamentation* (Kunsthistorisches Museum, Vienna), Hugo van der Goes has proved he was one of the most original artists of the Early Netherlandish era. In *The Fall of Man* he created a peculiar creature in the serpent, a hybrid being of nude woman and lizard who clutches the tree of knowledge and stares intently at Eve. This serpent is far more disconcerting than Michelangelo's serpent (in *The Garden of Eden*), or anything in Michelangelo's art. Eve, meanwhile, is still 'innocent': she is depicted as a nude Venus, belly forward, arm raised, displaying her nudity for the benefit of the spectator. In that simplistic but powerful poetic association of Renaissance art, a flower growing in front of Eve tactfully covers up her pubis from the viewer's glance. The petals of the gladioli are placed exactly over Eve's genitals, the age-old association of flower-womb and petals-labia are pointed up yet again.

XVI

Geertgen tot Sin Jans

GEERTGEN TOT SIN JANS, who may have died before the age of thirty, is one of the most idiosyncratic of Flemish painters. His paintings are instantly recognizable. As with Petrus Christus, Geertgen created figures and faces which were all his own. His figures have slanted eyes, tiny chins and noses, and little rounded, pointed faces, as if carved out of wood, like puppets. Eyes were definitely a problem for Geertgen: his *John the Baptist in the Wilderness*, for example, is successful on all counts (the landscape is particularly exquisite), but the eyes, too close together and lifeless, let the painting down.

Passionate emotion in the grand, gestural manner is not one of Geertgen's strong points, as he demonstrated in his *Lamentation* (in Vienna) which is of a much lesser power than any *Pietà* by Rogier van der Weyden or Petrus Christus. Despite all the gestures and poses of the figures surrounding Christ, Geertgen's *Lamentation* has none of the *gravitas* or tragedy of similar subjects by Gerard David, Robert Campin or Rogier van der Weyden. What is striking about Geertgen's *Lamentation* are details not seen in many other Early Netherlandish *Pietàs*: the large nails which made the holes in Christ's hands and feet are shown prominently in the foreground, while in the background the soldiers are taking the thieves down from the *tau* crosses, making certain they are dead by thrusting lances into their backs. This imagery is made all the more sadistic by apparently naïve way in which Geertgen paints it.

THE MAN OF SORROWS

Another of Geertgen's images of pain and suffering is his *Man of Sorrows*, where Christ is seen carrying his Cross surrounded by angels and the Virgin and Magdalene. The painting combines many moments from the Christian story. The central image is Christ's body: near-naked, it is lacerated with a multitude of wounds, which bleed profusely. Christ's expression as he stares imploringly and sorrowfully at the spectator invokes both pity and horror. It is a pathetic image in both the grand-tragic and the poor-paltry sense of the word.

THE NATIVITY AT NIGHT

What Geertgen tot Sin Jans lacks in the driving power of the big name masters of the Early Netherlandish era he makes up for in his idiosyncracies and small-scale innovations. *The Virgin in Glory*, for example, which may be by Geertgen, is a tiny but powerfully visionary depiction of the Virgin Mary in a *mandorla*, crowned, cradling the Christ child. Looking closer, one sees that the Madonna is being fêted by hundreds of little angels, blowing trumpets and horns, plucking harps and mandolins.

One of Geergten tot Sin Jans' best works is a minor masterpiece of

Early Netherlandish Painting

imagination. *The Nativity at Night* depicts just that: but why had so few painters before Geertgen tot Sin Jans depicted a true, deep night scene? There had been dawns and dusks previous to this painting, but relatively few black nights. Yet utter darkness is so central an experience for most humans (and plants, animals, etc). One of the great pleasures of Geertgen's tiny panel (34 x 25cm, in the National Gallery, London, is precisely this early evocation of the middle of the night. There is no pre-dawn glow altering the eastern horizon, and no afterglow of sunset perceptible in the heavens. This makes the light sources, which are both heavenly and 'natural', all the more eye-catching.

Essentially, Geertgen tot Sin Jans' *Nativity at Night* portrays a gathering of humans around the warming glow of a camp fire, all their faces lit from below. It is a primæval scene, one that hominids from two thousand or two hundred thousand years ago might recognize. Except here the generator of the reassuring illumination is the Christ child. Geertgen's *coup* here is to have the newborn child as the source of illumination in the interior of the stable. He even paints in the rays of divine light that issue from the naked baby. No wonder the gathering of angels, Mother and surrogate father (Joseph) look on with wonder. In the distance, the shepherd's bonfire is outshone by the airborne angel. While some of the angels around the crib act like well-trained and sober children, holding their hands together in pious prayer, one of them throws her/his hands up in joy. This gesture of wonderment is echoed by one of the shepherds on the hillside, seen from the window, in response to the glowing angel that hovers above the shepherds with the glad tidings. It doesn't matter, either, that Geertgen tot Sin Jan's sense of space and perspective is sometimes wayward (in the workshop *Relations of the Virgin in a Church*, Rijksmuseum, for example), for, in *The Nativity at Night*, the primal intimacy of the group of figures in this deep night scene nears profundity.

XVII

Jan de Beer

JAN DE BEER (d. *c.* 1535) was one of the so-called Antwerp Mannerists. Favoured subjects among the Antwerp Mannerists were Nativities by night and Adorations of the Magi. These were magical situations which allowed for all manner of flying angels, brooding clouds, lavish costumes, and general wonderment. Jan de Beer's *Adoration of the Magi Altarpiece* (Pinacoteca di Brera, Milan) teems with life – such a frenetically busy composition is quite a departure from similar works by Rogier van der Weyden or Petrus Christus. It is a painting that is resolutely 16th century, distinctly of the mannered, refined world of Italian Renaissance art. As with Jan Gossaert's later *St Luke Painting the Virgin Mary* or his *Malvagna Triptych*, the florid architectural splendour of de Beer's *Adoration* threatens to stifle any spiritual dimension.

Jan de Beer's *Nativity by Night* (Barber Institute, Birmingham) is nowhere near as magical as Geertgen tot Sin Jans' *Nativity at Night*, even though de Beer throws in more tricks and exaggerated gestures. Where Geertgen doesn't let the prayerful wonder of the angels around the crib detract from the Virgin's humility before Her child, de Beer smothers subtlety and goes for grandiloquent gestures. An angel soars over the manger, its wings and robes flapping in the supernatural breeze which Joseph has brought with him as he comes in from the night. The sound of flapping garments must be the acoustic accompaniment to de Beer's *Nativity by Night*: everyone's clothes in this painting are being lifted up and thrown about by the wind.

THE ANNUNCIATION

Jan de Beer's *Annunciation* (c. 1520, Thyssen-Bornemisza Collection) features a similarly airborne angel. If Sandro Botticelli's Uffizi *Annunciation* unsettled Leonardo da Vinci with its depiction of the Archangel Gabriel as a mass of billowing garments who threatens to push the Virgin Mary out of the picture, what would he have made of Jan de Beer's *Annunciation*? The angel in de Beer's image is excessively agile and kinetic: his robes flutter madly, his gold cape trailing wildly behind him, the scroll he carries curling like a snake in mid-air. The Virgin too is not free of this air-driven Baroque treatment: there is another scroll directly over Her head, spiralling in the room as if fired from a joke gun. What a development in a different direction these scrolls are in their twirling actions from the steady exchange of gold-embossed words in Trecento and Quattrocento *Annunciations*, such as Simone Martini's Uffizi *Annunciation*.

Jan de Beer's Munich *Annunciation* is even more flamboyant than the Thyssen *Annunciation*. As in the Madrid picture, there is the bed, the vase of lilies, the lectern and book, the sewing tools, the sumptuously tiled floor, and, oddly, a white cat. The Munich *Annunciation*, however, evokes a much larger and more opulent bedroom for the Virgin. It seems to be an impossibly grand dwelling for that 'obscure Jewish woman', as Geoffrey Ashe called the Virgin Mary before the Annunciation. In de Beer's *Annunciations*, and in many a Renaissance *Annunciation*, the Virgin Mary lives like a princess. She is like the princess who waits for her prince in fairy tales (in *Sleeping Beauty, Rapunzel, Cinderella, Snow White*). What, one wonders, does the Virgin need with an Annunciation, plus Archangel, plus giving birth to a Messiah, when Her living quarters are so luxurious? With a town house as grand as the one de Beer depicts in the *Annunciation,* the Virgin Mary could well do without all the aggravation of bringing up the Saviour of the world. Far better for Her to continue living in such luxury.

THE MARRIAGE OF THE VIRGIN

Other paintings by Jan de Beer are less pyrotechnical than *The Annunciation*. The reverse of the Thyssen *Annunciation*, for example, depicts *The Birth of the Virgin* as a gathering of women around the natal bed, comforting the baby, preparing candles, food, and busying themselves around the supine figure of the Madonna. Having recently given birth, She lies back on the pillows and does the one thing which all good Christians do: She prays. Even in Her post-natal exhaustion, after birthing a baby, She prays!

*

In *The Marriage of the Virgin* (in St Louis) the grandiose architecture adds rather than detracts from the subject of the picture. Opulent architectonics are of course par for the course in pictures of the Adoration or Nativity or Annunciation. Such joyous occasions call for extravagant architecture. The Adoration, of shepherds or Magi, occurs in a run-down stable, but Renaissance artists usually found ways of fitting the stable up into something more like a palace. During the course of Early Netherlandish art, the tendency to make the architecture in a painting more luxuriant increased. In the art of Jan Gossaert, Jan de Beer, Bernard van Orley, Quentin Massys and others, we can see how this grandiose architecture becomes the real subject of the painting. The theme, of Adoration or Annunciation, becomes secondary to the meticulous evocation of extravagant *mise-en-scène*. One can see the socio-political implications of this, related to the increased wealth of the patrons, the changing notions of economy, power, religion, the church and art in Renaissance times, and so on.

In Jan de Beer's *Marriage of the Virgin*, however, the sumptuous architecture for once works. Apart from a birth, a wedding is the one time when no expense should be spared. One sees this propensity for luxuriance in *Adoration of the Magi* paintings, where the birth of a child is the pretext for much gift-giving and general good feelings. In de Beer's *Marriage of the Virgin*, this desire for showy munificence is gratified. What is surprising is perhaps the relatively small number of portrayals of the Virgin's marriage. We see many more images of Her Annunciation, Her Nativity, Her anguish at the foot of the Cross and Her Death and Coronation. The wedding of the Madonna, though, is curiously absent from many painters' œuvres. We are more likely to see the 'mystic' marriage of St Catherine and the baby Jesus. But that is a strange pairing, the virginal saint and the year-old baby. One might expect many more *Marriages of the Virgin*, due to the omnipotence of bourgeois, heterosexual, romantic, erotic love in the West. Perhaps a wedding was too suggestive of erotic communion for the Church; perhaps the source in the *Gospels* made too little of it; perhaps painters and patrons preferred to have a superhuman being unite with the Virgin (Gabriel in the Annunciation) or Christ Himself (in the Coronation) rather than any one so obviously, fatally human as Joseph.

XVIII

Quentin Massys

THE ST ANNE ALTARPIECE

QUENTIN MASSYS, BORN in Louvain, the first great painter of Antwerp, produced some of the softest, most demure paintings of the Virgin, which recall the meekness of the Madonnas in the art of Fra Angelico and Sandro Botticelli. However, the humility of the Virgin Mary in paintings such as Massys' Brussels *Madonna and Child* is counterpointed by a massiveness about the treatment of the architecture, and the Virgin. In the Brussels *Virgin*, for example, the Mother of God has gigantic knees and legs: the top half of Her holy body is to scale and in proportion to the Child on Her lap. Her legs, which can be made out under Her cloak, as always in seated *Madonna and Child* pictures, are huge, as in Jan van Eyck's Madonnas.

Though he created a series of sweet, meek Virgins, Quentin Massys was also a student of Italinate architecture. His *The Holy Family*, in *The St Anne Altarpiece*, demonstrates Massys's Italianization graphically. The low viewpoint enables the architectonics to be spectacularly displayed. The right wing of this altarpiece, however, which depicts the Virgin's death, is more in keeping with Early Netherlandish composition, lighting, and emotion. The interior, again with a low viewpoint which makes the bed appear enormous, is Netherlandish, with few obvious Italianate references. Another *Madonna and Child* by Massys in London (National Gallery), again features resplendent half Gothic, half Renaissance architecture. Superbly crafted, the painting is let down by the focus of the image: the Virgin Mary's face. Rounded, with a long nose and a tiny mouth, Her face is not in keeping with the rest of the painting, which is showy and regal. The Virgin's face is a weakness in an otherwise accomplished painting. Italy breathes through Massys's moving *Entombment* (Antwerp), with a landscape background that recalls Giovanni Bellini and Andreas Mantegna. The painting is composed in a series of greys, a purpley grey, a blueish grey, a greeny-grey.

THE MADONNA AND CHILD

The Rattier Madonna (Louvre) depicts maternal *jouissance* in an dark Flemish interior. Mother and Child are shown embracing like lovers: She holds the baby up to Her face: their lips are touching. Here the Chid displaces any earthly, adult male lover, and becomes the bridegroom to the Virgin, Mother of the Church. Like Joos van Cleve, Hans Memling, Jan van Eyck and Gerard David, Quentin Massys depicts the mother-child relation as a sensual union. The signs of the Saviour's later fate (the grapes, for example, referring to Christ's Passion) are secondary to the central embrace of the Mother and Child.

Early Netherlandish Painting

STANDING MADONNA AND CHILD

The *Standing Madonnas with the Child and Angels* (such as in the Courtauld Institute, London and the Musée des Beaux-Arts, Lyon) are some of Quentin Massys's most typical works. Again, softness is one of the words that springs to mind when contemplating these *Madonnas Standing*. Massys's painterly treatment recalls some of the highpoints of Early Netherlandish art, including, most obviously, Jan van Eyck. The Madonna is seen standing in front of a portal to a cathedral, an image out of van Eyck's art. In Massys's image, however, the architecture shows as much influence from Florence or Rome as from Antwerp or Bruges. The sweetness of the attendant angels makes them some of the most exquisite in all Renaissance art. For sheer beauty Massys's angels vie with the most languid, liquiescent and child-like angels in the art of Raphael Sanzio, Fra Filippo Lippi, Sandro Botticelli or Petrus Christus. In the Courtauld *Madonna*, the sensuality of the painting as an object, with its rich gold-edged blue cloak (again recalling van Eyck), is underlined by the undeniable erotic treatment of the Virgin Mary. She has long, Pre-Raphaelite hair, three hundred and fifty years before the Pre-Raphaelite era.

Other long-haired women in Quentin Massys's art include the Philadelphia *St Mary Magdalene* and *St Mary of Egypt*, two of the most fervently penitent images of the Northern Renaissance. Both saints are shown in a darkened wilderness, naked, their below-waist-level hair hiding their sexuality. The pictures dramatically express the indignant Christian separation of erotic feelings, and the subservience to the moral and religious rectitude of monotheism.

Early Netherlandish Painting

ECCE HOMO

Quentin Massys is not all sweetness and light. His *Christ Presented to the People* (Madrid) rivals Hieronymous Bosch in the skill with which it portrays the mob mocking the Saviour. The jeering, leering crowds recall the thugs in Bosch's extraordinary *Christ Carrying the Cross* in Ghent. It's true that Massys's painting does not have the power of Bosch's hideously ugly, grimacing men. But then, hardly anybody could bring out the sheer, stupefyingly bestiality of humans like Hieronymous Bosch.

Like Christ in Bosch's Ghent painting, Christ at the centre of Quentin Massys's Madrid image is quiet, still, sorrowful, resigned to His fate. Massys's painting presents the mockery at a balcony overlooking a street: Christ has been brought outside onto the balcony for the hordes to mock him. The brutality of the occasion is emphasized by Massys's skillful rendering of caricature. The savagery of the mockery in Massys's *Ecce Homo* is also emphasized by the painter's placing of a carving directly above Christ of a Goddess tenderly suckling Her young. The bliss of the early, maternal union is a bitter contrast with the Saviour alone in the idiot throng.

XIX

Joos van Cleve

JOOS VAN CLEVE (Joos van der Beke, from Cleves in the lower Rhine region) was another Early Netherlandish painter who embraced Italian Mannerism. Some of Joos van Cleve's compositions are extraordinarily busy, such as his *Last Judgement* (c. 1520-5, Metropolitan Museum, New York), which presents the apocalyptical moment in a unified, Italianate space. Joos' Christ in judgement is a far less severe deity than in Rogier van der Weyden's *Last Judgement*.

THE DEATH OF THE VIRGIN

In Joos van Cleve's *The Death of the Virgin* (Munich) the problem of depicting someone lying back on a bed yet showing them to the viewer results in a piece of exaggerated perspective in an otherwise sophisticated painting. The interior setting reveals many architectural flourishes, from a recess with an elaborate carving over it, to the layered perspectival view of the town outside the building. The figures surrounding the bed are

Early Netherlandish Painting

caught in various stages of lamentation. Joos' *Death of the Virgin* in Cologne is much more satisfying as a composition, for the bed is seen side-on. The number of mourning participants is reduced, too, which reduces the number of distracting and competing features that were present around the death-bed in the Munich triptych.

THE VIRGIN AND CHILD WITH ANGELS

Some of Joos van Cleve's most accomplished works are his series of *Virgin and Child with Angels* paintings. These depict the Madonna seated on a throne against a cloth of honour, in the manner more of Giovanni Bellini and the Italian masters than, say, Jan van Eyck or Quentin Massys. Some art critics suggest the influence of Leonardo da Vinci on Joos: one can see the touch of Leonardo in some of Joos' characters' gestures. In *The Virgin and Child with Angels* (formerly at Lulworth Castle), the Virgin reaching for the grapes that one of the attendant angels offers recalls Leonardo's *Virgin of the Rocks*. The Vienna *Holy Family* also features a seated Madonna, but with an aged St Anne on Her right. As before an angel offers the Virgin, not the Child (as is usual), some grapes. The architectural setting here is much more elaborate than in the Lulworth *Madonna*. The throne is practically a mini Italianate church in its own right, with thick pillars and barrel vaulting.

Early Netherlandish Painting

MADONNA AND CHILD PAINTINGS

Joos van Cleve painted many Madonnas, and many of them show the Virgin happily suckling Her Child, as in the matronly Cambridge and the wistful Metropolitan Museum paintings. Fingers splayed over Her nipple, the Virgin smiles down at Her offspring, who drowses on Her breast in the Cambridge painting, while in the New York *Madonna* He stares vaguely into space, as babies so often do at the breast. Many of Joos van Cleve's pictures reveal his careful observation of people: the baby drowsing, the baby staring into the distance, and, an unusual touch in any *Madonna and Child* painting, the baby asleep with its mouth pressed open over its forearm (in the Lulworth *Madonna and Child with Angels*). Joos' paintings demonstrate how accurate he was in his studies of life. In the Detroit *Adoration of the Magi* one of the kings is privileged not only to kneel before the child god, but to cuddle His tiny body, which the Virgin solemnly offers.

THE REST ON THE FLIGHT INTO EGYPT

Joos van Cleve's *Adoration of the Magi* in Detroit is not particularly exceptional, and appears derivative and uninspired after the wonderful *Adorations* by Rogier van der Weyden and Petrus Christus. Joos' *Rest on the Flight into Egypt* recalls the expanse of landscape in the art of Jaochim Patinir and especially Gerard David. The Virgin is centre frame, a large pyramidal figure. The maternal bliss of a mother suckling her child is the central rite displayed here. Joseph is nowhere to be seen (though his staff and a basket are found in the foreground).

Joos van Cleve's *St Jerome* is a painting with a convoluted architectural design. Dominating the composition is a tree in the foreground. The bony old man is in the centre, atop a pile of rocks, while the lion skulks in the shadows on the left. Behind this already cluttered foreground, in the middle distance, is the saint's dwelling, a rocky cave, which looks like it's quite well-furnished, with its group of holy objects: an icon of the Virgin, the *Bible*, and a crucifix. The landscape itself in *St Jerome* is worthy of Joachim Patinir or David: a town, a pond, animals, trees, hills.

THE LAMENTATION OVER CHRIST

Joos van Cleve's *Lamentation* in the Musée du Louvre is a much more powerful image than the *Adoration* or other earlier works. As so often in Joos' art, certain objects are picked out and isolated in the foreground. In the *Lamentation* (not a time for subtlety), a human skull and bones are closest to the viewer. Christ's body shows the suppleness and ease of Italian art, and the range of gestures from the mixed company of mourners also shows an Italian input. The composition is fine, each figure is carefully harmonized with the ones on either side of it. The atmosphere of *gravitas* is lessened, however, by one of the female followers, who throws up both hands in sorrow: her fingers are splayed and the gesture seems over-emphatic. Go too far in a lamentation scene, and you ruin the credibility – as many actors as well as painters know.

XX

Anonymous and Other Early Netherlandish Painters

SOME OF THE best Early Netherlandish works are by anonymous painters. It seems odd that the artists could produce highly sophisticated artworks in a highly sophisticated European town of the 15th and 16th centuries, and yet no one knows their name. Some of these anonymous painters have names such as 'Follower of' such and such a painter. Others are called the 'Master of the Embroidered Leaf' or the 'Master of the Saint Bartholomew Altarpiece'.

THE MASTER OF THE EMBROIDERED LEAF

The Master of the Embroidered Leaf produced a sumptuous *Virgin and Child* set against a richly woven cloth of honour. The painting is based on the Madonna Enthroned types as found in the art of Rogier van der Weyden, Robert Campin/ the Master of Flémalle and Jan van Eyck. Mary sits in an enclosed garden which has the usual plants in it associated with the Virgin. As so often in Early Netherlandish painting, two angels fly above the Madonna with a crown. The Child, as in Rogier van der Weyden's Prado *Madonna*, ruffles the pages of a book. Beyond the garden are views of a park.

THE MASTER OF THE MAGDALENE LEGEND

The Master of the Magdalene Legend produced some poignant images, notably *The Holy Family*, which depicts the Child greeting Joseph as he returns from some errand (Antwerp). The Child pulls on his surrogate father's cloak eagerly, and points to His mother. The two adults indulge their Child quietly and somewhat sorrowfully. The Virgin in particular seems sadly introspective, as if contemplating the boy's tragic future. Yet the Master of the Magdalene legend captures so well a certain lightness of spirit of childhood, which is also found in *The Virgin and Child* in Brussels. The latter painting depicts the Madonna and baby against a flat, gold, punched background, The delicacy and tenderness of the mother-child bond is celebrated here in a timeless manner, as if children have been snoozing on their mother's laps for millennia.

Early Netherlandish Painting

THE MASTER OF HOOGSTRAETEN

The Master of Hoogstraeten created a *Madonna Enthroned with Saints Catherine and Barbara* (Uffizi) which draws on the influence of Italian Renaissance art, as in Gerard David, Bernard van Orley or Quentin Massys. The Uffizi painting takes the *sacra conversazione* of Italian art, with the hanging cloth of honour which is such a prominent feature of Giovanni Bellini's art, and sets distinctly Flemish-style figures in the space which is half Early Netherlandish and half Italian.

THE ST LUCY LEGEND MASTER

One of the extraordinary paintings of the Early Netherlandish era is the Master of the St Lucy Legend's *Mary, Queen of Heaven* (Washington). Rarely has the Virgin Mary been given such a grandiose and epic treatment. True, Spanish and Italian Renaissance painting, or more precisely, Baroque painting, did offer the Virgin Mary some wild and populous settings and treatments, but it is rare to see such a gloriously over-the-top exposition. The Madonna is surrounded by swarms of angels: some play musical instruments, some sing, as expected, and many of them are touching Her. They hold Her robes, Her arms, Her shoulders, all these hands are supporting Her. The angels' legs are bent backwards, so they look like mermaids flying in the air around the Virgin Mary. The painting is all movement and life, a crowd of faces and hands fluttering about the Madonna's enormous body as She hovers above the Earth.

Early Netherlandish Painting

THE VIRGO MASTER

The Master of the Virgo inter Virgines, also called the Virgo Master, was active *c.* 1470 - *c.* 1500. His name comes from *The Virgo inter Virgines* in Amsterdam. This is a familiar Early Netherlandish theme, but the Virgo Master's version of it is by no means the most accomplished. The paintings by the Master of the Lucia Legend and the Master of the Ursula Legend (both in Brussels) are more sophisticated examples of the *virgo inter virgines* theme. The spatial dynamics of the Virgo Master's painting are sometimes awkward – a light, open courtyard is given a crude sense of perspective and scale. This is very much inferior to Jan van Eyck or Rogier van der Weyden. One only has to compare paintings by the Master of the Virgo inter Virgines with those of van Eyck or Hans Memling to see how much more successful are the latter painters. The Philadelphia *Marriage of the Virgin Mary*, for instance, by the Virgo Master or a follower, contains an airy but unsatisfactory depiction of a church interior – compared to the churches of Rogier van der Weyden or Jan van Eyck.

The Master of the Virgo inter Virgines' *Lamentation* (in the Hospital of St Nicholas, Enghien, Belgium) is lit by an eerie illuminaton, something akin to the stormlighting that appears in some of his other paintings (such as the Vienna *Crucifixion*). The figures seem insubstantial and ghostly. Christ lies in the foreground. As so often in Renaissance art, the winding sheet is pulled back to reveal His body. It just covers His genitals, so that at times Christ in the post-Crucifixion scenes recalls male fashion models and pornographic imagery which plays with nearly revealing-not-revealing that holiest of objects, the phallus.

The Virgo Master's Liverpool *Entombment* shows one of painting's most emaciated Christs being carried to the sepulchre. The tenderness of the figures surrounding Christ's exhausted body is lyrically portrayed. The Virgin Mary kneels in front of the body, Her own slumped body echoing His. The Virgo Master's *Entombment* creates a sense of tragic irony, for the poses of the Madonna and Christ mock the positions they take up in *Assumption* and *Coronation* paintings. In this *Emtombment*, Jesus and Mary crumple towards each other, but this is not the union of lovers, but of one who is now dead, and one who suffers as much as He. Setting off this tragic event is the Virgo Master's sonorous colouration.

In his *Crucifixion* the brightest colours (chiefly red) are made all the brighter by the surrounding gloom. This *Crucifixion* really does look like it is occurring at the eleventh hour, or near it, for the sky is very dark, the fag end of dusk. The landscape is in shadow, the greens of the vegetation are mixed profusely with black. Rather than show the grieving women clutching the foot of the Cross, the Master of the Virgo inter Virgines shows the mob – noblemen riding horses, soldiers, scribes, priests, casual onlookers. The spear enters Christ's side. He is moments away from giving up the ghost. The jeering, chattering men in the foreground are much larger than the three crucified figures. The *chiaroscuro* and coloration deepens the tragedy of the scene.

The Virgo Master's *Annunciation* (in Rotterdam) is an intriguing depiction of the holy message. A pillar separates Virgin and angel, inside and outsider. Here the metaphor of the room as womb work well: the angel is shown as arriving from an outside door: his half of the painting is light-filled; the Virgin's room, meanwhile, is dark and enclosed. The soft and dark (womb-like) furnishings of the Virgin's quarter contrast dramatically and poignantly with the masculine, hard, rectangular edges of the angel's hallway.

Early Netherlandish Painting

THE MASTER OF MARY OF BURGUNDY

One must limit one's discussion somewhere: one could also study at length the miniaturists and painters of illuminations, and the complex and multi-faceted relationships between painters and miniaturists. Many of the Early Netherlandish painters also painted illuminations, and vice versa. Petrus Christus's tiny, jewel-like paintings spring to mind in this context: his *Christ as the Man of Sorrows* and *The Virgin of the Dry Tree* demonstrate amply his skill as a miniaturist painter. There are many extraordinary Northern Renaissance illuminations, many lovely *Books of Hours*. The Limbourg Brothers produced the famous *Book of Hours (Les Très Riches Heures) of the Duke of Berry* (1416), a series of images that have proved to be long-lasting; they still appear on Christmas and greetings cards each year.

The Master of Mary of Burgundy produced a distinguished *Book of Hours* (c. 1480, Vienna), probably made for Mary of Burgundy, the daughter of Charles the Bold. One illustration (MS. 1857, fol. 14v) shows Mary (?) reading in front of a church window: inside the vast church, sitting in the choir, is the Virgin and Child, attended by Her virgin companions. The scene is portrayed by a deep spatial perspective, making the illumination large in conception, even though it is but 7.5. by 5.3 inches. The lady and her surroundings, in the foreground (she is seen reading, with cloth, jewels, a dog and other objects around her) serve as a frame for the painting of the Virgin and Child in the cathedral, a job usually done by the floral, ornamental borders in manuscript illumination.

Early Netherlandish Painting

OTHER EARLY NETHERLANDISH PAINTERS

One can continue with the study of Early Netherlandish painting with a discussion of many other painters. There is JACQUES DARET (died after 1468), who should be noted here. He was a pupil of Robert Campin-the Master of Flémalle. Daret's *Adoration of the Magi* and *Visitation* (Berlin) and *Presentation in the Temple* are tender examples of early Early Netherlandish art. Sweet indeed are the arrays of golden spikes which emanate from St Anne's and the Virgin's heads in *The Visitation*. These golden shards do for haloes, marking out the holy participants in these early 15th century altarpiece images.

Jacques Daret's *Nativity* (Thyssen-Bornemisza Collection) is an Adoration-type image, in the Italian manner, with the Virgin kneeling before Her offspring. Though nowhere near as sophisticated as the Antwerp Mannerists' *Nativities*, Jan Daret's *Nativity* is a compelling image. The figures may all be of a different scale – the angels fluttering about the stable roof are really tiny, while the Virgin, as so often, is huge – but this does not detract from the emotion of the painting.

*

JAN MOSTAERT (*c*. 1475-1555/6) created some powerful images as idiosyncratic as painters such as Petrus Christus or Dieric Bouts. Mostaert's *Descent From the Cross* (Brussels) has none of the emotional expressivity of Rogier van der Weyden's Madrid painting, but it does have moments of interest. The facial expressions, for instance, are quite Mostaert's own: the protagonists stare out of the corner of their eyes at the other participants, more concerned, it seems, with their standing among their compatriots than with the central tragic act of taking down the dead Saviour. While the design follows Rogier van der Weyden's painting, the figures are derived partially from Geertgen tot Sin Jans. While Jan Mostaert is an intriguing painter, he is not in the front rank of Early Netherlandish and Dutch painters.

Early Netherlandish Painting

JAN VAN SCOREL'S (1495-1562) art is full of limpid, open spaces, in which figures move with ease and self-assurance. See, for example, the expansive landscape of *Entry of Christ into Jerusalem* (Utrecht), *The Baptism of Christ* (Haarlem) and *The Holy Kinship Altarpiece* (Obervellach). Van Scorel's *Presentation in the Temple* (Vienna) depicts the interior of a Roman church with an easy self-confidence. In this unusual view of the Presentation (the action occurs in the middle distance, behind some figures in the foreground), the representation of the architecture is a dramatic development on from such Early Netherlandish luminaries as the Master of the Virgo inter Virgines or Robert Campin. Van Scorel's rationalization of space and light makes the movement from North to South complete.

One should also mention JOOS VAN GHENT (d. c. 1480), whose *Crucifixion Triptych* in the Cathedral of St-Bavon in Ghent is an accomplished piece of work. Elements in the painting recall (the figures of) Dieric Bouts, while the landscape is suitably wintry and barren.

ADRIAEN ISENBRANDT (died 1551) is one of the late Flemish painters, in which the influence of Italy and Mannerism is very much in evidence. As with Bernard van Orley, Mabuse, and Quentin Massys, the architectural settings are crucial in Isenbrandt's art. There is nothing as audacious and ornate as Mabuse's *Malvagna Virgin and Child* in Isenbrandt's art, but paintings such as his *Virgin of Sorrows* (Bruges) reveal a heightened architectural imagination at work. The Virgin, showing Gerard David's influence in Her face and headdress, sits on an elaborate throne around which are arranged small paintings from the Virgin's life (the Flight into Egypt, the Presentation, the Pietà and so on). Isenbrandt's London *Mary Magdalene* has the softness of Hans Memling or Gerard David, combined with the landscape detail of Joachim Patinir. The Magdalene is seen kneeling and praying before the Holy Book and a crucifix, a scene familiar from the portrayal of male saints such as St Bernard or John the Baptist. Isenbrandt takes on this stereotype of iconography, and creates a marvellous Italianate interpretation, in which not the least aspect is the depiction of Mary Magdalene's eroticism.

*

JAN PROVOST (1465-1529) painted some powerful images – his *Death and the Miser* for example (Bruges) where a grinning skeleton exchanges bills with a miser. Provost's Baltimore *Madonna* has the heavy frontality of Jan van Eyck's *Madonnas*, while his *Martyrdom of St Catherine* (Antwerp) is a grim portrayal of the saint about to be beheaded by a muscular soldier. Many of Provost's other paintings, however, on closer inspection prove to be disappointing. He painted an alluring *Madonna and Child* (Piacenza), which has a post-van Eyckian fountain and flowery enclosed garden. The painting, though, is not as successful as similar images by Petrus Christus, Hans Memling, Massys or Gerard David.

*

JAN JOEST (born between 1450 and 1460, died 1519) produced a memorable *Lamentation* (Cologne), with the dead Saviour collapsed back onto Joseph of Arimethea and the Virgin Mary. In this *Pietà*, as in few *Pietàs*, the body of Christ actually falls and lies like a real body – it is not the stiff-limbed figure of earlier *Pietàs* by lesser artists, who made the dead God look awkward not because his tortured body was setting rigid in death but because they could not paint bodies properly. In Joest's *Lamentation* the artist has studied the human figure astutely, and has made a faithful rendering of it. While other paintings by Provost do not always demonstrate the same suppleness (for example, his *Flight into Egypt*, Palencia, and *Entombment*, Palencia), generally, Joest is one of the more graphic artists of the Early Netherlandish painters (in his *Baptism of Christ*, Kalkar, for example).

Early Netherlandish Painting

※ ※ ※

Early Netherlandish painting continues to fascinate and entrance for a host of reasons; one of the main ones is that is an incredibly beautiful art, an art that gives immense pleasure. And I'd always draw attention to the quality of the *light* in Early Netherlandish painters: somehow they managed to capture and transmit a truly glorious sense of light, and that deep, rich light is somehow an equivalence for being alive, or an expression of being alive. Or maybe it is life itself.

Notes

I The Early Netherlandish World

1. Michelangelo, in R. Goldwater, 68
2. The term 'Flemish' properly refers to the art of 15th century Flanders (M. Whinney, 27), and cultural centres such as Bruges and Ghent; other centres included Tournai, Brussels, Delft and Utrecht.
3. see Elizabeth Ardrey's report, in C. Eisler, 1989, 15

II Mysticism and Art in Mediæval Northern Europe

1. Rufus M. Jones: *Some Exponents of Mystical Religion*, Epworth 1930, 77
2. Michael Cox: *Mysticism*, Aquarian Press 1983, 99f
3. Meister Eckhardt: *Sermons*, tr. Evans, in F.C. Happold, 1970, 274
4. On Eckhart's monism, see R.C. Zaehner: *Mysticism Sacred and Profane*, Oxford University Press 1957, 207
5. see Sidney Spencer: *Mysticism in World Religion*, Penguin 1963, 166f
6. Jan van Ruysbroeck: *The Adornment of the Spiritual Marriage*, tr. Wynschenk, Dutton, New York 1916
7. see Erich Neumann, 44f

III Space, Light and Aesthetics in Early Netherlandish Art

1. see E. Neumann, 51, 261ff
2. see Pamela Berger, 89ff

3. St Bridget, in Lottlisa Behling: *Die Pflanze in der mittelalterlichen Tafelmalerei*, Cologne 1967, 3

4. see Paul Watson, 17, 23

5. see R. Graves, 1961, 255, 409f

6. Mircea Eliade writes: 'The presence of the goddess beside a plant symbol confirms one meaning that the tree possesses in archaic iconography and mythology: that of being an *inexhaustible source of cosmic fertility.*' 1958, 280

7. Master of the Lucia Legend: *Madonna and Child with Female Saints*, Master of the Ursula Legend: *St Anne, Virgin and Child Between Saints Catherine, John the Baptist and Barbara and Louis the Pious*, both in the Koninklijke Musea voor Schone Kunsten van België, Brussels

IV   *Robert Campin-the Master of Flémalle*

1. See M. Meiss: "Highlands' in the Lowlands: Jan van Eyck, the Master of Flémalle and the Franco-Italian Tradition", *Gazette de Beaux-Arts*, 57, May 1961

V   *Jan van Eyck*

1. See J.L. Ward: "Van Eyck's *Chancellor Rolin and the Blessed Virgin*", *Art Journal*, 28, Spring 1969

2. Rolin's seignorial holdings included properties at Pruzilly, Raismes, Virieux-le-Grand, Gergy, Muz, Chazeux, Ricey-le Bas, Polisot, Chailly, Saisy, Bragny, Salans, Savoisy and Beauchamp, among others. (C. Harbison, 111)

3. M. Friedlander, 1943, in C. Eisler, 1989, 59

VI   *Rogier van der Weyden*

1. W. Vogelsang: 'Van der Weyden's art is pre-eminently religious' (7)

2. Ruth Massey Tovell: 'Rogier is the last of the mystics of the Middle Ages. He chose to express his moods through the religious subjects so beloved of the period. His gentle, mannered Virgins, elegant and lucid, are symbolic, detached, a product of the imagination.' (1955, 50)

Early Netherlandish Painting

3. Ruth Massey Tovell: 'Rogier dramatized misery with an instinct for powerful harmonies. Supremely intelligent, he knew how to display emotions in a well-ordered composition; his was a perfect technique in the art of expressing deep grief; there is even a splendour in the agony of his subjects.' (50)

VII   *The Passion According to Rogier van der Weyden*

1. Carlo Ludovico Ragghianti writes: 'This marks the moment of the artist's maturity and is one of the most monumental conceptions.' (1969, 118)

2. J. Kristeva: "Stabat Mater", *Tales of Love*, 251

VIII   *Petrus Christus*

1. See M.P.J. Marten: "New Information on Petrus Christus's Biography and the Patronage of His Brussels *Lamentation*", *Simiolus*, 20, 1991

2. See E. Panofsky, 1953, 1, 311; J. Bruyn, 1957, 105; C. Cuttler, 1968, 132; B.G. Lane: "Petrus Christus", *Art Bulletin*, 52, Dec 1970, 393; C. Sterling, 1971, 11 n. 46; J. Upton, 1984, 23; P. Schabacker, 1974, 111

3. See H. Beenken: "The Annunciation of Petrus Christus in the Metropolitan Museum and the Problem of Hubert van Eyck", *Art Bulletin*, 19, June 1937

4. See J.M. Collier: "The Kansas City Petrus Christus", *Nelson Gallery and Atkins Museums Bulletin*, 5, 5, Sept 1979

5. See R.A. Koch: "Petrus Christus: *The Virgin and Child in a Gothic Interior*", in *Flemish Paintings in America*, Antwerp 1992, 52

6. See L.B. Gellman: "'The Death of the Virgin' by Petrus Christus", *Burlington Magazine*, 112, 1970

7. See Joel Upton, 1990, 76; Charles Sterling, 1971, 3

XI   *Hans Memling*

1. Otto Pächt: *The Master of Mary of Burgundy*, 1948, 54, note 23

Early Netherlandish Painting

XII Gerard David

1. See M.W. Ainsworth: "Gérard David's Workshop Practices", in *Le Dessin sous-jacent dans la peinture: Dessin sous-jacent et pratiques d'atelier*, Louvain-la-Neuve 1993.
2. (C. Cuttler, 195; M. Whinney, 112)

XIII Joachim Patinir

1. M. Conway: *Literary Remains of Albrecht Dürer*, 1889, 119

XV Hugo van der Goes

1. M. Whinney, 83; M. Friedländer, ib., 31.

Bibliography

Maryan W. Ainsworth: *Petrus Christus: Renaissance Master of Bruges*, Metropolitan Museum of Art, New York/ Harry N. Abrams, 1994

F. Ames-Lewis: "Fra Filippo Lippi and Flanders", *Zeitschrift für Kunstgeschichte*, XLII, 1979, 255-273

Emile de Antonio & Mitch Tuchman: *Painters Painting*, Abbeville Press, New York 1984

C.G. Argan: *The Renaissance*, Thames & Hudson 1969

Karen Armstrong: *The Gospel According to Woman; Christianity's Creation of the Sex War in the West*, Pan 1987

Geoffrey Ashe: *The Virgin: Mary's Cult and the Re-emergence of the Goddess*, Arkana 1987

—. *Discovering the Goddess: A Personal Testimony*, Crescent Moon 2007

Patrick Bade: *Femme Fatale: Images of evil and fascinating women*, Ash & Grant 1979

Ludwig van Baldass: *Jan van Eyck*, London 1952

Michael Baxandall: *Painting and Experience in 15th Century Italy*, Oxford University Press 1988

—. *Patterns of Intention: On the Historical Explanation of Pictures*, Yale University Press 1985

Germain Bazin: "Petrus Christus et les rapports entre l'Italie et la flandre au milieu du xve siècle", *Revue des Arts*, II, 1952

James Beck: *Italian Renaissance Painting*, Harper & Row, New York 1981

Ean Begg: *The Cult of the Black Virgin*, Routledge 1985

Hans Beltin & Dagmar Eichberger: *Jan van Eyck als Erzähler*, Worms 1983

Bernard Berenson: *The Italian Painters of the Renaissance*, Phaidon 1952/ Fontana 1960

—. *Looking at Pictures with Bernard Berenson*, selected by Hann Kiel,

Early Netherlandish Painting

Abrams, New York 1974
Pamela Berger: *The Goddess Obscured*, Robert Hale 1988
Bruce Bernard: *The Queen of Heaven: A Selection of Painting the Virgin from the Twelfth to the Eighteenth Centuries*, Macdonald/ Orbis 1987
—. *The Bible and Its Painters*, Orbis 1983
Carlo Bertelli: *Piero della Francesca*, Yale University Press, New Haven 1992
Jan Bialostocki: *Jan van Eyck*, Warsaw 1973
K.M. Birkmeyer: "The Arch Motif in Netherlandish Painting in the 15th Century", *Art Bulletin*, 43, June 1961
Shirley Nielsen Blum: "Symbolic Invention in the Art of Rogier van der Weyden", *Konsthistorisk tidskrift*, XLVI, 1977
—. *Early Netherlandish Triptychs: A Study in Patronage*, Berkeley 1969
Charles Bouleau: *The Painter's Secret Geometry: A Study of Composition in Art*, tr. Jonathan Griffin, Thames & Hudson 1963
Serge Bramly: *Leonardo: The Artist and the Man*, Michael Joseph 1992
Allan Brahama: *Italian Renaissance Painters of the Sixteenth Century*, National Gallery 1985
Helmut Brinker: *Zen in the Art of Painting*, Routledge & Kegan Paul 1987
Stephanie Brown: *Religious Painting*, Phaidon 1979
J. Bruyn: *Van Eyck Problemen*, Utrecht 1957
Jacob Burckhardt: *The Altarpiece in Renaissance Italy*, Phaidon 1988
Titus Burckhardt: *Sacred Art in East and West*, Perennial Book, Middlesex 1967
Anne Hagopian van Buren: "The Canonical Office in Renaissance Painting, Part II: More About the Rolin Madonna", *Art Bulletin*, LX, 1978
Caroline Walker Bynum: "The Body of Christ in the Later Middle Ages: A Reply to Leo Steinberg", *Renaissance Quarterly*, XXIX, 1986
Robert Cafritz *et al*: *Places of Delight: The Pastoral Landscape*, Weidenfeld & Nicolson 1989
Ritchie Calder: *Leonardo and The Age of the Eye*, Heinemann 1970
Joseph Campbell: *The Power of Myth*, with Bill Moyers, ed. Betty Sue Flowers, Doubleday, New York 1988
Lorne Campbell: *Van der Weyden*, New York 1980
—"Robert Campin, the Master of Flémalle and the Master of Mérode", *Burlington Magazine*, CXVI, 1974
Michael P. Carroll: *The Cult of the Virgin Mary*, Princeton University Press, New Jersey 1986
Richard Cavendish: *Visions of Heaven and Hell*, Orbis 1977

Andre Chastel: *Art of the Italian Renaissance*, tr. Peter & Linda Murray, Alpine Fine Arts Collection 1985
—. *The Studios and Styles of the Renaissance, Italy 1460-1500*, tr. Griffin, Thames & Hudson 1966
Albert Châtelet: *Van Eyck*, Bologna 1979
Herschel B. Chipp, ed. *Theories of Modern Art*, University Press of California, Los Angeles 1968
J.E. Cirlot. *A Dictionary of Symbols*, Routledge, London, 1981
Kenneth Clark: *Rembrandt and the Italian Renaissance*, John Murray 1969
Bruce Cole: *The Renaissance Artist at Work*, John Murray 1983
—. *Piero della Francesca: Tradition and Innovation in Renaissance Art*, Harper Collins, New York 1991
J.C. Cooper. *An Illustrated Dictionary of Traditional Symbols*, Thames & Hudson, London, 1978
Pierre Courthion: *Flemish Painting*, Thames & Hudson 1958
Paul Crossley: "Medieval Architecture and Meaning: The Limits of Iconography", *Burlington Magazine*, CXXX, 1988
Charles D. Cuttler: *Northern Painting From Pucelle to Bruegel*, Holt, Rineheart & Winston, New York 1968
Martin Davies: *Rogier van der Weyden*, Phaidon 1972
—. *The Early Netherlandish School*, London 1968
Valentin Denis: *Tutta la pittura di Jan van Eyck*, Milan 1954
Elisabeth Dhanens: *Hubert and Jan van Eyck*, New York 1980
G. Didi-Huberman: *Fra Angelico. Dissemblance et Figuration*, Flammarion, Paris 1990
Lene Dresen-Coenders, ed: *Saints and She-Devils: Images of Women in the 15th and 16th Centuries*, Rubicon Press 1987
Andrea Dworkin: *Pornography: Men Possessing Women*, Women's Press 1984
Donald Ehresmann: "Some Observations on the Role of the Liturgy in the Early Winged Altarpiece", *Art Bulletin*, LXIV, 1982
Colin Eisler: *Early Netherlandish Painting: The Thyssen-Bornemisza Collection*, Sotheby's Publications 1989
Mircea Eliade: *Ordeal by Labyrinth*, University of Chicago Press 1984
—. *A History of Religious Ideas*, I, Collins 1979
—. *Patterns in Comparative Religion*, Sheed & Ward 1958
—. *Symbolism, the Sacred and the Arts*, Crossroad, New York 1985
Joan Evans, ed: *The Flowering of the Middle Ages*, Thames & Hudson 1966
Giorgio T. Faggin: *The Complete Paintings of the Van Eycks*, Wiedenfeld &

Nicolson 1970

R.L. Falkenberg: *Joachim Patinir: Landscape as an Image of the Pilgrimage of Life*, Amsterdam 1988

George Ferguson: *Signs and Symbols in Christian Art*, Oxford University Press 1961

John Ferguson: *An Illustrated Encyclopaedia of Mysticism*, Thames & Hudson 1976

Peter Fingesten: *The Eclipse of Symbolism*, University Press of California 1970

John Fletcher & Andrew Benjamin, ed; *Abjection, Melancholia and Love: the Work of Julia Kristeva*, Routledge 1990

S.J. Freedberg: *Painting of the High Renaissance in Rome and Florence*, Harper & Row, New York 1972

Max J. Friedlander: *From Van Eyck to Bruegel*, Phaidon 1969

—. *The van Eycks, Petrus Christus, Early Netherlandish Painting*, vol. 1, tr. Heinz Norden, Sijthoff, Leyden, Netherlands 1967

—. *Hugo van der Goes: Early Netherlandish Painting*, vol. 4, tr. Heinz Norden, Sijthoff, Leyden, Netherlands 1967

—. *Memling*, Palet Series, 1949

Margaret Frinta: *The Genius of Robert Campin*, Paris 1966

Eugène Fromentin: *The Masters of Past Time: Dutch and Flemish Painting from Van Eyck to Rembrandt*, Phaidon 1981

Fred Gettings: *The Hidden Art: A Study of the Occult Symbolism in Art*, Studio Vista 1978

Matila Ghyka: *The Geometry of Art and Life*, Sheed & Ward, New York 1946

Marija Gimbutas: *The Language of the Goddess*, Thames & Hudson 1989

Carlo Ginzburg: *The Enigma of Piero: Piero della Francesca, The Baptism, The Arezzo Cycle, The Flagellation*, Verso 1985

F.M. Godfrey: *A Student's Guide to Italian Paintings 1250-1800*, Alec Tiranti 1965

Rona Goffen: *Giovanni Bellini*, Yale University Press, New Haven 1989

Robert Goldwater & Marco Treves, eds. *Artists on Art*, John Murray 1975

E.H. Gombrich: *Norm and Form: Studies in the Renaissance I*, Phaidon 1985

—. *Symbolic Images, Renaissance Studies II*, Phaidon 1985

Cecil Gould: *Leonardo: The Artist and the Non-Artist*, Weidenfeld & Nicholson 1975

—. "On the Direction of Light in Italian Renaissance Frescoes and Altarpieces", *Gazette des Beaux-Arts*, 6, XCVII, 1981

Early Netherlandish Painting

Rainald Grosshans: "Rogier van der Weyden, Der Marien altar aus der Kartäuse Miraflores", *Jahrbuch der Berliner Museen*, XXIII, 1981
John Hale: *Italian Renaissance Painting*, Phaidon 1977
James Hall: *A Dictionary of Subjects and Symbols in Art*, John Murray 1984
John Oliver Hand & Martha Wolff: *Early Netherlandish Painting*, National Gallery of Art, Washington DC 1986
F.C. Happold, ed. *Mysticism*, Penguin 1970
Craig Harbison: *Jan van Eyck: The Play of Realism*, Reaktion Books, 1991
—. "Realism and Symbolism and Art-historical Method", *Simiolus*, XIX, 1989
—. "Visions and Meditations in Early Flemish Painting", *Simiolus*, XV, 1985
Frederick Hartt: *History of Italian Renaissance Art: Painting, Sculpture, Architecture*, Thames & Hudson 1987
—. *Sandro Botticelli*, Collins 1954
Annemarie Vels Heijn: *Rembrandt*, tr. Weir, Scala Books 1969
P. Hendy: *Piero della Francesca and the Early Renaissance*, London 1968
Hans Hoftsatter: *Art of the Late Middle Ages*, Abrams, New York 1968
D. Hollanders-Favart & R. van Schouteeds: *Le Dessin sous-jacent dans la peinture, Le Problème Maître de Flémalle–van der Weyden*, Louvain-la-Neuve, 1981
William Hood: *Fra Angelico at San Marco*, Yale University Press, New Haven 1993
Michael Jacobs: *A Guide to European Painting*, David & Charles 1980
Charles Johnson: *Memlinc*, Faber, n.d.
Penny Howell Jolly: "Rogier van der Weyden's Escorial and Philadelphia *Crucifixions* and their relation to Fra Angelico at San Marco", *Oud Holland*, XCV, 1981, 113-126
Diane Kelder: *Pageant of the Renaissance*, Pall Mall Press 1969
Julia Kristeva: *The Kristeva Reader*, ed. Toril Moi, Blackwell 1986
—. *Desire in Language: A Semiotic Approach to Literature and Art*, ed. Leon Roudiez, tr. Thomas Gora, Alice Jardine & Leon Roudiez, Blackwell 1982
—. *Tales of Love*, tr. Leon S. Roudiez, Columbia University Press, New York 1987
Weston La Barre: *The Ghost Dance*, Allen & Unwin 1972
Barbara Lane: *The Altar and the Altarpiece: Sacramental Themes in Early Netherlandish Painting*, New York 1984
—. "Sacred vs Profane in Early Netherlandish Painting", *Simiolus*, XVIII,

1988

Robert Lawlor: *Sacred Geometry: Philosophy and Practice*, Thames & Hudson 1984

Leonardo da Vinci: *Selections from the Notebooks*, Oxford University Press 1952

Michael Levey: *High Renaissance*, Penguin 1975

—. *Early Renaissance*, Penguin 1967

Christopher Lloyd: *Fra Angelico*, Phaidon 1979

—. *A Picture History of Art*, Phaidon 1979

Robert Longhi: *Piero della Francesca*, Milan 1955

K.B. MacFarlane: *Hans Memling*, Clarendon Press 1971

Emile Male: *The Gothic Image*, Collins 1961

Elaine Marks & Isabelle de Courtivron, eds: *New French Feminisms: an Anthology*, Har-vester Wheatsheaf 1981

G. Marchini: *Filippo Lippi*, Electa Editrice, Milan 1975

James Marrow: "Symbol and Meaning in Northern European Art of the Late Middle Ages and Early Renaissance", *Simiolus*, XVI, 1986

Christine Hasenmueller McCorkel: "The role of the suspended Crown in Jan van Eyck's *Madonna and Chancellor Rolin*", *Art Bulletin*, LVIII, 1975

K.B. MacFarlane. *Hans Memling*, Clarendon Press, Oxford, 1971

M.B. McNamee: "The Origins of the Vested Angel as a Eucharistic Symbol in Flemish Painting" *Art Bulletin*, LIV, 1972

Milliard Meiss: "Light as Form and Symbol in Some Fifteenth Century Paintings", *Art Bulletin*, XXVII, 1945

J.C.J. Metford: *Dictionary of Christian Lore and Legend*, Thames & Hudson 1983

Toril Moi: *Sexual/Textual Politics: Feminist Literary Theory*, Routledge 1988

Edward Mullins: *The Painted Witch: Female Body, Male Art*, Secker & Warburg 1985

Peter & Linda Murray: *The Penguin Dictionary of Art and Artists*, Penguin 1976

Linda Murray: *High Renaissance*, Thames & Hudson 1977

Lawrence Naftulin: "A Note on the Iconography of the van der Paele Madonna", *Oud-Holland*, LXXXVI, 1971

Lynda Nead: *Female Nude: Art, Obscenity and Sexuality*, Routledge 1992

Erich Neumann: *The Great Mother*, Princeton University Press, New Jersey 1972

Shirley Nicholson, ed. *The Goddess Re-awakening: The Goddess Principle*

Today Theosophical Publishing House, New York 1989

Rudolf Otto: *The Idea of the Holy*, Oxford University Press 1958

Otto Pächt: *Van Eyck and the Founders of Early Netherlandish Painting*, Harvey Miller 1994

Erwin Panofsky: *Studies in Iconology*, Harper & Row, New York 1972

—. *Early Netherlandish Painting*, Harvard University Press, Mass., 1953

Geoffrey Parrinder: *Mysticism in the World's Religions*, Sheldon Press 1976

Walter Pater: *The Renaissance*, Oxford University Press 1980

Michael Payne: *Reading Theory: An Introduction to Lacan, Derrida, and Kristeva*, Blackwell 1993

Robert Payne: *Leonardo da Vinci*, Robert Hale 1979

Karen Petersen & J.J. Wilson: *Women Artists: Recognition and Reappraisal from the Early Middle Ages to the Twentieth Century* Women's Press, 1978

Lotte Brand Philip: *The Ghent Altarpiece and the Art of Jan van Eyck*, Princeton University Press 1971

J. Plummer & I. Lavin, eds: *Studies in Late Medieval and Renaissance Painting Presented to Millard Meiss*, New York University Press, New York 1977

Piero della Francesca: *The Complete Paintings of Piero della Francesca*, intr. Peter Murray, notes by Pierluigi de Vecchi, Penguin, 1985

John Pope-Hennessy: *Fra Angelico*, Phaidon 1974

Mario Praz: *The Romantic Agony*, tr. Davidson, Oxford University Press 1933

Carol Purtle: *The Marian Paintings of Jan van Eyck*, Princeton University Press, Princeton 1982

Leo van Puyvelde: *Flemish Painting From the Van Eycks to Metsys*, tr. Alan Kendall, Weidenfeld & Nicolson 1970

Carlo Ludovico Ragghianti, ed: *Great Museums of the World: Prado, Madrid*, Hamlyn 1969

D. Robb: "The Iconography of the Annunciation in the Fourteenth and Fifteenth Centuries", *Art Bulletin*, XVIII, 1936, 480-526

Jeremy Robinson: *Glorification: Religious Abstraction in Renaissance and 20th Century Painting*, Crescent Moon 1994

Heinz Roosen-Runge: *Die Rolin-Madonna des Jan van Eyck, Form und Inhalt*, Weisbaden 1972

Robert Rosenblum: *Modern Painting and the Northern Romantic Tradition*, Thames & Hudson 1978

Mark Roskill: *What is Art History?*, Thames & Hudson 1976
Peter H. Schabacker: *Petrus Christus*, Utrecht 1974
Wolfgang Schöne: *Dieric Bouts und seine Schule*, Berlin 1938
Anne Markham Schulz: "The Columba Altarpiece and Rogier van der Weyden's Stylistic Development", *Münchener Jahrbuch der bildenden Kunst*, 3rd series, XX, 1971
Larry Silver: "Fountain and Source: A Rediscovered Eyckian Icon", *Pantheon*, XLI, 1983
Alistair Smith: *Early Netherlandish and German Painting*, National Gallery 1985
Molly Teasdale Smith: "On the Donor of Jan van Eyck's Rolin Madonna", *Gesta*, XX, 1981
James Snyder: "Jan van Eyck and the Madonna of Chancellor Nicolas Rolin", *Oud-Holland*, LXXXII, 1967
Micheline Sonke & J. Folie: *Het werk van Rogier de la Pasture Van der Weyden*, Tournai 1964
J. Spencer: "Spatial Imagery of the Annunciation in Fifteenth-century Florence", *Art Bulletin*, XXXVI, 1955, 273-280
Sidney Spencer: *Mysticism in World Religion*, Penguin 1963
Oswald Spengler: *The Decline of the West*, ed. H. Werner, Allen & Unwin 1962
Wolfgang Stechow: *Northern Renaissance Art, 1400-1600, Sources and Documents*, Prentice-Hall, New Jersey 1966
L. Steinberg & S. Edgerton: "How shall this be? Reflections on Filippo Lippi's *Annunciation* in London", *Artibus et Historiae*, VIII, 1987, 25-53
Frank Stella: *Working Space*, Harvard University Press, Cambridge, Mass., 1986
Charles Sterling: "Observations on Petrus Christus", *Art Bulletin*, LIII, 1971
Victor I. Stoichita: *Leonardo da Vinci*, Abbey Library 1978
Peter Streider: *Dürer: Paintings, Prints, Drawings*, F. Muller 1982
Ruth Massey Tovell: *Rogier van der Weyden and the Flémalle Enigma*, Burns & MacEachern, 1955
Patrick Trevor-Roper: *The world blunted through sight: An inquiry into the influence of defective vision on art and character*, Thames & Hudson 1970
Walter Ueberwasser: *Rogier van der Weyden: Paintings From the Escorial and the Prado Museum*, B.T. Batsford, 1947
J.M. Upton: *Petrus Christus*, University Park 1990
Nicholas Usherwood: *The Bible in 20th Century Art*, Pagoda Books 1987

Early Netherlandish Painting

Lionello Venturi: *Renaissance Painting, from Leonardo to Dürer*, Skira/ Macmillan 1979
—. *Italian Paintings*, Zwemmer 1950
—. *Botticelli*, Phaidon 1964
T. Verdon & J. Henderson, eds: *Christianity and the Renaissance*, Syracuse University Press, Syracuse 1990
W. Vogelsang: *Rogier van der Weyden's Pietà*, Longmans, Green & Co, 1949
John Ward: "A New Attribution for the *Madonna Enthroned* in the Thyssen-Bornemisza Collection", *Art Bulletin*, L, 1968
—. "Hidden Symbolism in Jan van Eyck's Annunciations", *Art Bulletin*, LVII, 1975
Marina Warner: *Alone Of All Her Sex: The Myth and Cult of the Virgin Mary*, Picador 1985
—. *Monuments and Maidens*, Weidenfeld & Nicholson 1985
Paul Watson: *The Garden of Love in Tuscan Art of the Early Renaissance*, Associated University Press 1979
Margaret Whinney: *Early Flemish Painters*, Faber 1966
John White: *The Birth and Rebirth of Pictorial Space*, Faber 1957/87
Edward C. Whitmont: *Return of the Goddess*, Routledge 1987
Peter Lamborn Wilson: *Angels*, Thames & Hudson 1980
Mara R. Witzling: *Voicing Our Viions: Writing by Women Artists*, Women's Press 1992
Heinrich Wolfflin: *Classic Art*, Phaidon 1952/80
Marion Woodman: *The Pregnant Virgin: A Process of Psychological Transformation*, Inner City Books, Toronto 1989
Manfred Wudram: *Art of the Renaissance*, Weidenfeld & Nicolson 1985
J.E. Zeigler: "The Medieval Virgin as Object: Art of Anthropology?", *Historical Reflections*, XVI, 1989
Charles Zika: "Hosts, Processions and Pilgrimages: Controlling the Sacred in Fifteenth-Century Germany", *Past and Present*, CXVIII, 1988

CRESCENT MOON PUBLISHING

ARTS, PAINTING, SCULPTURE

The Art of Andy Goldsworthy
Andy Goldsworthy: Touching Nature
Andy Goldsworthy in Close-Up
Andy Goldsworthy: Pocket Guide
Andy Goldsworthy In America
Land Art: A Complete Guide
The Art of Richard Long
Richard Long: Pocket Guide
Land Art In the UK
Land Art in Close-Up
Land Art In the U.S.A.
Land Art: Pocket Guide
Installation Art in Close-Up
Minimal Art and Artists In the 1960s and After
Colourfield Painting
Land Art DVD, TV documentary
Andy Goldsworthy DVD, TV documentary
The Erotic Object: Sexuality in Sculpture From Prehistory to the Present Day
Sex in Art: Pornography and Pleasure in Painting and Sculpture
Postwar Art
Sacred Gardens: The Garden in Myth, Religion and Art
Glorification: Religious Abstraction in Renaissance and 20th Century Art
Early Netherlandish Painting
Leonardo da Vinci
Piero della Francesca
Giovanni Bellini
Fra Angelico: Art and Religion in the Renaissance
Mark Rothko: The Art of Transcendence
Frank Stella: American Abstract Artist
Jasper Johns
Brice Marden
Alison Wilding: The Embrace of Sculpture
Vincent van Gogh: Visionary Landscapes
Eric Gill: Nuptials of God
Constantin Brancusi: Sculpting the Essence of Things
Max Beckmann
Caravaggio
Gustave Moreau
Egon Schiele: Sex and Death In Purple Stockings
Delizioso Fotografico Fervore: Works In Process 1
Sacro Cuore: Works In Process 2
The Light Eternal: J.M.W. Turner
The Madonna Glorified: Karen Arthurs

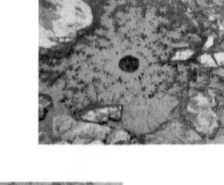
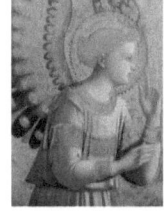
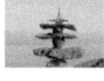
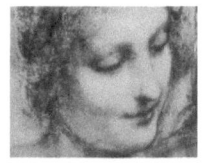
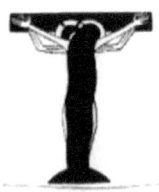
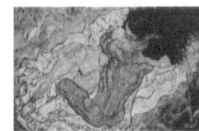

LITERATURE

J.R.R. Tolkien: The Books, The Films, The Whole Cultural Phenomenon
J.R.R. Tolkien: Pocket Guide
Tolkien's Heroic Quest
The *Earthsea* Books of Ursula Le Guin
Beauties, Beasts and Enchantment: Classic French Fairy Tales
German Popular Stories by the Brothers Grimm
Philip Pullman and *His Dark Materials*
Sexing Hardy: Thomas Hardy and Feminism
Thomas Hardy's *Tess of the d'Urbervilles*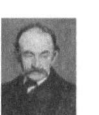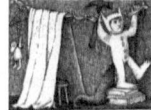
Thomas Hardy's *Jude the Obscure*
Thomas Hardy: The Tragic Novels
Love and Tragedy: Thomas Hardy
The Poetry of Landscape in Hardy
Wessex Revisited: Thomas Hardy and John Cowper Powys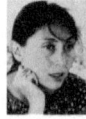
Wolfgang Iser: Essays and Interviews
Petrarch, Dante and the Troubadours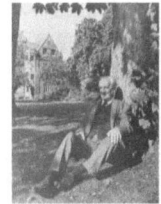
Maurice Sendak and the Art of Children's Book Illustration
Andrea Dworkin
Cixous, Irigaray, Kristeva: The *Jouissance* of French Feminism
Julia Kristeva: Art, Love, Melancholy, Philosophy, Semiotics and Psychoanalysis
Hélène Cixous I Love You: The *Jouissance* of Writing
Luce Irigaray: Lips, Kissing, and the Politics of Sexual Difference
Peter Redgrove: Here Comes the Flood
Peter Redgrove: Sex-Magic-Poetry-Cornwall
Lawrence Durrell: Between Love and Death, East and West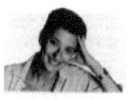
Love, Culture & Poetry: Lawrence Durrell
Cavafy: Anatomy of a Soul
German Romantic Poetry: Goethe, Novalis, Heine, Hölderlin
Feminism and Shakespeare
Shakespeare: Love, Poetry & Magic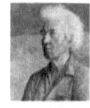
The Passion of D.H. Lawrence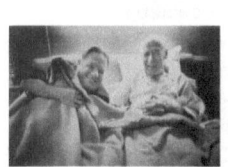
D.H. Lawrence: Symbolic Landscapes
D.H. Lawrence: Infinite Sensual Violence
Rimbaud: Arthur Rimbaud and the Magic of Poetry
The Ecstasies of John Cowper Powys
Sensualism and Mythology: The Wessex Novels of John Cowper Powys
Amorous Life: John Cowper Powys and the Manifestation of Affectivity (H.W. Fawkner)
Postmodern Powys: New Essays on John Cowper Powys (Joe Boulter)
Rethinking Powys: Critical Essays on John Cowper Powys
Paul Bowles & Bernardo Bertolucci
Rainer Maria Rilke
Joseph Conrad: *Heart of Darkness*
In the Dim Void: Samuel Beckett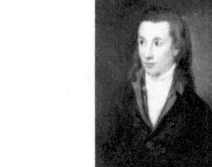
Samuel Beckett Goes into the Silence
André Gide: Fiction and Fervour
Jackie Collins and the Blockbuster Novel
Blinded By Her Light: The Love-Poetry of Robert Graves
The Passion of Colours: Travels In Mediterranean Lands
Poetic Forms

POETRY

Ursula Le Guin: Walking In Cornwall
Peter Redgrove: Here Comes The Flood
Peter Redgrove: Sex-Magic-Poetry-Cornwall
Dante: Selections From the Vita Nuova
Petrarch, Dante and the Troubadours
William Shakespeare: Sonnets
William Shakespeare: Complete Poems
Blinded By Her Light: The Love-Poetry of Robert Graves
Emily Dickinson: Selected Poems
Emily Brontë: Poems
Thomas Hardy: Selected Poems
Percy Bysshe Shelley: Poems
John Keats: Selected Poems
Joh n Keats: Poems of 1820
D.H. Lawrence: Selected Poems
Edmund Spenser: Poems
Edmund Spenser: Amoretti
John Donne: Poems
Henry Vaughan: Poems
Sir Thomas Wyatt: Poems
Robert Herrick: Selected Poems
Rilke: Space, Essence and Angels in the Poetry of Rainer Maria Rilke
Rainer Maria Rilke: Selected Poems
Friedrich Hölderlin: Selected Poems
Arseny Tarkovsky: Selected Poems
Arthur Rimbaud: Selected Poems
Arthur Rimbaud: A Season in Hell
Arthur Rimbaud and the Magic of Poetry
Novalis: Hymns To the Night
German Romantic Poetry
Paul Verlaine: Selected Poems
Elizaethan Sonnet Cycles
D.J. Enright: By-Blows
Jeremy Reed: Brigitte's Blue Heart
Jeremy Reed: Claudia Schiffer's Red Shoes
Gorgeous Little Orpheus
Radiance: New Poems
Crescent Moon Book of Nature Poetry
Crescent Moon Book of Love Poetry
Crescent Moon Book of Mystical Poetry
Crescent Moon Book of Elizabethan Love Poetry
Crescent Moon Book of Metaphysical Poetry
Crescent Moon Book of Romantic Poetry
Pagan America: New American Poetry

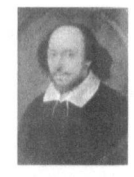
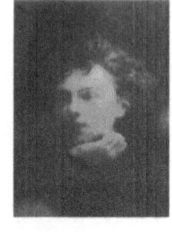
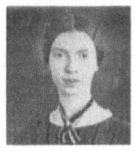
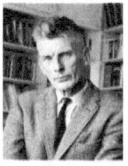
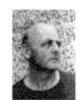
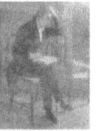
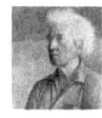
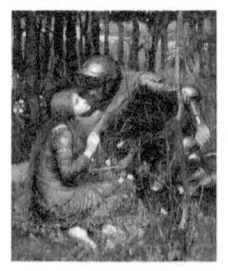
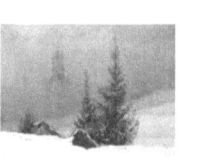
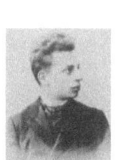
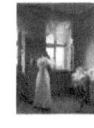
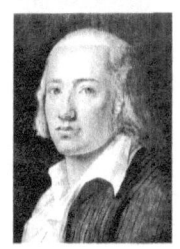
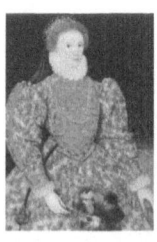

MEDIA, CINEMA, FEMINISM and CULTURAL STUDIES

J.R.R. Tolkien: The Books, The Films, The Whole Cultural Phenomenon
J.R.R. Tolkien: Pocket Guide
The *Lord of the Rings* Movies: Pocket Guide
The Cinema of Hayao Miyazaki
Hayao Miyazaki: *Princess Mononoke*: Pocket Movie Guide
Hayao Miyazaki: *Spirited Away*: Pocket Movie Guide
Tim Burton
Ken Russell
Ken Russell: *Tommy*: Pocket Movie Guide
The Ghost Dance: The Origins of Religion
The Peyote Cult
Cixous, Irigaray, Kristeva: The *Jouissance* of French Feminism
Julia Kristeva: Art, Love, Melancholy, Philosophy, Semiotics and Psychoanalysis
Luce Irigaray: Lips, Kissing, and the Politics of Sexual Difference
Hélene Cixous I Love You: The *Jouissance* of Writing
Andrea Dworkin
'Cosmo Woman': The World of Women's Magazines
Women in Pop Music
Discovering the Goddess (Geoffrey Ashe)
The Poetry of Cinema
The Sacred Cinema of Andrei Tarkovsky
Andrei Tarkovsky: Pocket Guide
Andrei Tarkovsky: *Mirror*: Pocket Movie Guide
Andrei Tarkovsky: *The Sacrifice*: Pocket Movie Guide
Walerian Borowczyk: Cinema of Erotic Dreams
Jean-Luc Godard: The Passion of Cinema
Jean-Luc Godard: *Hail Mary*: Pocket Movie Guide
Jean-Luc Godard: *Contempt*: Pocket Movie Guide
Jean-Luc Godard: *Pierrot le Fou*: Pocket Movie Guide
John Hughes and Eighties Cinema
Ferris Bueller's Day Off: Pocket Movie Guide
Jean-Luc Godard: Pocket Guide
The Cinema of Richard Linklater
Liv Tyler: Star In Ascendance
Blade Runner and the Films of Philip K. Dick
Paul Bowles and Bernardo Bertolucci
Media Hell: Radio, TV and the Press
An Open Letter to the BBC
Detonation Britain: Nuclear War in the UK
Feminism and Shakespeare
Wild Zones: Pornography, Art and Feminism
Sex in Art: Pornography and Pleasure in Painting and Sculpture
Sexing Hardy: Thomas Hardy and Feminism

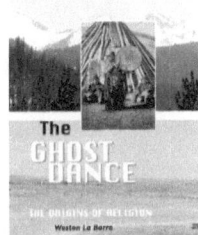
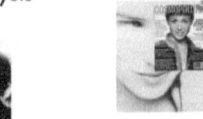
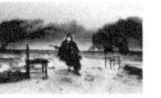
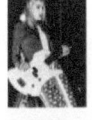
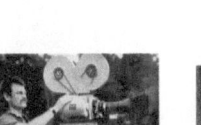
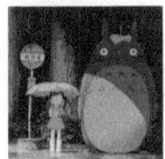
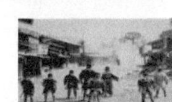
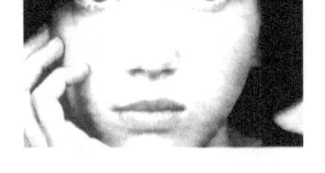

In my view *The Light Eternal* is among the very best of all the material I read on Turner. (Douglas Graham, director of the Turner Museum, Denver, Colorado)

The Light Eternal is a model monograph, an exemplary job. The subject matter of the book is beautifully organised and dead on beam. (Lawrence Durrell)

It is amazing for me to see my work treated with such passion and respect. (Andrea Dworkin)

CRESCENT MOON PUBLISHING
P.O. Box 1312, Maidstone, Kent, ME14 5XU, Great Britain. www.crmoon.com

www.ingramcontent.com/pod-product-compliance
Lightning Source LLC
Chambersburg PA
CBHW031615210526
45464CB00004B/1583